One House

The Unicameral's
Progressive Vision
for Nebraska

SECOND EDITION

Charlyne Berens

With a new introduction by the author

University of Nebraska Press
Lincoln and London

Contents

List of Illustrations   vi

Acknowledgments   vii

Introduction   ix

1. One of a Kind   1

2. Power to the People   18

3. Let the Sun Shine In   42

4. Forty-nine Independent Contractors   72

5. We, the People   115

6. "You Lie, You're Gone"   147

7. Promises Fulfilled?   170

Appendix 1. Survey Results   181

Appendix 2. George Norris's 1923 Article in the *New York Times*   189

Appendix 3. George Norris's 1934 Model Legislature Speech   195

Notes   209

Bibliographic Essay   219

Index   221

Illustrations

Following page 102
The Sower being readied for its perch atop the Nebraska capitol
The Nebraska capitol during construction
The 133 members of the two houses posing in joint session
The unicameral chamber
The Nebraska capitol
U.S. senator George Norris and Dr. John Senning

Acknowledgments

I just can't seem to get enough of the Nebraska unicameral. Even before I began studying the legislature in an organized manner, I was fascinated by the way it worked and, like many other Nebraskans, felt very close to this small, accessible institution.

The more I've studied it, the more interested I've become and the more I've wanted to continue investigating how it works: thus, this book, which tries to determine whether the promises made for the one-house, nonpartisan legislature by its 1930s proponents have been kept.

Many people helped make this book possible. Patrick O'Donnell, clerk of the legislature, was an extremely patient and helpful resource. Current and former state senators and lobbyists were generous with their time, completing surveys and granting interviews.

Terri Diffenderfer spent hours with the microfilm reader, helping track down newspapers' references to unicameral history, and hours at the computer, helping organize and analyze survey data. She deserves a medal.

Will Norton encouraged me to undertake this project and continued to nudge me along throughout its progress. And, of course, my husband, Dennis Berens, has been my biggest cheerleader. I simply couldn't have done this without his unquestioning support.

I am, indeed, blessed to have such friends and family.

Introduction

At first glance, the idea of term limits appears to be a natural for Nebraska: a populist notion, reflecting the spirit on which the Nebraska unicameral was founded. One of the advantages Nebraska's U.S. senator George Norris stressed as he campaigned for the one-house body in 1934 was that it would be closer to the people, more responsive, a true "citizen legislature."

U.S. Term Limits—the national group that contributed hundreds of thousands of dollars to help pass term limits legislation in Nebraska and many other states during the 1990s—made similar promises. According to the group's website: "Term limits encourage regular, competitive elections; they improve citizen access to the process; they bring a broader range of experience and perspectives to the legislature; they improve the incentives faced by sitting legislators and they widen the circle of those with intimate knowledge of state government. In sum, term limits bring the legislature closer to the people."[1]

The idea sounded good to plenty of Nebraskans, and after several failed attempts to change the state constitution to make term limits a reality for the unicameral, proponents finally got a measure passed in 2000. The two-term, eight-year limit was the state's biggest institutional change since the voters adopted the one-house, nonpartisan structure in 1934.

The first senators forced out of office by term limits left the legislature in 2006. By 2012, no senator had served more than two terms. A ballot measure that would have increased the number of four-year terms from two to three failed at the polls on November 6, 2012. While it may be too soon to know the long-term effects term limits will have on Nebraska, some trends seem already to be developing.

Specifically, the Nebraska legislature as an institution appears to be growing weaker for several reasons. The governor, political parties, and special interest groups have been able to take advantage of the large number of inexperienced senators to exert increased influence over the policymaking process. And while equality among senators may have increased because no one is able to accumulate seniority, senators also experience a sharp learning curve and difficulty developing leadership expertise. Also, many of the policies the term-limited senators make tend to address short-term needs without always looking at long-term problems—and the policies often seem to be more driven by the executive branch than was the case before 2006.

While George Norris valued and promoted openness, responsiveness, and equality among members as advantages of his "model legislature," he also wholeheartedly believed that the legislature was the people's branch of the government. Thus, he promoted independence from political parties, lobbyists, and the executive branch as well as efficiency and expertise. It looks as if term limits' early effects on the institution he fathered are mixed at best.

Nebraska Adopts Term Limits on the Fourth Try

It is probably safe to say that Americans have never been satisfied with their government—and that their dissatisfaction is one thing that has helped keep that government honest and kept it adapting to citizens' changing needs and demands. Citizen unhappiness has manifested itself in demonstrations both peaceful and unruly, in challenges to state or federal legislation that sometimes go all the way to the U.S. Supreme Court, in attempts to form third parties to represent specific interests, and in limits to the number of years an elected representative can serve.

In the 1990s, adopting term limits became the protest of choice in twenty-one states, Nebraska among them. California, Colorado, and Maine passed citizen initiatives limiting legislative service in 1990. Subsequently, eighteen other states adopted term limits measures, but in Oregon, Washington, Massachusetts, and Wyoming, state supreme courts overturned the measures. In Idaho and Utah, the legislatures repealed them. That leaves fifteen states with legislative term limits in place.[2]

Nebraska was the last to make term limits a reality when 56 percent of voters approved a ballot initiative in 2000. U.S. Term Limits made a broad case that appealed to many in Nebraska who thought the legislature simply was not listening to the people on a variety of matters. But proponents had been trying to get the job done since 1992, each time through the initiative petition process, which the state had adopted in 1912.

In the early 1990s, a group of Nebraskans formed the Concerned Citizens Committee to defend the right of initiative and referendum from what it saw as unconstitutional encroachment by the unicameral. It wasn't long before the committee's attention turned to term limits as one potential solution. "We could see that the problem was career politicians who got in and stayed on to accumulate an inordinate amount of power," Bob Wright, a member of the Concerned Citizens Committee, said in 2002.[3] The group launched a term limits petition campaign in 1992 focusing on Nebraska's congressional delegation, although, Wright said, "We thought we could help the legislature by throwing it in, too."

The committee got enough petition signatures to place the Term Limits Act on the 1992 ballot, and Nebraskans approved the measure with a healthy 68.2 percent of the vote. It was an ambitious measure, amending the Nebraska Constitution to limit legislators and statewide officials to two consecutive four-year terms, U.S. representatives to four consecutive two-year terms, and U.S. senators to two consecutive six-year terms.[4]

The proponents' success was short-lived, however. When the ballot measure was challenged in court, the Nebraska Supreme Court ruled in 1994 that not enough signatures had been collected to place the question on the ballot. In *Duggan v. Beermann* the court said that a 1988 change to Nebraska's constitution had increased the number of signatures required and that proponents of the 1992 ballot initiative had come up thirty thousand names short. The court did not touch on the major constitutional issue raised by the proposed amendment: whether a state could limit terms for its members of Congress who serve at the federal level of government.

So proponents went out and got more signatures on their petitions and placed a nearly identical measure on the 1994 ballot. That amendment passed with 67.7 percent of the vote. This time the legal challenge was based on the constitutionality of such a mandate. In 1995 the U.S. Supreme Court ruled in *U.S. Term Limits v. Thornton*, a case involving a similar term limits measure in Arkansas, that states cannot limit federal terms of office. That ruling also made unconstitutional parts of Nebraska's 1994 ballot initiative. In 1996 the Nebraska Supreme Court ruled in another case, also titled *Duggan v. Beermann*, that the remaining portions of the measure were so interwoven with the unconstitutional parts of the amendment that they, too, must be declared void.

Taking a different approach, term limits proponents got a proposal on the 1996 ballot that was a form of what is often called a "scarlet letter" law.[5] In this case, the proposed amendment to the state constitution would have instructed Nebraska's members of Congress and state legislators to support passage of an amendment to the U.S. Constitution that would put term limits on members of both houses of the U.S. Congress and require all candidates for Congress and the state legislatures to make their positions on that amendment known to the voters. Failure to support such a measure, it was implied, would mark the recalcitrant candidate with a scarlet letter of shame.

Voters passed this ballot initiative with 58.3 percent of the vote, although a district court judge immediately found the measure an unconstitutional infringement on free speech. Then in 1997 the U.S. Supreme Court declined to review an Arkansas Supreme Court ruling that had found Arkansas's scarlet letter law to be unconstitutional, allowing the ruling against the law to stand (*Donovan v. Priest*). As a result, all state scarlet letter laws were considered unconstitutional.

Four years later, though, Nebraska's term limits supporters found success. Nebraska Initiative 415 was approved by 56 percent of voters—a lower total than any of the previous attempts but easily clearing the simple majority needed for passage. It amended the Nebraska Constitution to limit members of the legislature to two consecutive terms. A state senator who wanted to run for a third term would have to sit out four years before he or she could file for reelection to the unicameral. The first senators affected were those who had served at least part of one term before January 1, 2001, and were reelected in 2002. They became ineligible to run again in 2006. By 2008, any senator in office when the voters approved Initiative 415 would be gone from the legislature.

That staggered approach to implementing term limits makes the numbers somewhat confusing. In 2006 nineteen senators were scheduled to be forced out by term limits, but one had already resigned from the legislature in 2004, so eighteen of the open seats in the 2006 election were open due to term limits. Sixteen more senators were on the term-limited list for 2008, but one of those, Mike Foley, had left in 2006 to become state treasurer.

The impact was smaller in 2010, when five were scheduled to lose their seats to term limits. Two of those had declined to run for reelection in 2006, and one had resigned in 2008. In 2012 nine senators became ineligible to run for reelection; however, one of those had already dropped out in 2008 after serving only one term. In 2014, all those elected in 2006 are barred from running for third terms.

Of the fifteen states where term limits are currently in effect, Nebraska and nine others limit their legislators to eight years. Oklahoma, Louisiana, and Nevada legislators may serve up to twelve years; those in Arkansas and Michigan may serve only six; California's state senators may serve eight years and members of the lower house six. However, Nebraska's is the only unicameral legislature, the only one where senators term-limited out of service in one house do not have the opportunity to run for election to the other house. The result has been a rapid and significant decrease in experience and institutional memory, a detriment that term limits opponents decry but proponents appear to believe worth the price.

Taking on the Incumbents

"Throw the bums out!" is the unofficial rallying cry for those who favor term limits. The thinking is that legislators who stay in office for a long time become, in effect, "career politicians." Because they want to keep getting reelected, they try to bring the bacon home to their own districts and to pass regulations to address any perceived problem their constituents may have in order to build support for the next election.[6] Those who favor more limited government often accuse long-serving officials of expanding government and its reach and scope, of becoming too comfortable in office—no matter how often they must run for reelection. It can be difficult for a newcomer to unseat a senator who becomes popular and entrenched in her district. The solution, some say, is simply to make it impossible for anyone to become entrenched, to become a career politician.

The power of incumbency is one of the primary factors U.S. Term Limits and its supporters say term limits can change. Too many good candidates who would like to run for office, they say, find themselves facing incumbents with enormous advantages: name recognition, the resources of the office, substantial campaign contributions, and opportunities to claim credit for making or blocking policy. As a result, few challengers are willing to take on an incumbent, instead opting to wait until the incumbent decides not to run and *all* candidates are newcomers.[7] Nebraskans did see evidence of that trend in 2006 when eighty-three candidates filed for twenty-two open seats; eighteen seats were being vacated by senators who were not allowed to run again and four by senators who would have been eligible to run but declined to do so or had already left the legislature.

The growing power of the incumbency in the past fifty years has been well documented. According to the National Conference of State Legislatures, for example, 92 percent of legislators running for reelection in 1994 were successful. The number in Nebraska was 90 percent.[8] In 1996 six new members (about 12 percent of the total) joined the legislature; in 2002 it was seven new members (about 14 percent of the total).[9] According to a 2002 study, one-fourth of the unicameral's membership, on average, turned over every two years, and the average state senator spent seven years in office.[10]

Those numbers indicate that not nearly all legislators were running for election three, four, or more times. In fact, in Nebraska, of the 139 senators who served between 1980 and 2005, twenty-three (16 percent) served more than two terms but only sixteen (about 10 percent) more than three. While the power of incumbency may have been strong in Nebraska in the two decades before term limits took effect in 2006, it did not lead to a legislature clogged with career politicians who came and stayed—and stayed some more.

Because only three legislative elections have taken place in Nebraska since 2006, it's not possible to draw any firm conclusions about term limits' impact on incumbents' reelection rate. Of the twenty-two senators elected for the first time in 2006, all but two ran for a second term in 2010. And of those twenty who ran for a second term, eight ran unopposed. The remaining incumbents all had at least one challenger, but only two were not reelected.[11]

In 2012, term limits prevented nine members from running again. Of the sixteen senators first elected in 2008 and eligible to run again in 2012, one chose not to run for reelection, and two had already left the legislature. Their replacements, appointed in 2011, were both on the ballot in 2012; one was reelected, the other defeated. Four of the remaining thirteen ran unopposed in 2012.

On the first two times out of the barn, term limits seem not to have had much impact on the power of the incumbency where incumbents were allowed to run again; almost everyone who sought a second term got one. In 2012 all but two of the seventeen incumbents were reelected.

But proponents have other reasons for embracing term limits. They say the limits will make it more likely that more ethnic minorities and women will be elected and that legislators will represent a wider variety of occupational backgrounds, making legislatures more responsive to the people, an echo of Norris's populist call.[12] It is true that, in some states, ethnic diversity has increased since term limits were adopted, although the limits alone were probably not responsible for all the changes. On the other hand, term limits have not made significant impacts on the numbers of women in state legislatures or in the occupational backgrounds of those who serve.[13]

The Nebraska legislature has historically been dominated by white males with a few women added to the mix and only a handful of people of color. In fact, while Dr. Matthew O. Ricketts, an African American, was elected to Nebraska's legislature in 1892, his legislative service was something of an anomaly. Only one other person of color served in the unicameral before Ernie Chambers, an African American, was elected in 1970 and repeatedly reelected to represent North Omaha—until term limits made him ineligible to run for reelection in 2008. Chambers's successor, Brenda Council, is an African American woman, although she served only one term before being defeated by Chambers himself, who had sat out the requisite four years before running again. Tanya Cook, elected in 2008, also is an African American woman.

Ray Aguilar was elected to represent the Grand Island area in 2000 and was reelected in 2004; term limits made him ineligible to run for a third term in 2008. No one else with Latino heritage has served in the legislature before or since.

The first woman member of the legislature was elected in 1955; the 1965–66 session included two women and the 1967–68 session three. Women's ranks grew slowly, and it wasn't until 1989–90 that they reached a total of ten. Nine women were members in 2001–2 and 2003–4. That number jumped to fifteen in 2005–6—before term limits took effect—but decreased again to nine in 2007–8. Ten women served during the 2009–10 term and eleven during 2011–12.

Women were candidates in six of the races for the nine seats open in 2012 because of term limits and in four of the races that involved an incumbent. Of the eleven new senators elected in 2012, three were women. A total of six women won election in the twenty-six legislative races that November. With only three elections since term limits took effect, it is too soon to identify a trend, but the mandatory decrease in incumbents running again has not yet seemed to have a significant effect on the gender balance in the legislature.

Perhaps term limits have fulfilled another of the original proponents' goals and made it possible for people from a wider variety of careers to be elected, but a fall 2010 survey of state senators who served in the legislature since 2000 doesn't give much support to that proposition. Survey respondents were asked to identify their occupations as "farmers/ranchers," "attorneys," "professionals," or "other." Of the forty-one respondents, twenty-eight were elected before 2006 and thirteen in 2006 or after. Of those elected before 2006, eight identified themselves as professionals, eleven as farmers, three as attorneys, and six as "other." Of the thirteen elected since 2006, a larger percentage—eight—identified themselves as professionals, one as a farmer, one an attorney, and three as "other." If term limits proponents were hoping that more turnover would bring more blue-collar workers into the mix, they have yet to see that come to pass in Nebraska (see table 1).

For many Nebraskans, though, a vote in favor of term limits may have been motivated less by a desire to increase the diversity of the membership or to hold senators more accountable to the voters or to allow them the freedom to think broadly than it was to get rid of one member whose North Omaha district just kept sending him back to the legislature term after term. Ernie Chambers was first elected to the unicameral in 1970 and holds the record as the longest-serving senator. The man who listed his occupation in legislative handbooks and other documents as "defender of the downtrodden" became a force in the legislature not because he ever served as speaker or chair of a powerful committee but because he knew the legislature's rules and how to use them better than nearly anyone else. He often introduced legislation that was often unpopular and often blocked legislation he thought was misguided. His efforts got a lot of attention from his colleagues, from the media, and from citizens. Even citizens who knew little about the unicameral knew about Ernie Chambers. Some defended him because, as the body's most liberal senator, he championed ideas and opinions that might otherwise never have been raised in the generally conservative body. But many saw him as an obstructionist—at best.

Trouble was, he just kept coming back. The voters in his district were apparently satisfied with his performance in the capitol and kept reelecting him term after term. Many observers have concluded that "getting rid of Ernie" was a big reason many Nebraskans voted for term limits.[14] Chambers himself suggested as much in an interview with National Public Radio in January 2006.[15] However, as noted above, Chambers reappeared on the ballot in 2012, challenging incumbent Brenda Council, the woman who had filled his seat in 2008. And he won, ironically subverting the intentions of those who may have voted for term limits primarily to get rid of him.

Whether their intent was practical or ideological, Nebraskans in the waning years of the twentieth century decided they wanted new faces in their legislature and passed a constitutional amendment to make it happen. It is a truism that term limits are certain to bring new faces to the legislature, and even some who don't support the concept appreciate the results.

Annette Dubas of Fullerton, elected in 2006, said in 2011 that one benefit of term limits is that "I'm here." Running for an open seat is more attractive to a newcomer than challenging an established veteran, she said.

Mike Gloor of Grand Island also found that opportunity attractive. "There's truth to the power of incumbency," he said, adding that he knew his predecessor, Ray Aguilar, well enough that he would not have challenged him had Aguilar not been forced out by term limits in 2008. Gloor ran unopposed for reelection in 2012.

An informal survey of twelve senators elected to the legislature in 2012 supports this notion. Only one respondent said he would have run against an incumbent while ten respondents said they would have sat out the race rather than face someone running for reelection. The twelfth respondent actually beat an incumbent in 2012: Bill Kintner defeated Paul Lambert, appointed by Governor Dave Heineman just a year earlier to fill a vacancy. Lambert ran afoul of the governor when he voted with the majority to override Heineman's veto of a sales tax bill, and the governor campaigned successfully against his own appointee when Lambert had to run for the seat in 2012.

Bill Avery, elected in 2006 from the Lincoln district long represented by Chris Beutler (who went on to serve as mayor of Lincoln), said the new people bring new ideas, "sometimes better ideas." When all senators are new or nearly new, none of them have long records of supporting or opposing particular policies, and that can allow the legislature to "re-set the table."

Kathy Campbell, elected in 2008 and reelected in 2012, noted the same thing. All the new people bring new perspectives and "concentrate more on what's happening now," she said. And Governor Dave Heineman mentioned the same advantage: "We have new faces, new ideas, new excitement. New people are not bound by the old ways. They can look outside the box. They don't say, 'We've always done it that way.'"

Even veterans of the legislature speak well of the new blood injected into the body since 2006. Ron Withem was a state senator from 1983 to 1997, was speaker during his last four years in office, and now works for the University of Nebraska as a lobbyist. He had general praise for the senators elected since term limits took effect. "They're a pretty high-quality group," he said.

Walt Radcliffe, who has lobbied in the unicameral since 1977, agreed: "We were really lucky in the early rounds of term limits. We got some good people."

In the short term, then, term limits may have brought new people with new ideas and perspectives—whether or not they increased ethnic, gender, and career diversity. And observers say the new senators are generally talented. Indeed, some studies have found that rookie legislators are as capable as their predecessors in terms of their sheer abilities.[16] But one thing is certain: term limits, on purpose, have decreased the level of experience and institutional memory among the state senators.

Learning on the Fly

Of all the arguments made against term limits, the one usually at the top of everyone's list is the obvious: no one will accumulate long experience in the legislature. And that fact, opponents say, can lead to all kinds of unintended consequences: increased lobbyist influence, increased staff influence, short-term thinking, and a shift in the balance of power between the legislative and executive branches of government, all of which go against the populist/progressive ideals that hatched Nebraska's nonpartisan unicameral legislature in the first place.

The senators themselves—past and present—recognize that term limits have affected institutional memory. For example, Senator Annette Dubas said that institutional memory, important for a variety of reasons, has been weakened by the term limits turnover.

Bill Mueller agreed. Mueller, partner in the firm Mueller and Robak, has lobbied the unicameral for twenty-seven years and said the idea of bringing in new people and new ideas sounds great but concluded that it's actually harmful—and worse in Nebraska than it might be in other states. "We can't fix mistakes made in the other house," he said. And he thinks the laws passed since term limits took effect are not as well drafted as they should be, in part thanks to the lack of institutional memory.

"I'm not questioning competence and intelligence of the new senators," Mueller said. "But you don't get more experience by being intelligent. You get better by doing it," by debating and questioning and piling up knowledge as similar issues come up again and again.

Lowen Kruse, who was elected in 2000 and was term-limited out of office at the end of 2008, recalled a specific benefit of institutional memory. When he arrived in the legislature, Kruse served on the Appropriations Committee of which Roger Wehrbein was the longtime chair. Kruse said the members of the committee and other senators "would come up with great ideas." Wehrbein would listen to the proposals and then tell his colleagues that the legislature had tried just such a policy "back in 1992, but the agency heads wouldn't follow the procedures." And that would save the current committee members from trying again to do something that had proved unworkable in the past. "It saved time and frustration," Kruse said. Wehrbein was first elected in 1986 and served four terms.

Some scholars' findings support Kruse's observations, asserting that experienced legislators are important if a body is to produce any kind of innovative policies. New members have to learn the ropes, and when a large number of members are new, their lack of expertise lowers their productivity.[17]

Patrick O'Donnell, clerk of the legislature since 1978, has had plenty of opportunity to observe what constant and significant turnover can do to senators' productivity. "It takes time to learn the necessary skills even to ask the right questions," he said. "It really takes four years before you know what to ask." O'Donnell said members often ask him for advice because of his longevity in and knowledge of the institution, and he's happy to help when he can. "But they often don't even know what to ask," he said, "and, anyway, I'm still not a member."

O'Donnell has traditionally provided several days of training and preparation for new senators, but he now finds himself doing a lot more teaching, both formally and informally. He spends time on the floor of the legislature, suggesting ways to make the process work better. In the past, freshman senators would usually sit next to experienced members who would serve as mentors for the newcomers. "Now they're all inexperienced," O'Donnell said.

Senator Tom Carlson, elected in 2010, said it takes a lot of time and effort to become familiar with the issues, the constitution, and the rules of the legislature as well as its customs and norms. Calling committee hearings the "second house," Carlson said how a senator behaves in those hearings is very important. "We want to be sure people feel comfortable testifying, and we want to be sure to listen." Abrupt exchanges between politicians are fine, he said, but members of the public must be treated politely. It's a behavioral norm that must be learned by observing, and that takes time.

Then there's the matter of figuring out how to form coalitions, identify opposition, find compromise. "It's a long, complicated process," Carlson said. "Nobody can be effective right away." Simply learning how the legislature functions is an intense process with a steep learning curve, he pointed out. It takes time to learn how to use the process to make effective law and policy.

So when it comes to efficiency, one of Norris's goals for the unicameral back in the 1930s, it seems likely that, while they have not deeply wounded the institution, term limits haven't been particularly helpful.

Listening to the People

Being responsive to the people of the state was another thing Norris said a nonpartisan unicameral would do well. Over the decades, observers argued about just how well that was working out—and how well it *should* work out.

Back in the late seventeenth century, Edmund Burke, when he was a member of the British Parliament, argued that an elected member ought to be not just a delegate who serves as a conduit for his constituents' expressed preferences but rather a trustee, someone who represents his constituents' interests. A member should also be expected to use his own knowledge, experience, and expertise for the good of all citizens.

Burke outlined a dilemma that members of democratically elected bodies still face: how to be responsive to their constituents' desires but not at the expense of the broader citizenry or of their own educated judgments. Populism, with its fundamental understanding that "a people" exists and the people's wishes must be served, demands more of a delegate approach. But society is complicated and complex, and the laws passed in the legislature affect the state as a whole, so members also must struggle with their obligations to be trustees.

Studies indicate that term-limited senators may tend to be less responsive than senators whose terms are not restricted. Perhaps it is simply a matter of time: that a senator in office for no more than eight years simply doesn't have as many years of contact with her constituents and, thus, feels less pressure. Perhaps it is a matter of fewer election cycles: that once a senator is elected, she must mount only one more campaign in which she must make extensive efforts to know her constituents and their concerns. For whatever reason, term limits seem to dampen the responsiveness of legislators to their constituents and incline them toward more of a statewide perspective.[18]

Is that good or bad? Dave Landis, who represented the 46th district in Lincoln from 1978 to 2006, thinks it's both. Term limits promoters, he said, argue that anyone who is elected over and over can lose touch with the voters' concerns and agenda. After all, incumbents don't have to work all that hard to be reelected, and they may simply be able to muzzle any opposition.

Landis admits he was most attentive to the voters in his district during his very first term in office. He had campaigned door-to-door, looking people in the eye and hearing what they had to say. "What you get from meeting people and building alliances the first time is vivid and powerful," he said.

During that first session, a constituent would contact him and say, for example, "I don't know what I'll do if you vote for a sales tax increase." How will I be able to manage the increased expense? And because Landis had met so many constituents during the campaign, the question was "immediate and personal," he said. "Later on, the relationship was more arm's length." He would receive checks from special interests and endorsements from groups he didn't even know. He never felt that same intense personal connection again.

"That's both a virtue and a vice," he said.

Don Wesely remembers seeing the same changes during his two decades in the legislature, from 1978 to 1998. During his first term, he said, he responded as quickly as possible to his constituents' concerns. But after he was reelected the first time and from there on, he began to focus more on the bigger picture, balancing his responsibilities to his district with those to the state. "Some never grow out of that constituent focus," Wesely said, and having only one chance to run for reelection may intensify that trend.

"The first time I ran, it was about my hopes and dreams, what I wanted to accomplish. Then you run for reelection, and it's about the incumbent," an incumbent with a legislative record to defend. Someone who successfully defends that record and is reelected develops a strength that allows him or her to shift focus toward the bigger picture, to take more chances. Each reelection intensifies that move toward a broader perspective, Wesely said. Senators who are allowed to run for reelection only once can't take advantage of that effect and may, instead, continue their close attention to their own district and constituents through their entire eight years.

So, national studies to the contrary, perhaps a new senator in Nebraska is a more responsive senator. Bill Lock has been a staff member at the unicameral most of the past thirty-five years, and he finds it interesting that Norris and the other unicameral sponsors promoted their model legislature as one that would be both more responsive *and* more responsible.

Lock thinks the body is still plenty responsive to the people. He also thinks it's possible for an elected body to be overly responsive. It's possible to "just do what a small group of completely interested people want you to do" without enough consideration for how a policy will fit into the long-term strategy for good government for the entire state. "It's easier to be responsible when you have more experience," Lock said.

A 2002 survey of legislators asked them to agree or disagree with the statement "As a state senator, I listen(ed) to my constituents' opinions and ideas when making my decisions about laws and policy." That year, 95 percent agreed "strongly" or "somewhat" with the statement. A 2010 survey of senators who had served since 2002 asked the senators to rank themselves on the same scale, and forty of the forty-one respondents—98 percent—agreed either "strongly" or "somewhat," not a significant difference. Although term limits proponents said one advantage to quick turnover and new faces in a legislature would be more responsiveness to the people, it looks as if Nebraska legislators have always listened carefully to their constituents or, at least, are reluctant to admit it if they do not.

Or course, not every constituent will bother to get in touch with his or her senator. It's the few most attentive and outspoken constituents who are likely to make their voices heard. And a senator who knows he will be around no longer than eight years may feel rushed to pursue legislation his constituents are pushing, legislation that may address high-profile issues that draw headlines and provide quick returns instead of long-term benefits.[19] The shorter-run perspective imposed by term limits may lead to weaker public policy—and it may actually reduce the amount of leverage constituents have over their senators by denying use of reelection as an incentive to keep the representatives politically responsive.[20]

Thus far in Nebraska, it looks as if the results are mixed. Both survey data and close observers indicate that members of the unicameral continue to pay attention to their districts, something George Norris would applaud. But if, over time, that responsiveness makes it harder for legislators to draft good statewide policy, Norris would probably shake his head over the irresponsibility of such a legislature.

Balancing Power

Independence from the governor was one thing the reformers of 1934 didn't really push as they set out to sell the idea of a new legislative institution, but many legislative observers and participants today say maintaining that independence is one of their biggest concerns. An increase in the power of the executive branch was the item most often cited by survey respondents and interviewees as the biggest early effect of term limits in Nebraska.

Norris and his compatriots wanted a strong legislature, but when they campaigned for the new structure in 1934, they often found themselves defending the elimination of a second house by reminding folks that the governor would still be around to provide a check on the legislative branch. But some critics of the unicameral proposal saw it differently. They said a one-house body would be at the mercy of the governor, who possessed patronage, the power of publicity, and popular appeal. Already in the 1930s, the influence of the executive at all levels of government was becoming obvious—and was a concern to some who feared the balance of power was shifting away from the legislative branch.

John Senning, chairman of the political science department at the University of Nebraska and one of the major planners and promoters of the proposed new system, shared some of the critics' concerns on that point. He thought the legislature had lost power to the governor during the 1920s and '30s and said the new system might provide a better balance between the two branches. He said the new system would be so much simpler and more transparent that it would be harder for the governor to shift blame to the legislature. And that, Senning said, would give the direct representatives of the people as much power as is held by the chief executive.

Power in the legislature, the people's branch, was the essence of democracy, Senning said.[21] Ernie Chambers, who served thirty-eight years in the unicameral, told the *Omaha World-Herald* much the same thing in August 2010. The judiciary and executive branches, Chambers said, *serve* the people, but "only the legislature *represents* the people." Chambers said that is why setting term limits on legislators is "profoundly different from and of greater consequence than term-limiting executive officers."[22]

Robert Cochrane, who was governor when Nebraska made the switch to the nonpartisan, one-house body, said before the 1937 session that he wasn't worried that the absence of political parties would make much difference in how he worked with the legislature. At the end of the session, though, he saw things differently. For one thing, he complained that the senators had passed an appropriations bill significantly higher than what he recommended. He said the governor had become simply "advisory" when it came to budget matters.[23]

It only became harder for successive governors over the years. No longer could the executive work through the legislative leaders of his or her party to direct legislation through the system. Without party structure and party discipline in the body, partisan appeals or threats had little or no effect. The only real clout left to a governor was the veto, something many governors have tried with mixed success. Often the vetoes stand, but sometimes the legislature overrides, as it did with some high-profile appropriations and revenue vetoes in 2002 and 2003 and with several prominent vetoes in 2012.

With the advent of term limits, though, power may be returning to the governor's office. In fact, the increased influence of the governor was cited frequently in the open-ended questions on the 2010 survey about what the unicameral does poorly or what it could improve. Nine of the forty-one respondents suggested in one way or another that the executive branch's influence has grown since term limits took effect—and that such a shift in power is not a good thing.

Joel Johnson was a senator from 2002 to 2008. In his survey answers, he drew a direct connection between the legislature's loss of historical knowledge and increased executive power. When newcomers don't have long-timers to go to for information and advice, "the senators then rely on the governor's office; therefore, the legislature becomes the weakest link in a three-part government. The governor's office becomes much stronger," Johnson wrote in comments that were echoed by other respondents.

Cap Dierks served twice in the legislature, once before (1986–2002) and again after term limits (2006–10). Simple inexperience among senators has added to the imbalance between the two branches, he said. "It takes a while to know which door to knock on, which knob to turn," Dierks said. "With new people having to learn the ropes, that puts more influence or power in hands of the exec branch." Tom Carlson, the senator who introduced the failed 2012 constitutional amendment to extend the number of terms from two to three, said much the same thing.

Studies of term limits' effects in other states support that idea. A 2000 study writes: "It may be that the influence lost by elected legislators is being widely and unevenly redistributed, with the governor gaining most."[24] Nearly all of the more than twenty-five legislative participants or observers interviewed for this introduction volunteered the same thing. When asked what they saw as benefits and costs of term limits thus far, both former and current senators, lobbyists, and people of both parties often said the balance of power has shifted from the legislative to the executive branch.

The governor himself admits that lots of people seem to think his office has gained power as term limits decrease the collective experience in the legislature, but he said in a 2011 interview that he doesn't see it that way. The governor's strength is to suggest the right policies, policies people want to support, Heineman said. "When I articulate those policies with proposals in the legislature, that tends to pass. If I'm in sync with the citizens, we're likely to get things done."

But the governor's view is the minority view. Most participants and close observers say the executive branch has gained power. The most frequent reason cited in support of that shift is the lack of experience among state senators who are not permitted to have more than eight years in office. The imbalance evidences itself in a number of ways.

For one thing, executives have more access to and control over information and the technical expertise of the state government bureaucracy. If information is power, the executive has an abundance of it compared to the legislature. New senators have relatively few resources to help them get up to speed on every new issue that confronts them. A governor—even a relatively inexperienced governor—has far more resources at her disposal and will be more quickly prepared to negotiate effectively with the legislature.[25] That imbalance of knowledge and resources can intimidate a new legislator who has not yet gained the confidence that comes with experience.

Mike Gloor, elected to the unicameral in 2008, made exactly that point: Power has shifted away from the legislature to the executive branch, "where the knowledge and information resides."

For another thing, the executive branch is a unitary and united institution; even a small legislature like Nebraska's is not. Senator Kathy Campbell, elected in 2008, noted that the governor has always had a bully pulpit from which to try to influence legislators and the public but added, "That's even more true now."

Legislative leadership is a primary way a body comes together as an institution, but the norms of leadership are weakened in a term-limited body. Inexperienced lawmakers tend to show less respect to committee chairs and other leaders, knowing that those folks haven't been around much longer than they themselves.[26] Against a relatively uninformed and often divided legislature—which Senator Gloor described as trying to get "forty-nine falcons to fly in formation"—an executive can often get his way. Studies show that term-limited legislators challenge fewer items in a governor's budget and ask fewer questions of statewide agencies than do their less restricted counterparts.[27]

That's exactly what appears to have happened in the 2011 budget negotiations. Governor Dave Heineman's proposed budget passed with nary a skirmish, much less any kind of pitched battle. Some of the apparent amicability in 2011 may have been a result of an Appropriations Committee membership that Speaker Mike Flood described as conservative and ideologically inclined to fall in line with the conservative governor regarding budgets and spending. But scholarly studies of term-limited legislatures have found similar results: Such legislatures play a diminished role in crafting the state's budget because inexperienced legislators are "less politically canny" and inclined to give up more ground to the executive.[28] Whatever the reasons in Nebraska in 2011, the situation was far different from the standard in the 1990s, when long-time Appropriations chair Jerome Warner said that, when it came to budgets, "the governor proposes but the legislature disposes."[29]

Lowen Kruse isn't happy that Warner's quote no longer holds up. He says it is proper and helpful that the governor works with his agency heads to prepare a budget for the legislature to consider. "But *we* are the ones who hold the public hearings and debate the thing and hear from the public," Kruse said. "Any governor fears that process." In recent years, though, Kruse thinks the governor has had less to fear.

The governor himself agrees that turnover in the legislature has helped him negotiate a budget to his liking. The people in office now are "willing to take a second look," Heineman said. That may have been less likely when the unicameral included some long-serving leaders, he added.

Under term limits, even the legislative leaders—themselves inexperienced—may be unwilling to take on the governor. They, too, have less access to information than the executive and, as a result, less information to pass along to their colleagues as they try to lead policy development.[30] While the vast majority of survey respondents indicated they believe legislative leaders like committee chairs and the speaker help the body reach its goals, many of those positions in today's unicameral have been filled by members with four or sometimes just two years of experience. While their positions may confer additional gravitas, they still are likely to be less informed and knowledgeable than the governor they are expected to complement but sometimes also confront.

In the early days of term limits' effects in Nebraska, though, leadership apparently has been less a problem than it might have been. One after another of the sources interviewed for this introduction volunteered that Mike Flood, elected to the legislature in 2004 and elected speaker in 2006, 2008, and again in 2010, was a strong force both within the body and against the executive. "He's the guardian of this branch," Senator Campbell said in a 2011 interview, sometimes bluntly counseling his colleagues that a particular action or procedure they are pondering will strengthen the executive and asking the senators to consider carefully whether they want to do that. Of course, Flood's leadership was lost at the end of 2012, when he reached the end of his second term in the unicameral.

Greg Adams, Flood's successor as speaker, had served six years before taking that leadership post—considerably more than Flood himself when he became speaker. But Adams had the opportunity to put his experience to work for only two years before term limits would force him from the legislature in 2014. Flood was something of an anomaly; almost no senator has been elected speaker who had not served at least four years in the legislature, which means no speaker is likely to occupy the body's highest leadership post for more than four years before being term-limited from office.

Additionally, as Nebraska's political parties become more involved in recruiting people to run for the legislature and helping raise money for their campaigns, the governor, as titular head of his party, has become more involved, too. Newly elected members who are of the same party as the governor—and between thirty and thirty-five members have been Republicans in every session since 2003—may feel obligated to go along with what the governor makes clear he expects. As Senator Campbell said, "Sometimes senators feel more allegiance to a governor who helped them get elected than they do to the institution of the legislature."

Annette Dubas made the same point: "You can assume someone helped you get elected, and there's no free lunch."

Lobbyist Bill Mueller reinforced that notion: "When you try to talk to lots of senators about a bill, [many] say, 'The governor opposes it,' and that's the end of the discussion."

Several senators and observers said they thought the governor's political influence with senators was enhanced by the fact that he is a Republican and a solid majority of senators are also Republicans, making it easier to pass the administration's policies. In addition, Heineman will have been one of Nebraska's longest serving governors, moving up from lieutenant governor in 2004 to fill the last two years of Mike Johanns's term when Johanns took a job in the federal government, then winning election on his own in 2006 and again in 2010. Besides being more experienced than the majority of senators, Heineman is a skilled politician who, multiple sources said, would likely be influential in any setting.

Bill Avery, part of the first wave of post–term limits senators elected in 2006, said Heineman's political acumen definitely helped him shift at least some power from the legislative to the executive branch when about 40 percent of the senators were new. But Avery added that the legislators seemed to find their voices in 2012, overriding vetoes of two bills regarding issues against which Heineman had taken a strong stand: restoring prenatal health care for immigrant women, regardless of their legal status, and allowing municipalities to adopt a local option sales tax. The legislature was not willing simply to roll over and give in to the governor on every high-profile issue.

But the governor's growing influence may still be quite real. It seems safe to say that individuals choose to run for legislative office in the first place because they believe they have something to offer, something that will make their state and its citizens better off. Some may be content to go back to their regular careers after eight years in the unicameral, but others may want to continue in public service. Because they can't run for another house of the legislature, they may consider serving in an appointed position in government. And it may well be the governor who appoints them. The idea of opposing the person who may give them their next career opportunity may make senators less inclined to oppose the governor or his policies.[31] Several Nebraska legislators gave credence to that idea, saying that the governor has declined to reappoint people he believes have not gone along with his policies and directives.

The evidence shows that, for a variety of reasons, the balance of power has begun to shift away from the legislative and toward the executive branch in Nebraska. Certainly, the situation is far from a constitutional crisis, but the effects on the institution of the unicameral bear watching.

"The institution is weakened significantly," said Bill Mueller, who has lobbied the legislature since the early 1980s. He echoes the opinion of scholars and other observers that the governor's office with its staff and agencies has always been powerful but adds that long-time senators were less likely to be intimidated by all of that. "Without the longevity advantage, the legislature as an institution is less powerful."

A number of senators serving in the early years of term limits agreed with that concern for the institution. "The legislature must guard itself as a branch of government," Kathy Campbell said.

The institution is important not because of its members' egos but because a strong legislature is essential to preserving the balance among branches, a balance that Americans for centuries have agreed results in the best public policies. In the years since term limits took effect, Nebraska's governor and legislature seem to have gotten along quite well, said DiAnna Schimek, senator from 1988–2008. "But you don't always get the best policy that way." The debate and argument and give-and-take within the legislature itself and between the legislative and executive branches are integral to developing policies that best serve the people of the state, she said in 2011.

In Nebraska's early years under term limits, the effects of legislative inexperience may have been magnified by the fact that the governor had served longer than the usual two-term limit and that he was a particularly skilled politician. But it seems clear that, for all the reasons discussed above, power has shifted away from the legislative and toward the executive branch.

That was not what George Norris and his fellow unicameralists had in mind. They saw the legislature as the people's branch of government and, thus, to their populist/progressivist way of thinking, the most important branch. They wanted their model legislature to be close to the people and to exercise power on the people's behalf. They would probably lament any shift in power toward the executive branch.

Lobbying Goes On

When Americans express their frustrations with government, the politicians themselves usually come in for the first criticism, but lobbyists are a close second. Citizens mistrust lobbyists as much today as they did in the 1930s, when George Norris promised that a nonpartisan unicameral legislature would help to reduce the influence of special interests. A one-house body with no conference committees and no party apparatus would give lobbyists nowhere to hide, Norris said. In fact, decreasing lobbyists' influence was one of the cornerstones of Norris's campaign for his model legislature.

During the decades since Nebraskans approved the unicameral amendment, the lobby has not gone away. Early sessions of the unicameral restricted lobbyists' access to the legislative chamber, and in 1976 the legislature passed the Accountability and Disclosure Act, mandating that lobbyists make public where they get their money as well as what they spend and on whom. Senators, too, are governed by the act; they are required to make public what they receive and from whom and are prohibited from accepting gifts from lobbyists of more than a certain value. (The amount has been adjusted upward periodically to reflect inflation.)

Much as it may be publicly derided, lobbying is not inherently evil or corrupting. In fact, scholars recognize that lobbies and special interests represent the legitimate interests of ordinary people—often in conflict with other legitimate interests of other ordinary people.[32] Information is lobbyists' stock in trade. Their goal is to influence politicians to support or oppose legislation important to the folks who hire them, and they foster that influence by providing information that helps educate a senator about the issue in question. Yes, lobbyists may wine and dine legislators. They may spend money to support campaigns and hope that such support will incline a legislator to be sympathetic to their goals—or, at least, to listening to what they have to say. As noted in chapter 6, lobbyists concentrate on building relationships of trust with legislators. Nothing is likely to go a lobbyist's way if a senator does not trust what the lobbyist has to say.

Supporters of term limits said regular legislative turnover would prevent senators from becoming cozy with lobbyists.[33] Opponents said new, inexperienced legislators would lean more heavily on the lobby for information, would be more easily influenced.[34] Studies of term-limited legislatures, though, have found little statistical difference in lobby influence between states with and those without term limits.[35] Comments from senators and lobbyists interviewed for this introduction tend to support that notion.

Asked to identify which sources they rely on most heavily for information as they develop and advance legislation, survey respondents elected before and after term limits both ranked lobbyists as relatively unimportant—well below their own experience and personal knowledge, their constituents, staff, and other legislators (see table B). That appears to be similar to what happened in other states. For example, a 2006 story in *The Economist* noted that after term limits took effect in Ohio, "many of the new politicians would not even meet with lobbyists for the first few months. But eventually they tended to give in."[36]

In interviews, a number of senators said they think the lobby still has considerable influence in the unicameral, although the level of influence may not have changed much since term limits took effect. Lowen Kruse, who served from 2000–2008, said lobbyists' campaign contributions make them influential and give them access to senators. But he added that he never thought a lobbyist had been dishonest with him. He "learned everybody has an interest group. It's not necessarily bad."

Governor Heineman said it's likely the lobby is more influential than it was twenty years ago, partly because issues have become increasingly complex. Echoing Kruse's observation, he added, "Everybody has an interest group," representing a particular point of view.

Kathy Campbell said special interest influence may have increased simply because senators need a lot of information and need it in a hurry: "In the past, you could have dug stuff out for yourself more." Now, it may be easier to rely on lobbyists to provide background and facts.

And those facts had better be accurate. Lobbyists know that if they deliberately provide misleading or false information, senators will never listen to them again. As a result, even someone like Cap Dierks, who deplores the pressure lobbyists can bring to bear on an issue, respects them for the information they provide—on both sides of the issue if a senator asked for that. Tony Fulton, who served from 2007–2012, said much the same thing: "If a lobbyist can give you the other side of the argument, too, you can trust him more."

Mike Gloor said he thinks lobbying is more effective when so many senators are newcomers. "Knowledge is power," he said. Gathering that knowledge during the heat of the legislative session is difficult, Bill Avery said. The pace is frantic, and any senator—much less a relatively new one—has trouble learning the issues quickly enough. The senators simply have to rely on lobbyists and staff for information.

But lobbyists see things very differently. They say term limits have made it infinitely harder to build relationships with senators, and it's those relationships that make lobbying effective. Bill Mueller said new senators are more suspicious of lobbyists and less likely to listen to the information they offer. "They don't have to believe or accept what they're told, but they won't listen." Too many newcomers think listening to someone explain the other side of a question is "a weakness."

Don Wesely was a state senator from 1978–98 and has been a lobbyist since 2004. "Lobbying is built on relationships," Wesely said, "and they don't happen overnight." Building those new relationships takes a great deal of time and effort, and Wesely and others noted that several long-time lobbyists retired after 2006 rather than put in the time and effort needed to build relationships with large batches of new senators. Of course, plenty of veteran lobbyists remain.

Wesely pointed out that, like him, a number of other former senators now lobby. "The lobby is the group with the most experience," Wesely said, "but the lobby is not stronger" than it used to be. He said current senators do ask questions and use the institutional memory the former-senators-turned-lobbyists can provide. "But the power has not shifted." Today, because they haven't yet developed relationships with lobbyists, senators often look at the information the lobbyist provides as just one more factor to consider, no more or less helpful than information from any other source, Wesely said.

Herb Schimek, who lobbied for the Nebraska State Education Association from 1974–2009, agrees with Mueller and Wesely that lobbying has gotten harder since the advent of the term limits effect. He chalks up some of the problem to new members' tendency to be suspicious of lobbyists and their information and some of it to what he sees as an increase in partisanship. The latter means that, on some issues, some senators simply don't want to hear anything at all from a representative of an organization they associate with the "other" party.

Historically, one prime source of information for new senators has been their veteran colleagues, the relatively few people who had served three terms or sometimes more. Senators still tend to ask their colleagues for information and help, but today none of them has much experience, either. "To an extent, it's the blind leading the blind," Bill Mueller said. In general, he said, the quality of legislators is high, but people new to a complicated process and a complicated set of issues "don't even know what they don't know."

The absence of veterans has, indeed, made a difference, said Dave Landis, a state senator from 1978–2006. With so much to absorb, new senators have to defer some learning to others, and lobbyists are often the first source of information. But then "there are no veterans to turn to after you hear from the lobby," Landis said. Colleagues used to help each other even if they disagreed, even if they were from different political parties. "You get less of that now."

The change in the lobbying climate since term limits came about has pushed lobbyists to become more involved in election campaigns than they were in the past, said Walt Radcliffe, who has lobbied since 1997. Lobbyists have always been active in campaigns on behalf of their clients, but now, Radcliffe said, he has gotten more involved at the primary campaign level. "That's where the pro–term limits argument falls apart," he said. "People like me will be involved sooner and with more resources."

Radcliffe and Landis also suggest that the climate at the capitol is a bit less open than it once was. "Significant issues are decided off the floor," Radcliffe said. "People don't have the ability or desire to make reasoned decisions on complex matters," and they may prefer not to seek out more information or to debate that information in open sessions.

Landis said lobbyists become frustrated when they identify ways bills might be improved but senators tell them that the decision is already made. "They've moved away from floor debate to a less public space" for making decisions, Landis said. And once the agreement is made, they prefer not to stir things up by adding more ideas to the pot.

Bill Mueller made the same observation. "Even when we agreed with the intent of a bill, we couldn't get them to clean up the language"—to make it clearer and be sure it reflected the legislators' intent.

Overall, the effect of term limits on lobbyists' power and influence seems to be a wash. On the one hand, senators seem to need lobbyists and their information more than ever. On the other hand, it takes more than just a few years for lobbyists to build relationships of trust with senators. When so many senators are new, the lobbyists' efforts are diffused, and any gains in relevance are pretty well wiped out by the losses in relationships. The fact that so many lobbyists are frustrated by the situation would probably be just fine with George Norris, who was reacting to the cozy deals and even outright corruption that characterized much of lobbying in his day. But it may not be an optimal situation for a legislator who needs to learn a lot and learn it fast.

In short, institutional structure and function affect policy. Just as Norris promised that the institutional switch to a nonpartisan unicameral would have an effect on policy for the people of Nebraska, the institutional change that denies legislators the opportunity to build experience and make a career in the body has had an effect on how policy is made.

Leadership: Equality versus Efficiency

The constitutional amendment that created the unicameral set up its broad structure, but the senators who met in the first session in 1937 established its fine points. Mindful either consciously or instinctively of the populist ideal of the unity of the people, the Rules Committee set up a system whereby no senator would have much more power or influence than any other. Under those early rules, the speaker was merely a figurehead. Committee chairs had a little more authority, largely because they were able to develop expertise in the topics that were the focus of their committees, but even they were relatively weak.

Theoretically, it sounded great. In practice, it rapidly became unwieldy. Over the years, as the workload got heavier and the issues more complex, the legislature was forced to increase the power of its leaders. Committee chairs and the executive board became somewhat more influential, but the position that changed most was that of speaker.

For decades, the speaker did not set the unicameral's agenda; bills were simply considered in the order in which they were reported from committees to the floor. It wasn't until the 1970s and then the mid-1990s that the senators decided to grant the speaker power to control the calendar and agenda, to decide in what order bills would be considered and the order of amendments and motions filed during debate. Even so, the speaker still cannot demand that the legislature cease debate and vote on a bill, only that senators set one debate aside temporarily while picking up another. The speaker also may designate some bills as "super priorities," bills guaranteed to be debated and considered and not lost in the legislative stampede. However, his super priorities must be chosen from among the bills already set by other senators as their own priority bills.

When the senators increased the speaker's power in 1996, their debates indicated an instinctive understanding that they were giving up some equality for the sake of the efficiency the new rules were designed to enhance. The debate reflected the populists' distrust of elitism; senators only reluctantly allowed the speaker to become a bit more elite, recognizing that leadership is essential if a legislature is to have a chance of dealing with all the business confronting it.

Term limits, too, have been touted as a populist notion, allowing no senator to develop much more experience than any other, keeping everyone on more equal footing than in the days when a few senators served twenty years or more and held leadership positions for many of those years. The unicameral still has a speaker, executive board, and standing committee system, but the people elected to those posts often bring with them minimal legislative experience—because the term limits law gives them no choice.

After the 2006 election, the first affected by term limits, the unicameral had a new speaker—Mike Flood, elected to the legislature just two years earlier. His immediate predecessor had served ten years before becoming speaker; the three speakers before that had each served nine or ten years before taking the leadership post. Despite his inexperience as he entered the office, Flood would become the first speaker in the legislature's history to serve three two-year terms before being forced out of office by term limits at the end of 2012. Also elected in 2006 were new chairs of twelve of the fourteen standing committees. Four of the new chairs had been elected to the legislature just two years before, in 2004. Two were elected in 2002 and three in 2000. By contrast, the reorganization after the previous election—in 2004—had resulted in a new speaker, who had been elected in 1994, and new chairs of five standing committees: two elected in 2002, one in 2000, one in 1998, and one in 1992.

After the 2008 election, nine committee chairs and the chair of the executive board were new. The speaker and five committee chairs were reelected to additional two-year terms. After the 2010 election, the leadership stabilized considerably. The speaker and eleven committee chairs were reelected; only three committee chairs were new, as was the chair of the executive board.

By 2010, no senator serving in a leadership position had more than six years of service in the legislature. Two of the new chairs in 2010 had been elected just two years before. After the 2012 election, the situation was somewhat reversed: while the speaker and nine of the committee chairs were new to their leadership positions, six of the committee chairs had served in the legislature four years, but the speaker and two chairs had served six years. The norms that had generally assured that a senator had substantial experience in office and was a "senior" member with at least eight years of service before taking a leadership post had no alternative but to change. Senator Tom Carlson laments that term limits mean turning people out of their leadership posts just when they can become most effective.

Of course, the unicameral's small size provides opportunities for plenty of senators to serve in leadership positions. With fourteen standing committees, a speaker, and a chair of the executive board, sixteen senators—almost a third of the total body—can and must hold elected leadership posts at any one time. In the past, almost no one would be elected to fill those positions during her first term in office or even two years later, the next time the body would reorganize. Since term limits have taken effect, though, senators can find themselves leading a committee or even serving as speaker after just two years—or certainly four years—on the job.

The 2010 survey of current and former legislators supports the notion that expectations are different. Forty percent of the respondents who were first elected before 2006 said eight years were required before someone could be counted as a "senior" member of the unicameral, although 35 percent said four years were enough. The remainder indicated more than eight years were necessary. Of the respondents elected in 2006 or after, 82 percent said four years were sufficient, reflecting the reality of limited terms.

Those responding to the survey did agree that leadership is important to the institution. Nearly all the respondents elected before or after 2006 agreed strongly or somewhat that committee chairs help the body achieve legislative goals. A strong majority also agreed that members of the legislature should specialize, developing policy expertise in a specific area or areas. That is a time-honored way of becoming a leader,[37] especially in the nonpartisan unicameral, where party hierarchy—the only sure way to leadership in most partisan bodies—doesn't exist.

But the confines of term limits can reduce legislators' incentives to specialize, to invest the necessary time to become experts and leaders, scholars say. In many term-limited bodies, studies have found that by the time a legislator has enough expertise to take a leadership role, she is often in her last term.[38] That has not always been the case in Nebraska, however, where a number of senators with only two years of experience have been elected to leadership positions. Perhaps the specific way term limits took effect here, eliminating nearly half the body in the 2006 election, was a primary reason behind the meteoric rise of some leaders. The same number of seats will be empty in 2014, so it may be that seniority and leadership will be somewhat cyclical over time and become particularly salient when the twenty-member cohort departs every eight years. Fifteen seats were vacated by term-limited members in 2008 and two in 2010. (Five seats would have come open because of term limits, but three senators who would have been prevented from running again had already left the legislature.)

Other studies find that leaders in term-limited institutions are working hard, are doing a pretty good job, and are influential players in the chamber. But they are not as powerful as their predecessors because limited time in office means limited knowledge and expertise and, thus, limited influence.[39]

Joel Johnson, who saw term limits take effect in the middle of his two terms, has a different point of view. He thinks the unicameral's committee chairs are actually more influential now. Senators elected to those positions are "at least thought to be the ones who understand the system and the needs of the state best," he said. He pointed out that even though Republicans have always had about a two-to-one advantage over Democrats in the officially nonpartisan body and could, if they wanted to, stack all the leadership posts with Republicans, that hasn't happened. Instead, the ratio of Republicans to Democrats in leadership positions has been about the same two-to-one distribution over the years with an occasional lopsided ratio in favor of the Republicans—or even the other way around. In 2012, the legislature's thirty registered Republicans, seventeen Democrats, and two independents elected five Republicans, eight Democrats, and one independent to committee chairmanships, reinforcing Johnson's assertion that the members are really trying to elect leaders with the most expertise and ability.

Plenty of senators appear to be eager to fill that need. With only four years in office guaranteed and eight years the most to be hoped for, newly elected senators waste no time. "There's a real rush to acquire leadership positions," said Don Walton, *Lincoln Journal-Star* reporter and columnist and longtime observer of state government and politics. Ambitious members move quickly to take the lead.

Former senator Marian Price said she sees members scrambling for committee chairmanships. "There's a frenzy to make your place in the legislature," she said, adding, "Term limits gives the process an air of desperation."

Senators know they won't be around long, so they need to be fast starters and make an impression early, said Senator Mike Gloor. Despite general collegiality among the senators, "We're not around long enough to develop a real comfort level with each other," Gloor said. "You could be a brilliant person, but no one figures it out for four to five years—or a blithering idiot and no one figures that out, either." So choosing leaders is a bit of a risk.

Even with its populist emphasis on the equality of all its members, the unicameral has a generally strong committee system, made more so by the absence of political party caucuses and party discipline. Every bill is referred to a committee, and that committee must give every bill a hearing before deciding whether—and in what form—to send the bill to the full legislature. While the chairs are granted automatic authority by virtue of being elected to their positions, committee members are also expected to pull their weight and provide leadership within the committee.

"Leadership is distributed," Senator Kathy Campbell said. No one, including committee chairs, has the time to develop expertise in every area. Several other senators made the same point. "You can take the lead even if you're not a chair," thanks to the egalitarian unicameral system, Senator Annette Dubas said.

Scholars say a legislature with a strong committee system relies heavily on stability and members' experience for creating and retaining expertise in their jurisdictional area. When term limits force consistent churn in committee membership, the decrease in experience can translate into a decrease in expertise. Both members and chairs are less knowledgeable about the issues and about general legislative procedures and may also be less concerned about fine-tuning legislation, which is considered a standard committee role.[40] Experience doesn't just confer authority and power; it also makes legislators more effective.[41]

Whether or not they are as effective as they might be, committees are still the place where the fundamentals of policy are hammered out in the unicameral. Committee chairs can be influential within the committee by virtue of their convening and scheduling authority and in the body at large because they usually speak on behalf of the committee. Senators say some chairs have more power than others because of the subject matter with which their group deals. The "money" committees, for example—Appropriations and Revenue—tend to have the most influence and their chairs the most clout. Beyond the authority granted by the institutional structure and rules, though, today's committee chair's influence is a function of the person's abilities and personality, according to senators Mike Gloor and Deb Fischer in 2011 interviews. That has undoubtedly always been part of the equation, but with term limits removing the opportunity for a chair to develop lengthy experience and expertise, it may be that innate abilities and personality play a larger role today.

While committee chairs are definitely leaders in the unicameral, it's the speaker who is considered to be the most influential leader. That was especially true of Mike Flood, the first speaker in the body's history to serve three two-year terms in that position. Flood won election to the unicameral in 2004 and served his first two years with people he calls "the last of the long-termers": Kermit Brashear, Ed Schrock, Dave Landis, Pam Brown, and others. "I hardly spoke on the floor for two years," Flood said, but he spent a lot of time with the veterans, learning from them about policymaking and procedures. "It really had a benefit." Even so, Flood said he worried about taking on the speaker's job after only two years in the legislature. He was moving quickly into a position with growing influence.

After the rules changes of the mid-1990s officially gave the speaker more power, some subsequent speakers found ways to enhance that power unofficially, through norms and procedures. For example, Flood said, Kermit Brashear, speaker during the 2005–6 session, confronted a legislative bottleneck; in the process of unstopping it, he also increased the power of the speaker's office.

The problem was related to priority bills and the way bills were ordered to be debated on the legislative floor. Most years, Flood explained, the speaker set a date on which he would begin accepting priority designations—and he would find senators lined up down the hall outside his door way before 8 a.m. on that date. Priority bills were designated for consideration in the order in which they were received, and many senators wanted to be sure their bills would be considered early. It could be that a bill was still in committee at the time a senator designated it his or her priority; in that case, it would be inserted into the list in its "designated spot" once it was reported out of committee and after a three-day waiting period.

Senators whose priority bills were likely to be controversial got in line to be early on the designation list so their bills would be ensured debate whenever they got out of committee. "For instance," Flood said, "a bill like concealed carry or motorcycle helmet repeal would not get out of committee right away but could jump to the top of the list of priority bills once it was advanced out of committee." That could hold up more routine bills indefinitely, to the frustration of those bills' sponsors.

To make matters worse: "We could be close to debating one of those noncontroversial bills, and a major 'show stopper' could get out of committee and jump in front of a bill that had been shown on the agenda for days," Flood said. "And since there was only one list, holding up bills ten, eleven, and twelve would impact when bill thirteen was debated and provided an incentive to drag out debate on noncontroversial measures if a senator strongly opposed a later bill."

In order to streamline the process, Brashear created multiple lists of "divisions" with four bills or fewer in each; no bill could be held up by any more than the few bills ahead of it in the division. If a particular bill within a division ran into trouble on the floor, the speaker could move that division to a different slot on the agenda, Flood said.

Brashear's new procedure did not require a change in the rules, and it became part of the speaker's routine way of managing legislative business. Flood said he continued that process and added some new procedures of his own. "You can do new things now," he said. "It's a new era."

Perhaps because individual senators are too new to have developed expertise in policy areas or procedures or to have developed strong working relationships with their colleagues, they appear to have gravitated toward a capable speaker, virtually inviting Flood to take on additional power. For example, in 2010 Senator Lavon Heidemann, chair of the Appropriations Committee, proposed creation of an ad hoc committee to address the possible 10 percent budget shortfall the legislature was anticipating. The committee, to be chaired by the speaker and composed of the Executive Board members plus the chairs of the fourteen standing committees, would direct a major effort to review all state government programs. Each committee was charged with finding potential cuts within its subject-matter jurisdiction, identifying programs that would be considered for reduction or elimination during the legislature's 2011 budget debate.

At first, Flood said, he had qualms about the special committee itself and about making the speaker the chair. But because of the serious budget problems the legislature was about to face, he agreed to the plan. And it worked, he said.

But when two resolutions came along in 2011 proposing the creation of similar groups that the speaker would lead, Flood dissuaded the sponsors from moving forward with their plans. "The speaker here is not a 'quarterback' like the speaker in some other states. I don't decide what the budget cuts should be," he said. "But in this era of term limits, the members ask the speaker to handle a lot of things."

Sometimes Flood's job was to protect the institution from itself. For example, some senators floated a plan to form task forces on particular issues, task forces that would include members from the executive branch and the judicial branch, an agency head, and a senator. "That's letting the other branches decide policy. It's a breach of our sovereign authority." Flood said a firm no to that one, and the proposal was dropped.

But the speaker understood that a leader in the egalitarian unicameral has to be careful how he exercises his authority. "It's not my call to make decrees for the legislature," he said. "That's the province of the committees. If a speaker is seen as horning in on committees' power, you're done."

Ron Withem, himself a former speaker and now a lobbyist, had high praise for Flood's leadership but noted that the legislators, unfamiliar with the rules, are willing to give the speaker more authority than he really has according to legislative rules. That was fine as long as Flood was in the office. However, as Withem cautioned in a 2011 interview, "Mike hasn't used that to punish people, but the next speaker may not be so altruistic."

Patrick O'Donnell, the longtime clerk of the legislature, agreed that the speaker's office grew stronger under Flood. "He's the go-to guy" for the other members, O'Donnell said in 2011. "He's done well. The next speaker may not."

Flood was conscious of the conflict between willingness, ability, and opportunity to lead—not to mention demands by members that he do so—and the populist intentions behind the legislature. If he took advantage of the situation in which he found himself, "the speaker would be in ten years what George Norris never wanted," he said: a powerful elite in what was intended to be a body of powerful equals.

So committee chairmanships go to inexperienced senators and turn over frequently, but there's little evidence at this point to determine whether the chairs are more or less influential than chairs who served longer both in the legislature itself and as leaders. Regarding the speaker, though, the evidence seems clearer. Rather than weakening the speaker's office, term limits in Nebraska, at least at first, promoted a strong speaker who was asked to provide more and more leadership in a body of relative novices. Part of it may be attributable to the personality of the man who was speaker during the first six years after term limits took effect, but it is unlikely that all the additional influence that accrued to the office during Flood's tenure will slip away again under his successors.

A slightly different problem arises at the other end of the two-term limit. In Nebraska, where they are limited to only two terms, senators become lame ducks in their second four years. By the time leaders have begun to build the expertise and knowledge that allows them to be most effective, they're on their way out the door. Some studies have found that lame duck leaders are weakened by the fact that their colleagues know they soon will be gone and, thus, see few long-term consequences from offending or not cooperating with the leaders.[42]

And the lame ducks themselves may be looking for their next job and not focusing intently on the business of the legislature.[43] As Bill Avery observed, the situation "affects how they legislate." Depending on just how that plays out, some term limits proponents would be happy to hear it. After all, removing the chance to run for another term was designed to also remove political pressures and encourage officials to think bigger and smarter.

Pat O'Donnell, the legislature's clerk, said he hasn't seen evidence of that. "The shackles of their districts have not been lifted," he said. Even those who won't be able to run again for the unicameral are caught up in the election cycle, especially if they aspire to be leaders. "Today, political consequences are first and foremost in their minds" as senators shape policy.

In California, which adopted legislative term limits in 1990, the chair of the Republican Party said lame duck status has hurt good policymaking. It has given rise to a "get out of town" budget, Bob Naylor said in a 2010 newspaper interview, a budget made by people who know they will be out of office before the budget takes effect and who won't be held accountable.[44]

Senator Deb Fischer said that hasn't happened in Nebraska. She said in 2011 that she continued to work during the session and between sessions just as she did before she won a second term, and she thought her colleagues were doing the same. "Most people are still out serving their districts," she said, even when they know those constituents can't vote to reelect them and that the policies they make now often won't really affect their constituents until after the senators are out of office. It remains to be seen whether that attention to voters and to good policy will continue over time as lame duck status becomes institutionalized.

Term limits are designed to eliminate seniority, to cut all legislators down to approximately the same size in the belief that such equality will allow for policies more likely to serve the entire state rather than specific districts. In Nebraska, though, equality is already enshrined in the unicameral via its institutional structure and its rules and norms. Granted, committee chairs and the speaker have gradually gained additional influence over the decades, and those who manage quickly to acquire knowledge and expertise on particular subjects can be particularly influential. But compared to leaders in states with large, partisan legislatures, the unicameral's leaders are on a short leash. Term limits in Nebraska appear to have had mixed effects on leadership. Logically, inexperience may have made committee chairs somewhat less influential, but the need for someone to provide guidance and direction appears to have made them somewhat stronger—and made the speaker considerably stronger—at least for the time being.

Partying in the Nonpartisan Unicameral

The idea of moving from two houses to one was one item Norris had to sell when he set out to change Nebraska's legislative structure in 1934. Nonpartisanship was another and more difficult item to deal with. Even those who served with Norris on the committee to restructure the legislature weren't enthusiastic about the nonpartisan idea and were afraid it would sink the entire amendment. It did not, of course.

Scholars, though, often have criticized nonpartisanship. For one thing, it removes party labels from the ballot, depriving voters of a piece of information that might make their vote choice easier.[45] For another, lack of party structure within the legislature means no easily organized voting coalitions and a greater degree of uncertainty about how issues will be decided, as a 2002 study points out: "It seems almost as though each bill is considered anew rather than in the context of established sides and coalitions. Rather than having a partisan/ideological cleavage to block out other possible bases for division, members can, and apparently do, focus on any aspect that strikes them."[46]

Somehow, that sounds like a perfectly fine idea to most Nebraskans. Legislative scholars may criticize nonpartisanship, but Nebraskans themselves remain devoted to it. A solid majority of citizens surveyed in 2000 opposed the idea of returning to a partisan body, and a solid majority of current and former senators surveyed in 2010 said the same thing. So did every person interviewed for this introduction—current and former senators, lobbyists, legislative observers, and the governor—although one or two senators and the governor said going back to a partisan legislature might be something to consider in the future. And even though Nebraskans realize that their senators do belong to political parties, citizens and senators who responded to both the 2000 and 2010 surveys said they believe the legislature gets more done without party labels. "In partisan legislatures, [governing] is a sport. That's not true here," said lobbyist Bill Mueller in a 2011 interview.

If term limits have made a difference to partisanship in the legislature, it has, thus far, been a subtle change. No informal party caucuses have formed. The speaker has not become the leader of his party in the legislature. One increase in partisanship that observers do point out goes back to the perceived increase in the governor's influence on new and inexperienced senators. Some see it as fairly blatant, others as fairly benign.

"I haven't sensed any party pressure to vote a certain way," Senator Kathy Campbell said. She added that the governor did tell senators, on a couple of issues during the 2011 session, what he thought they should do. "But it wasn't couched in party politics."

Perhaps the governor did not specifically tell his fellow Republicans to vote with him because of their shared political affiliation, but "Heineman tells people how to vote more than other governors I've worked with," noted Pat O'Donnell, the legislature's clerk. "If he doesn't like something, he's quick to get on the phone" and let a senator know.

Heineman's expectations of cooperation from his fellow Republicans became clear in fall 2012. Just a year earlier, in October 2011, Heinemann had appointed Paul Lambert to fill out the term of a senator who had resigned. When Lambert ran for election to the seat in 2012, Heineman actually endorsed Lambert's opponent, saying the freshman senator had lost his trust by voting to override the governor's May 2012 veto of a bill that allowed municipalities to levy an additional half-cent sales tax.

Heineman said that, before he appointed Lambert, he asked him twice whether he would oppose that bill, and Lambert had agreed both times that he would do so. But Lambert ultimately voted in favor of the bill and to override Heinman's veto because, the senator said, the bill turned out to be different from what the governor had originally asked him about. What the legislature actually passed includes a provision requiring a vote of the people before a city can increase its sales taxes.[47] Heineman was not favorably impressed by the new senator's independence, and he campaigned actively against him in 2012. The governor succeeded; Lambert was not elected.

Partisanship comes up most often in campaigns where parties, sometimes led by the governor, raise funds and line up endorsements for candidates who are members of the party even though that label won't show up on the ballot to elect senators to the unicameral. Scholars say that is exactly the way party influence has grown in other term-limited legislatures, all of which are partisan to begin with. Parties in states with term limits are more active in recruiting candidates, and campaign contributions channeled through the political parties increased dramatically after term limits.[48]

Lobbyist Walt Radcliffe said he's seen that trend in Nebraska. Knowing for certain when a seat will come open gives parties a chance to recruit and start to raise funds for candidates earlier. "Term limits contribute to the defeat of the nonpartisan legislature," Radcliffe said.

Lobbyist Bill Mueller agreed and added that he thinks party support during a campaign spills over to how people govern. "After all, [the party] are the people who got you here."

Nearly everyone interviewed agreed with Radcliffe and Mueller that parties have ramped up their involvement in election campaigns since term limits became state law. Getting elected costs more each year, and the need for more campaign funds would seem to be a logical place for parties to get involved. However, the evidence in the early years of the term-limited legislature indicates very few direct contributions from the Republican or Democratic parties. A number of candidates who ran in 2012 received $500 or $1,000 contributions from other politicians' political action committees: from U.S. Senator Ben Nelson, Governor Dave Heineman, county or city officials, or former members of the legislature. Only a few received money from the parties themselves. Several senators said what they did get from the parties was non-monetary support: the work of volunteers, help motivating supporters to go to the polls, and so forth.

Despite the help parties may provide during elections, Speaker Mike Flood said in 2011 that the parties' campaign support didn't seem to have much effect after the election. "You'd think that would give them influence on senators [during the session], but I haven't seen it."

Cap Dierks, who served both for 15 years before term limits and again from 2006-10, said parties have always been involved in getting senators elected. "But when we got into the session, nobody paid attention to party pressure. We just did what we had to do." In 2012, Paul Lambert was an obvious example of that philosophy—and paid a price for ignoring his governor's and his party's wishes.

In contrast, the 2011 legislature dealt with several high-profile issues that found the senators split along party lines. Only one proved to be a triumph for the state's Republicans.

Several senators cited the 2011 legislative battle over the way Nebraska's electoral college votes are distributed as an example of one of the legislature's most partisan moments. Since 1991, Nebraska has allowed its five electoral college votes for president to be split among the districts so that it's possible for a Republican to win some of the electoral votes and a Democrat the others. (Maine is the only other state that allows the split; the other forty-eight give all their electoral votes to the candidate who wins the popular vote in the state.)

In 1995 and again in 1997, the legislature passed bills that would have returned the state to the "winner take all" system, but both bills were vetoed by then-Governor Ben Nelson, a Democrat. But the state did not actually take advantage of the opportunity to split its electoral college votes until 2008 when the Second Congressional District's vote went to Barack Obama. That prompted another attempt to change the 1991 legislation. The debate was intensely partisan.

Mark Fahleson, chair of the state Republican party, said publicly that senators would lose their seats in the next election if they didn't vote to return to the "winner take all" system. Despite that threat, it was Senator Paul Schumacher of Columbus, a Republican, who apparently split from the party's position in the Government, Military, and Veterans Affairs Committee. The committee's vote on whether to advance the bill to the floor for consideration by the entire legislature resulted in a 4–4 tie, with Schumacher declining to toe the party line. An article in the March 10, 2011, *Lincoln Journal Star* reported that Schumacher had said members of the unicameral are accountable to their constituents, not their political party.

The highly partisan issue that proved to be a triumph for Republicans during 2011 involved congressional and legislative redistricting, which must be done every ten years after census results become available. Redistricting, many legislative scholars and observers say, has always been partisan—even in Nebraska—as the two political parties jockey to draw district lines in ways that will increase the likelihood that their own candidates will be elected.

Negotiations over redistricting began in January 2011 but ran right through the last day of the session in May when the senators had to vote twice before the matter was settled. A redistricting committee that included senators of both parties was assigned to come up with a plan. They got as far as establishing procedures and standards, "but that was out the window when it was time to do [a redistricting plan]," Senator Bill Avery said. The committee voted 5–4, entirely along party lines, to advance the plan to the legislature. "The governor predicted the outcome of the committee's work before we even did it," Avery said.

Don Walton, writing in the May 30 *Lincoln Journal Star*, also recognized Heineman's influence. "The governor's fingerprints are all over that congressional redistricting map," he wrote. Walton said he wasn't criticizing Heineman, simply noting reality. Because the governor is his party's leading tactician, it was no surprise he would be engaged in the process behind the scenes, Walton wrote. The fact that the redistricting process was a partisan affair was no surprise, either, continuing the pattern established by past legislatures. If term limits made the 2011 struggle more partisan than ever, it was probably, again, by way of the governor and his influence on some inexperienced senators. One of the Republicans on the special committee was elected in 2008, two in 2006, and two in 2004.

Partisanship undoubtedly played a role in the budget debate too, as many observers assert, and to some extent in more issues than just the high-profile debates. On the other hand, although the 2011 legislature failed to override any of the governor's vetoes, the override votes did not simply split along party lines. While a supermajority of thirty votes would be needed to override a veto, several failed attempts split the senators closely—twenty-one to twenty-three and twenty to nineteen—despite the fact that thirty-three members were Republicans and sixteen Democrats. It looked as if any increase in partisanship had yet to become significant.

It's something the legislature must guard against, said Avery, a registered Democrat. "We have a responsibility to protect and maintain nonpartisanship." Besides the fact that nonpartisanship is written into the constitution thanks to the 1934 amendment, Avery said, he thinks the unicameral would not function as well if it were partisan. It would be harder to uphold the important norm of collegiality that guides the senators' actions and makes debates over thorny issues less rancorous.

Some observers believe the legislature already is partisan in practice if not in name. In his "Chairman's Report" in late 2012, Mark Fahleson, state Republican Party chairman, told members of his party to contact their state senators and encourage them to support only conservatives for leadership positions when the legislature reorganized in early 2013, not to break ranks with their party or their governor. The *Lincoln Journal Star* quoted Fahleson in a December 2012 story that "to say that the Nebraska legislature is non-partisan is a façade." He accused the Democrats in the body of caucusing regularly—as a political party.

Avery said that simply is not true. "I've *never* heard of caucuses by party," he said. "Republicans and Democrats don't even necessarily hang out together." He added that many of his best friends in the unicameral are Republicans. In the same December 2012 article, Senator Greg Adams, a registered Republican, said he thought most senators put partisan politics aside when they undertake legislative business, including electing people to leadership positions. In fact, when the new legislature chose its committee chairs in January 2013, eight of the fourteen were Democrats even though the body itself included a solid majority of thirty Republicans.

Partisanship is not totally absent from the body, Avery said, but he added that the unicameral has rejected outside pressure from the political parties who want to "tell us how to behave." George Norris would be pleased that, within the institution itself, at least, decisions continue to be made not at the direction of party leaders but by the give-and-take of debate among relative equals.

Influential Staff—or Not

A true progressive, George Norris wanted the legislature to take advantage of experts and their expertise as senators considered and made policy. Adding staff wasn't part of the amendment that created the unicameral, but adding staff was one of the first things the newly structured body did in 1937. The senators that year made the clerk of the legislature's position a year-round job and added an assistant clerk. They created the Office of Constitutional Reviewer to improve the technical aspects of bills. They expanded the services of the bill drafter into the Legislative Reference Bureau and hired a director of research to run the bureau.

In the 1970s, the unicameral moved from a total of nine secretaries who served all forty-nine senators to two year-round staff members per senator: an administrative assistant and a legislative assistant. The body also added a committee clerk, a research analyst, and legal counsel for each standing committee. The intent of all the staff additions was to give senators sources of information other than lobbyists.

When term limits were proposed, however, opponents said one result would be that senators would rely too heavily on staff. No one implied that staff were inadequate or untrustworthy; the point was simply that staff members are not elected, not chosen by the people. Term limits opponents expressed doubts that the elected officials, who should be making their own policy decisions, would be able to get up to speed fast enough without leaning on the expertise and institutional memory of long-time staff.[49]

In Nebraska, though, that does not seem to have happened. Those who responded to the 2010 survey said they do rely somewhat on staff members to gather information that helps them decide how to vote on a bill: 46 percent of those elected before 2006 but only 36 percent of those elected in 2006 or after. By contrast, 87 percent of those elected before 2006 and 90 percent elected after that date said they rely on their own personal knowledge and experience. Those elected after 2006 also said they rely more on friends in the legislature and constituents than they do on staff (see table 2).

Perhaps heavy reliance on staff has not materialized because the same thing seems to have happened here as happened in California after term limits: As turnover of legislators increased, so did turnover of legislative staff. Newly elected people often want to hire as staff the people who helped get them elected.[50]

A number of senators interviewed for this chapter said that's been true in the unicameral. Administrative aides, especially, seem to come and go with senators. On the other hand, committee staff seem to stay around longer, and they definitely can be influential. "People don't realize how term limits have affected staff influence," Senator Bill Avery said of the long-time staff members. "They were here when I got here, and they'll be here after I'm gone. They have the real institutional memory."

Senator Annette Dubas praised the staffers who have learned to know the unicameral and its processes over time. "They're incredible," she said. "They love and appreciate the institution."

Avery has no problem with senators relying on staff because, he says, most staff have no political agendas or ambitions. What they provide is solid history and background that can help a senator learn an issue and make an informed decision.

From George Norris's progressive point of view, legislators ought to rely on staff members and their expertise. But that point of view is slightly at odds with another of Norris's goals: that the legislature would be closer to and more directly responsive to the people. As term limits play out in Nebraska, senators' reliance on staff could shrink if staff turnover keeps pace with legislative turnover, or it could grow if staff stay on to provide the institutional memory the novice senators lack.

Learning to Live with Limits

The clamor to install term limits as a cure for what ails American politics seems to have subsided; no state has adopted such a measure since Nebraska did so in 2000. Periodically, people have suggested trying to repeal the state's amendment, but that would be a steep uphill battle. On Jan. 4, 2012, the first day of the legislative session, Senator Tom Carlson introduced a resolution for a constitutional amendment that would keep term limits in place but extend them to twelve years, three four-year terms instead of the current two. In a one-house body, where senators cannot take their legislative experience to the other house, a twelve-year limit would, at least, allow them to put their hard-earned expertise to work a bit longer, Carlson told the *Omaha World-Herald*.[51]

He should have had support from his colleagues. Nineteen of the thirty-six senators who answered the open-ended questions on the 2010 survey said one way to improve the unicameral would be to extend term limits to at least twelve years; four others suggested abolishing them altogether. In interviews, too, the possibility of limiting people to three terms instead of two came up frequently. The loss of institutional memory puts the legislature at a disadvantage vis-à-vis the executive branch, the lobby, and interest groups, senators said.

When Carlson decided to introduce the constitutional amendment, he said he focused on the thirty votes needed to get the measure to the ballot. Some senators, he knew, were in favor of the idea but "couldn't act like it" for fear of alienating constituents. Before the vote on final reading, Carlson said he thought he would have thirty-two votes; he ended up with thirty-one, enough to send the amendment to the people with one vote to spare. But when the voters of Nebraska had a chance to weigh in, Carlson's proposal to extend a senator's potential length of service to twelve years went down in resounding defeat with 65 percent voting "no."

The other suggestion for improvements that came up most often in the 2010 survey was increasing legislators' salaries, which have not changed from the $12,000 approved in 1988. Higher pay would make it easier for a larger variety of people to serve, senators said, but a constitutional amendment to increase annual salaries to $22,500 failed on the 2012 ballot with only 32 percent of the voters in favor of the increase. If a person listened hard enough, he could almost hear George Norris sighing that one of his goals for the model legislature—decent pay to attract good legislators from varied backgrounds— did not have support from the people of his state.

Another way to allow legislators to accumulate more experience would be to return Nebraska's legislature to a two-house body. That idea, however, was dismissed out of hand by nearly everyone responding to the 2010 survey or to an interview question. "I'd never support that," Annette Dubas said. "The positives for a unicameral far outweigh the negatives."

Mike Flood pointed out that a return to two houses would require a return to conference committees, the very thing George Norris probably disliked most about the two-house model when he proposed changing it. "Conference committees are ripe for backroom deals," Flood said, echoing Norris's own argument. "They wouldn't be transparent, and we wouldn't require a public hearing on every bill."

Tony Fulton said that having two houses would take a little of the pressure off the senators to be sure to get a policy right but added that it would cost more. Mike Gloor said he thought two houses might lead to more partisanship. Kathy Campbell said one house made the body more accessible to citizens. Dave Landis recalled that Norris wanted the legislature to function as a corporation. Ron Withem said the cure would be worse than the disease. To top it off, passing a constitutional amendment to recreate the bicameral system would probably be even more difficult than passing an amendment to set term limits at twelve years instead of eight.

In the meantime, term limits have changed the Nebraska unicameral legislature, albeit not drastically—at least not yet. One of the most basic benefits George Norris promised from his model legislature is still intact. The legislature is still relatively straightforward and easy to follow: one house, no conference committees, not a lot of members, a hearing required on every bill.

Another benefit Norris promised was responsiveness, something he believed was fostered by the elimination of political parties from elections and from the day-to-day workings of the body. On that count, things have changed a bit. The parties appear to have become more deeply involved in recruiting, financing and electing candidates to their liking, building at least some sense of loyalty in the senators they help elect. During the actual sessions, the legislature's business is still not run by party hierarchies, and no party caucuses have formed—even unofficial ones. But it seems that party, primarily in the form of the governor, has gained influence over senators who don't have the self-confidence born of experience and may be inclined to go along with whatever the head of their party requests. As a result, senators may be increasingly attentive to party and somewhat less responsive to their constituents.

Equality and efficiency were also part of Norris's benefits package, and term limits have had some impact on both. Committee chairs have always been influential, and that hasn't changed. The speaker's office, however, does seem to have changed. It seems as if the senators have encouraged the speaker to increase his authority, probably because leadership born of long experience is lacking and because a strong speaker, a designated leader, seems to be the best hope for keep a fluctuating membership moving in the right direction.

As for efficiency, it appears that the essentials are still getting done and done on schedule. In fact, the legislature actually finished its business and adjourned a few days early in 2011. But some observers say the term-limited legislature sometimes moves too fast and that inexperienced senators rush legislation along without enough attention to all the possible consequences. True efficiency demands not only speed but also quality and effectiveness.

Norris also hoped that a small, one-house, nonpartisan body would be better able to fend off the meddling of the lobby. Lobbyists didn't vanish when the new unicameral met in 1937, nor have they vanished since term limits were installed, but their influence does not seem to have grown a lot, either. Yes, lobbyists have more experience and more information than the senators they work with, information that can be valuable to senators trying frantically to learn their job. But lobbyists also have no long-term relationships with those senators and relatively little time to build them and the resulting trust that would allow them more influence.

Term limits' effects will become more clearly evident as time goes on. New faces and new ideas may come to offset lack of experience and increased partisanship, or the balance may tip the other way. In the meantime, chances are good most Nebraskans are not too concerned about the situation.

Dave Landis, forced out of the legislature in 2006, said he predicted at the time that term limits would be invisible to the public. The legislature would still hold hearings, introduce bills, pass a budget. "I said that, to the extent there's a change in the nature of the institution, it will be invisible to anyone but an experienced observer." Looking back in 2011, he said, "I think I was right. Term limits have not disturbed any underlying tectonic forces."

Table A

Year first elected to the legislature	Profession				
	Farmer/Rancher	Attorney	Professional	Other	Total
1978	0	0	1	0	1
1984	0	0	0	1	1
1986	2	0	0	0	2
1988	0	0	0	1	1
1992	2	0	2	0	4
1994	2	0	0	1	3
1996	0	1	0	0	1
1998	1	0	1	2	4
1999	0	1	0	0	1
2000	1	0	0	0	1
2001	0	0	1	0	1
2002	0	0	1	1	2
2003	1	0	0	0	1
2004	2	1	2	0	5
2006	1	1	5	1	8
2008	0	0	2	2	4
2009	0	0	1	0	1
Total	12	4	16	9	41

Table B

Sources relied on for information when voting on a bill	Elected before 2006	Elected 2006 or after
Personal knowledge/experience	87%	90%
Constituents	68%	85%
Staff/aides	46%	36%
Friend in the legislature	18%	78%
Lobbyists	25%	18%

Notes

Unless otherwise noted, all quotations and comments in this introduction from senators, lobbyists, and other observers are from personal interviews conducted in 2011 and 2012.

1. U.S. Term Limits, http://www.termlimits.org/.

2. National Conference of State Legislatures, http://www.ncsl.org/default.aspx?tabid=14849.

3. Francis L. Partsch, Rich Jones, and Reed Branson, "Term Limit Tenacity Pays Off in Nebraska," *State Legislatures Magazine* (July/August 2002): 37.

4. Ballotpedia, http://ballotpedia.org/wiki/index.php/Term_limits_in_Nebraska.

5. Doug Bend, "Term Limits for Nebraska State Senators: A Challenge to the Future Effectiveness of the Nebraska State Legislature," *Creighton Law Review* (December 2006): 27.

6. John M. Carey, Richard Niemi, and Lynda Powell, *Term Limits in the State Legislatures* (Ann Arbor: University of Michigan Press, 2000), 3.

7. Karl T. Kurtz, Bruce Cain, and Richard G. Niemi, *Institutional Change in American Politics: The Case of Term Limits* (Ann Arbor: University of Michigan Press, 2007), 188.

8. National Conference of State Legislatures, http://www.ncsl.org/default.aspx?tabid=16506.

9. National Conference of State Legislatures, http://www.ncsl.org/default.aspx?tabid=16563.

10. Partsch, Jones, and Branson, "Term Limit Tenacity Pays Off in Nebraska," 37

11. *Nebraska Legislative Journals*, 2007 and 2011.

12. Bend, "Term Limits for Nebraska State Senators," 11.

13. Kurtz, Cain, and Niemi, *Institutional Change in American Politics*, 187; Marjorie Sarbaugh-Thompson, Lyke Thompson, Charles D. Elder, John Strate, Richard C. Elling, *The Political and Institutional Effects of Term Limits* (New York: Palgrave Macmillan, 2004), 3; Carey, Niemi, and Powell, *Term Limits in the State Legislatures*, 39.

14. Scott Bauer, "Impact of Term Limits on State's Unicameral Government Feared," *Lincoln Journal Star*, March 25, 2006.

15. National Public Radio, http://www.npr.org/templates/story/story.php?storyId=5170002.

16. Thad Kousser, *Term Limits and the Dismantling of State Legislative Professionalism* (Cambridge UK: Cambridge University Press, 2005), 210.

17. Kousser, *Term Limits and the Dismantling of State Legislative Professionalism*, 202, 207.

18. Carey, Niemi, and Powell, *Term Limits in the State Legislatures*, 49.

19. Bend, "Term Limits for Nebraska State Senators," 18.

20. Bernard Grofman, ed., *Legislative Term Limits: Public Choice Perspectives* (Norwell MA: Kluwer Academic Publishers, 1996), 5.

21. *Congressional Record*, April 25, 1938.

22. *Omaha World-Herald*, August 11, 2010.

23. *Lincoln Star*, December 28, 1936.

24. Carey, Niemi, and Powell, *Term Limits in the State Legislatures*, 67.

25. Carey, Niemi, and Powell, *Term Limits in the State Legislatures*, 71, 72; Kousser, *Term Limits and the Dismantling of State Legislative Professionalism*, 207.

26. Kurtz, Cain, and Niemi, *Institutional Change in American Politics*, 8.

27. *The Economist*, http://www.economist.com/node/5636402.

28. Kousser, *Term Limits and the Dismantling of State Legislative Professionalism*, 207.

29. Charlyne Berens, *Leaving Your Mark: The Political Career of Nebraska State Senator Jerome Warner* (Lincoln: Nebraska Times, 1997), 150.

30. Kurtz, Cain, and Niemi, *Institutional Change in American Politics*, 86.

31. Bend, "Term Limits for Nebraska State Senators," 17.

32. Alan Rosenthal et al., *The Case for Representative Democracy* (Washington DC: National Conference of State Legislatures, 2001), 27.

33. Kurtz, Cain, and Niemi, *Institutional Change in American Politics*, 116.

34. Kurtz, Cain, and Niemi, *Institutional Change in American Politics*, 8; Sarbaugh-Thompson et al., *The Political and Institutional Effects of Term Limits*, 5.

35. Carey, Niemi, and Powell, *Term Limits in the State Legislatures*, 83.

36. "Term Limits and Democracy: Out with the Old," *The Economist*, March 16, 2006.

37. Victor Kamber, *Giving Up on Democracy: Why Term Limits Are Bad for America* (Washington, DC: Regnery Publishing, Inc., 1995), 70.

38. Kousser, *Term Limits and the Dismantling of State Legislative Professionalism*, 205–6.

39. Kurtz, Cain, and Niemi, *Institutional Change in American Politics*, 67, 68; Sarbaugh-Thompson et al., *The Political and Institutional Effects of Term Limits*, 5.

40. Kurtz, Cain, and Niemi, *Institutional Change in American Politics*, 76, 79–80.

41. Kamber, *Giving Up on Democracy*, 81.

42. Kurtz, Cain, and Niemi, *Institutional Change in American Politics*, 68.

43. Carey, Niemi, and Powell, *Term Limits in the State Legislatures*, 42.

44. Bob Nelson, "Term Limits' Disadvantages Emerge," *Omaha World-Herald*, August 13, 2010, 1B.

45. Samuel Popkin, *The Reasoning Voter: Communication and Persuasion in Presidential Campaigns* (Chicago: University of Chicago Press, 1991), 51.

46. Gerald Wright and Brian Schaffner, "The Influence of Party: Evidence from the State Legislatures," *American Political Science Review* 96, no. 2 (June 2002): 376.

47. *Omaha World-Herald*, October 15, 2012.

48. Grofman, *Legislative Term Limits*, 4; Sarbaugh-Thompson et al., *The Political and Institutional Effects of Term Limits*, 2.

49. Carey, Niemi, and Powell, *Term Limits in the State Legislatures*, 79.

50. Nelson, "Term Limits' Disadvantages Emerge."

51. Joe Duggan, "Lawmaker: Ease Term Limits a Bit," *Omaha World-Herald*, December 31, 2011.

1 / One of a Kind

What George Norris Said a Unicameral Would Do

Nebraska may look like just one long stretch of interstate highway, lined by cornfields and "Go Big Red" signs. But Nebraskans will tell you they have a unique claim to fame: theirs is the only state in the nation with a one-house, nonpartisan legislature.

It wasn't always that way. In fact, when the state entered the Union in 1867, it adopted the partisan, two-house legislative model that had become the norm in the United States. It was seventy years later, in 1937, that the first unicameral legislature met at the state capitol in Lincoln in an experiment that some predicted would not last long but which most Nebraskans today simply take for granted. In fact, the institution quickly became so firmly entrenched in Nebraska's state culture that, for decades, citizens have referred to their legislature as "the unicameral."

By a two-to-one majority, Nebraskans passed a 1934 constitutional amendment that created the new model. It was a peaceful revolution, achieved at the ballot box, and it didn't jettison the state's fundamental democratic structure. Nonetheless, a revolution it was. For the first time in more than a century and a half, one of the United States had decided it could manage just fine with a one-house, nonpartisan legislative branch.

Adoption of the unicameral was not born out of any political or social crisis but followed nearly thirty years of discussion and consideration fostered by the state's political leaders. The unicameral seems to have had its roots in the populist/progressive philosophy that had been a major influence in the state from the 1880s on. Not that Nebraskans voted for the new system because they recognized themselves as populists or progressives, but when they followed the recommendations of those who were promoting the nonpartisan, one-house body, they were responding to arguments grounded in the populist/progressive ideal.

George Norris was the most prominent person making those arguments. In a 1934 interview with a Washington DC newspaper, Norris, Nebraska's U.S. senator, a well-known progressive and a leading advocate for the new legislative structure, talked about why he thought Nebraska should make the switch: "The bicameral house is cumbersome, defeats the will of the people and is fundamentally and unnecessarily expensive."[1] Conversely, then, a unicameral legislature would be more efficient, would serve the will of the people and would be cheaper for the state to operate.

The argument reflects the populist/progressive belief that an identifiable entity known as "the people" exists and that its will should be carried out via government. Historically, the populist movement originated in the latter decades of the nineteenth century as the common people—especially farmers in the Midwest and South, suffering under harsh economic conditions—began to insist that government ought to serve them, too, not just the wealthy business classes. Americans began to question the liberal democratic model that kept the people at arm's length from a government designed to negotiate conflicting interests and, mostly, to keep its hands off the business of its citizens. The populists asserted their faith in classical republicanism, which proposed a unitary people with a discernible will.

By the end of the nineteenth century, many in Nebraska and other Plains states believed that "the people" should be in control. They were angry with a government they believed was no longer democratic, no longer representative of common folk. They believed the "plain people" of America were in basic agreement about what was right and wrong, fair and foul, and that majority rule should be majority rule. Period.

Populism was succeeded, historically, by the progressive movement, which adopted and developed many populist ideals, including the emphasis on more direct democratic participation and a belief that "the people" exist and have a discernible will.

The progressives wanted to open government to inspection and participation by the people. They decried policy manipulation and party bosses' power. They wanted the expression of popular sentiment to be accurately reflected in the policy making process. They encouraged the use of experts and specialists in government, people who would help articulate and realize the will of the people in public policy. To oversimplify, where populists were revolutionaries, progressives were reformers. But many of both groups' goals were the same: to use government to do the people's will, which they believed should be discerned without too much difficulty.

George Norris considered himself a progressive, and so did his contemporaries. Norris was a true believer in the populist/progressive philosophy, dedicated to making government more efficient and more connected to the people it was designed to serve. His interest in reforming the bicameral system went back to 1880s when he was a lawyer in Beaver City, Nebraska, and an avid observer of his state's legislature. In 1902 he was elected to the U.S.

House of Representatives, where he earned a reputation as a reformer. In 1923 he announced his intent to apply some of his skills to his own state by reforming its machinery of government. He saw the unicameral legislature as a way to restore political responsibility among governmental officials and to make them more accountable to the people, who were and should be their bosses.

Norris believed in the wisdom of the common people and in the progress of civilization. "To get good government and to retain it, it is necessary that a liberty-loving, educated, intelligent people should be ever watchful, to carefully guard and protect their rights and liberties," Norris said in a 1934 speech titled "The Model Legislature." The people were capable of being the government, he said, affirming his populist/progressive credentials.[2]

Norris and the other Nebraskans who led the charge to remake Nebraska's legislature sold the idea to the voters on the basis of that populist/progressive philosophy. They insisted one house would be more straightforward in its proceedings and, thus, easier to follow. They said parties only got in the way of government by the people, giving power to elites at the expense of the common good. They said a smaller legislature would be more responsive and responsible; it would be cheaper and more efficient, more businesslike in its approach to policy making. Furthermore, a streamlined legislature would sidestep the problems inherent in a more complex structure and take swift action in the people's interests.

Whether or not they thought of the unicameral model as a manifestation of populism or progressivism, the voters of Nebraska bought into the claims proponents made for the new system and have supported their one-house, nonpartisan system for more than sixty-five years. But some question whether the unicameral has lived up to its billing, whether the Nebraska legislature in the early years of the twenty-first century is still true to the populist/progressive philosophy and the promises Norris and others made for it: that it would be open, accountable, egalitarian and efficient. This book takes a look at the "model legislature" today, compares it to the one created in 1937, and tries to measure just how well the unicameral has fulfilled the promises made on its behalf.

Power to the People!

As a historical and political movement, the populism of the late nineteenth century had its roots in agrarian radicalism, the passing of the frontier, the excesses of railroads and other business monopolies, and the desperate economic conditions facing farmers in the Plains and the South in the 1880s and 1890s. In the Plains, farmers victimized by drought and low prices flocked to farmers' alliances, educational groups, and political groups. Their eventual collective outcry came to be known as the populist revolt.

Many "common people" of the day believed their problems were caused by interests that were trying to destroy the revered Protestant work ethic on which the settlement of the Plains was founded. Many believed those elite interests had taken over the government and were wielding power for private benefit. Gradually, in the decades following the Civil War, both major political parties had come to be controlled by business and financial entrepreneurs, and the "plain people" felt left out in the cold.

Citizens suspected, with some justification, that big businesses were manipulating government, using their wealth to secure privileges, block regulation, and maintain their monopolies.[3] The people of Nebraska and other states on the Plains saw powerful private interests as a danger to the public's interests and believed that democracy in an industrial era was not best served by rampant individualism. These "radicals" wanted government to restrain the wealthy elites and return authority to "the people," in whom they had complete faith and trust and who, they believed, existed as the unitary entity Thomas Jefferson had envisioned at the nation's birth.

Like others who espoused their philosophy before and since, the populists of the late nineteenth century believed the political community was a single organic whole, a virtuous, united people bound together by a shared public good.[4] The elite few, the populists believed, had corrupted that public good and used the institutions of government for their own power and aggrandizement.

Traditionally in the United States, any discontented group with strong enough grievances and big enough numbers turns to political action for redress, and that is exactly what the populists did. The Farmers' Alliance, which gave birth to populism in Nebraska, Kansas, and other states, encouraged its members to redefine the form and meaning of life and politics in the United States. But its approach was evolutionary: no one advocated complete overthrow of the system.

Instead, the populists wanted their democratic government to do more, to intervene in the economy to make people's lives better, to regulate economic affairs and assure that equality of opportunity was a reality for everyone. Their goal was to speak not for any class or group but for all the people.

The populists did not question the heart of the democratic process, but they did question the institutional structure they believed enabled oppression of "the people." Some talked of direct government, replacing legislatures with the initiative process, and called for the nationalization of railroads and utilities.[5] Paradoxically, their efforts to enhance popular, democratic control of government—like those of reformers before and since—also enhanced the scope and authority of the state.[6]

Populists believed political structures and processes should change, should be designed to encourage widespread, informed citizen participation, allowing citizens to work toward the common good. In summary, the populists had "large democratic hopes" for change.[7] Ultimately, those hopes led to the formation of a separate political party, the People's Party, in the last decade of the nineteenth century.

The People's Party reached out to use the existing political system, turning to partisanship in a maneuver that proved to be its downfall as a movement. Through a process known as "fusion," the People's Party was ultimately absorbed into the Democratic Party and ceased to exist as a separate organization. But while the party itself may not have survived, many of its doctrines did. The populist philosophy boiled down to two fundamental propositions: that government must restrain the selfish tendencies of those who profited at the expense of the poor and that the people, not the plutocrats, must control the government. The latter proposition has always been part of American democratic thought, and both propositions became fundamental to American political thinking and rhetoric in the twentieth century.

The progressive era began approximately where the populist era left off; the two overlapped in the last decade of the nineteenth and first decade of the twentieth centuries. Progressivism picked up many of populism's goals, trying to insure the survival of democracy in the United States by boosting government's authority to control and offset the power that private economic groups had over the nation's institutions and life.

Like the populists before them, the progressives wanted fairer distribution of the economic and political power of the nation. Like the populists, they were mightily aware of the contrast between political freedom and material progress on the one hand and economic inequality and poverty on the other. Also like the populists, progressives thought one of the chief evils in American life at the turn of the century was the collusion between big business and laissez-faire government. Progressives saw wealthy men getting cozy with politicians in order to get special treatment for their businesses and industries. In response, the progressives wanted some societal control and regulation of private utilities that were supposed to be serving the public. And they wanted to reestablish political responsibility among public officials. They distrusted the politicians who operated what they viewed as entrenched, elitist institutions. Progressives in the Plains protested against machine politics controlled by interests manipulating the system for their own ends. Progressives wanted honest, efficient representative government.

Progressives believed wholeheartedly that they could make things better, could reform government and society for the benefit of all. They shared with the populists a firm faith in and trust of the popular majority. Their point of view may seem naive, but it was a product of what Wesser calls America's "inherent belief in the perfectibility of human institutions."[8] True to their name, the progressives believed in the inherent good of progress.

Many of progressivism's goals sound a lot like populism's goals, particularly the belief that government should be returned to the people and used for their good. Progressives urged the citizens to reclaim the power they had abdicated. They wanted to pass new laws to fix what was broken and to see to it that existing laws were enforced. They believed representative government had become less representative of the people than it should be, that some method should be available to express the political will of the majority. Progressives insisted the channels between citizens and the state were corrupted and urged a return to the "first principles" of democracy, a return of government to the hands of the people.[9]

But the people were to be assisted in the process of governing by experts and specialists in the form of a professional bureaucracy. Progressives stressed constant watchfulness and continuous management by experienced, responsible professionals, acting on behalf of "the people." The institutionalized bureaucracy Americans take for granted today is a product of the progressive era, the outcome of administrative changes linked to reforms that promised to revitalize democracy and return power to the people.[10]

In Nebraska, progressivism stimulated "an intensive interest in social reform" and made citizens think about how the machinery of their state government could be adapted to promote social and economic change.[11] The progressives were committed to simplifying legislative procedures, and unicameralism gradually became an important part of the reforms they were advocating.

A joint legislative committee appointed in 1913 concluded that representative government should be direct and responsible. The committee recommended simplifying the legislature's rules of procedure and then made a radical suggestion: a constitutional amendment to create a one-house legislature. The 1915 legislature did adopt the recommendations for a revision of procedural rules—but then didn't actually make many revisions. And the legislature refused to take action on the recommendation for a unicameral body.[12]

The reform attempts in Nebraska coincided with movements on the national front. Woodrow Wilson, elected president in 1912, pushed Congress to enact major progressive reforms during his first years in office. By 1916 the progressives had pushed through the passage of direct primary legislation, had established the initiative and referendum, had passed an amendment of the Constitution to provide for popular election of senators, and had passed numerous corrupt-practices acts. Many Plains states had placed much of business under government control. Most people agreed that the function of government should include the social and economic welfare of the people at large, and significant legislation had been passed relating to health, employment, and safety.

On both the federal and state level, political institutions had changed. In Nebraska, for instance, party loyalties were weaker by 1914, and more voters split their tickets. Nebraskans proved to be independent voters, frequently crossing party lines and voting on state issues as if they had nothing to do with national issues.[13] Nebraska voters appeared not to take their party adherence seriously. That attitude may help explain why they were eventually willing to eliminate parties from their legislature.

Progressivism seemed to be rolling toward a comprehensive overhaul of American politics and society. Then disaster struck in the form of World War I, billed as a campaign to make the world safe for democracy. The war was horrifying, and the outcome didn't live up to its billing. The general disgust and disillusionment that followed made Americans want to roll up the oceans and stick to themselves. They slipped easily back into the belief that their business was business. Progressives in the 1920s had a hard time selling their philosophy of social improvement to folks who just wanted to be left alone.[14]

On the other hand, Wilson's New Freedom, combined with previous reforms, had cemented some basic progressive principles into the American system. "The people" were still important, but administrators would deal with them day by day in rational subdivisions. Progressives had recognized that the processes of modern technology made organization, specialization, hierarchy, and discipline absolutely necessary, but they fought to preserve the people's values as they adopted the benefits of organization.

Important elements of the progressive movement remained in full vigor during the 1920s. Farmers, for instance, were better organized and more powerful than they had ever been. The development of a program of aid to farmers, and the formulation of plans for public power—in which Nebraska's George Norris was a leader—were significant progressive achievements in the 1920s. In addition, a remnant of the previously large army of independent radicals, social workers, and preachers continued to push for reform.

Perhaps the 1920s, an economic boom period, should be considered not the end of progressivism but simply a decade in which the movement went underground. Progressivism would resurface in many of the programs of

Franklin D. Roosevelt's New Deal, his response to the Great Depression, which engulfed the nation by 1930. In his campaign, FDR reached out to the "plain people" whose welfare was at the center of both the populist and the progressive ideals. His speech accepting the Democratic nomination for president announced the New Deal and denounced the despotism of industrial dictatorship and private enterprise he said was too private to benefit the public. Although FDR had not been known as a progressive before the 1932 campaign, the New Deal began to emerge as a long-range, sweeping political, economic, and social reorganization that eventually absorbed many of the progressives of the decade. FDR shared with the progressives a willingness to use the machinery of government to meet the needs of the people. Like the populist and progressive movements, the New Deal set out to reform capitalism, not to replace the economic system with something else. The aim was to control government for the common good; economic justice, it was assumed, would naturally follow.[15]

The progressive movement may have gone underground in Nebraska during the 1920s as it did on the national scene. But progressives continued to push for legislative reforms throughout the decade. No doubt Nebraska's progressives were influenced by national talk about returning to one-house state legislatures.

The idea of a unicameral legislature had been an important part of the progressive reforms suggested in numerous states between 1912 and 1930. Alabama tried—and failed—to install a unicameral by constitutional amendment in 1915, the same year Nebraska's legislature declined to deal with the proposal. Arizona's governor urged his state to make the switch, but the people rejected the proposal in 1916. California, Arkansas, Colorado, Kansas, Minnesota, New York, Ohio, Oklahoma, Oregon, South Dakota, Tennessee, and Washington all considered a one-house body by one means or another but none adopted it. However, the debate continued in at least one state every year through 1934.

In Nebraska the idea officially resurfaced in 1923 when an initiative petition was circulated to put a one-house legislature on the 1924 ballot; the petition failed to get enough signatures. In January 1924 the Farmers Cooperative and Educational Union, with a membership of thirty-five thousand adopted a resolution to promote a one-house, nonpartisan legislature of a hundred members. And proposals for a unicameral body were introduced in the 1925 and 1933 legislative sessions.

The campaign that culminated in the adoption of the unicameral in Nebraska is closely identified with the progressive movement. One of the progressives' goals was to make legislatures more democratic. They promoted sunshine reforms, to open the state's business to public scrutiny, and open committee hearings. They attacked elaborate rules that concentrated legislative power in the hands of a few individuals or interests. The reforms they suggested added up to a systematic, coherent vision of democratic participation: minimize the role of intermediaries like parties, legislators, private interests—even politics itself. The progressives' vision was of a single, united, consensual people, beyond competition and politics, and was mobilized in opposition to the concentration of private power. It was a vision the unicameral's promoters said could be a reality in Nebraska.

Selling the Unicameral

In 1923 Senator Norris chose a national forum in which to describe and defend his plan for a one-house, nonpartisan legislature. His full-page piece in the January 28 issue of the *New York Times* was widely reprinted in Nebraska, and the points Norris made there became the foundation for the campaign to adopt the constitutional amendment eleven years later.

He wrote that the traditional two-house legislature had been "unsatisfactory in its results" and blamed a great deal of the trouble on the conference committees that are necessary to reconcile measures passed in two different houses. That complex system, Norris said, made it impossible for a citizen to follow and pass judgment on his representative's actions. In addition, one house often passed the responsibility for failure to the other house, allowing individual legislators to "cover up their own tracks." One house would eliminate the need for conference committees and make the legislature's workings far more open, and individual legislators far more accountable.

A contemporary assessment of unicameralism comes to the same conclusion. Alaska's Legislative Research Agency says the bicameral process is "mysteriously complex to everyone but those who are involved in it (and who profit directly from it)." Bicameralism tends to favor quiet deals and symbolic gestures over open deliberation. As a result, no one can be held accountable "for what finally emerges, or fails to emerge, from the murky labyrinth of committees." Unicameralism, the paper says, demystifies the process and opens it to more participation. [16]

Bicameralism is definitely at odds with the populist or direct democracy approach. The two-house system complicates representation and promotes access for elites and special interests and makes it harder for ordinary citizens to watch and influence their government. The sentiment was expressed eloquently by Centinel, an Anti-Federalist, in the eighteenth century:

The highest responsibility is to be attained in a simple structure of government, for the great body of the people never steadily attend to the operations of government, and for the want of due information are liable to be imposed upon. If you complicate the plan by various orders, the people will be perplexed and divided in their sentiment about the sources of abuses or misconduct; some will impute it to the senate, others to the house of representatives and so on, that the interposition of the people may be rendered imperfect or perhaps wholly abortive . . . . (In a unicameral) whenever the people feel a grievance, they cannot mistake the authors and will apply the remedy with certainty and effect, discarding them at the next election.[17]

Whether or not he ever read the passage, Norris would undoubtedly have agreed with Centinel that the people's involvement in the governing process was essential and that unicameralism was one way to make that participation more likely. The commonplace two-house system, he and his fellow reformers said, cried out for simplification.

Norris also said most state legislatures were too large and that cutting their size would allow for more direct participation by all members and for higher salaries for the fewer members. The result would be a two-fold payoff: better-qualified legislators and a lower dollar figure for total salaries. Smaller size would also make possible closer citizen observation.

The ideal legislature, according to this way of thinking, should have both a structure and rules that would make it "an effective and responsible agency of the public will." It should be uncomplicated and should give every bill a full hearing—in public—so the people could get involved in the legislative discussions and decision making.[18] If the people were more involved, the legislature would be more likely to serve their needs rather than those of powerful special interests.

But that wasn't the end of Norris's recommendation: legislatures also should be nonpartisan. "The business of the Legislature of a State is in no sense partisan," Norris wrote in the *New York Times* piece. State legislators' duties "have nothing to do with the National Administration or with the welfare or success of any political party." The senator believed it was "illogical to elect a man to the Legislature . . . because he belongs to some political party and will follow that party regardless of what course it takes" when his duties as a state legislator had nothing to do with partisan questions. Instead of being run on a partisan basis, a state, Norris said, should function like a "gigantic corporation, and the members of the Legislature would be members of the Board of Directors." Again, the result would be a system that was more fair to the people it was supposed to serve.

Each of those selling points was part of the campaign to install a nonpartisan unicameral legislature in Nebraska.

"Evil" Conference Committees

"The greatest evil of a two-house legislature is its institution of the conference committee," Norris wrote in his autobiography.[19] John Senning, another prominent supporter of the unicameral, called it a "necessary evil" that would be eliminated if a legislature had only one house.[20]

The conference committee, its critics said, was essentially a third chamber, and a secret one at that. When the two houses passed bills that were not identical, the leaders in each body would appoint several members to a conference committee. The committee would work out a compromise between the two versions, sometimes coming up with an entirely different proposition than what had been passed by the two houses. The conference committee would report the amended bill under a closed rule that allowed only a yes-or-no vote by the legislators. No more negotiating or amending allowed. Members often had to take "what they believe to be bad in order to get what they believe to be good," Norris said in his 1934 Model Legislature speech. It just wasn't fair.

More powerful than either house or both houses combined, the conference committee was downright undemocratic, Senning said.[21] In a brochure urging voters to approve the one-house legislature, proponents said about 15 percent of all bills and, more significantly, about 75 percent of all "important measures" enacted into law were the product of conference committees, not of the truly representative legislative houses.[22]

Franklin Burdette studied Nebraska conference committee reports from 1921 to 1933 and found the same pattern. During that time period, Burdette said, many of the most significant bills, including every biennial appropriation, were referred to a conference committee, usually toward the end of the session. In 63 percent of the cases, the conference committee made major changes in the content of the bill or its amendments. In several instances, conference committees presented entirely new bills.

Furthermore, citizens had no voice in naming people to these powerful conference committees. The five or six members of the committees were appointed by party leaders, often with an eye to improving their own party's advantage. That meant the party leaders wielded tremendous power to shape legislation to their own preferences without much, if any, accountability to the citizenry.

But that wasn't all. The committees met in secret, keeping no records of their proceedings, and their reports could not be amended by the entire legislature—exactly opposite of the open procedures the unicameral promoters said people were entitled to and would get in a one-house body.

Norris said in his Model Legislature speech and elsewhere that conference committees amounted to "a legislature of four or five men," with decisions often controlled by as few as two. Handing any individual or small group that kind of authority turned Norris's populist stomach.

Clearing the Muddy Waters

Elimination of conference committees was high on Norris's list of benefits offered by a unicameral, but simplifying the legislative structure in general was also important. Reflecting the populist/progressive ideal, Norris wanted the people to be the government, but that would be impossible if they were not able to watch and understand what their representatives were doing.

"One of the fundamental requisites that should always exist in any legislature where universal suffrage prevails is to enable the citizen to properly place responsibility either for the success or failure of legislation," Norris told a Lincoln newspaper in 1933.[23] That was pretty tough to do when the system was complex and secretive.

Pointing out that the United States did not recognize a hierarchical society in which different legislative houses represented different classes, Norris said he saw "no excuse whatever for a double-branch legislature." Members of both branches had to meet the same qualifications, were elected by the same people and had the same jurisdiction. Opponents of the unicameral said eliminating one house would eliminate an important check on ill-considered legislation. But rather than serving as checks upon each other, Norris said, the two houses simply served to muddy the legislative waters and allow for underhanded skullduggery by legislators themselves and by lobbyists.

Furthermore, in a one-house legislature, a citizen wouldn't have to be an expert in parliamentary procedure to see what his representative's record was, Norris said. Voters would not have to work as hard to remain informed about legislative activities. And legislators would not be able to shift responsibility for their actions—or inactions—to the other house; instead, their records would be open to the pitiless light of publicity because of roll call votes, public hearings, and press scrutiny.

Critics of bicameralism complained that the complex procedures of the two-house legislature "stint[s] every power of the legislator except that to evade responsibility."[24] For instance, members of one house might pass a measure to appease their constituents, knowing all along the other house would defeat it. So the legislator could seem to be voting as his constituents expected but still get the result he really wanted, avoiding the political fallout that might come if he couldn't "hide" his true loyalties. Observers said legislators had, indeed, used the two-house process in precisely that way. Two houses, they said, resulted in vote trades and shirking of real responsibility. In one house each member would be more conspicuous, and bills would be more open to public inspection.

Lobbyists would be more conspicuous in a one-house body, too. The unicameral proponents accused lobbyists of representing the interests of the elites at the expense of the common folk. They admitted not all lobbyists were corrupt or sinister, but they believed the complexities of two houses made it easier for any lobbyist, including an unscrupulous one, to hide his machinations. The simplified processes of a one-house body would open the procedures "so that publicity can attend every step" and keep the legislators accountable to the people.[25] Lobbyists—and the legislators they lobbied—would have no place to hide, no possibility of "covering their tracks."[26]

Small Is Beautiful

Norris and his compatriots promoted a smaller legislature for many of the same reasons they used to sell a one-house body. Primarily, proponents said a small legislature would be more responsive and responsible to the people, more easily held accountable for its actions.

Norris was particularly adamant that the legislature should be small. In his *New York Times* piece in 1923 and again in his 1934 Model Legislature speech in Lincoln, Norris asserted that one of the evils of the Nebraska legislature—133 members in the two houses—was that it was too big. In theory, he said, a larger legislature would provide better representation of the entire citizenry. But in order to get anything done, a large body must give up too much authority to a few leaders and must limit individual members' right to debate and to offer amendments. Norris wanted to see a nonhierarchical body in which every member would participate equally and openly in the decision-making process.

A large body, too, would be likely to create more committees in order to keep all its members occupied and satisfied with their jobs. A smaller legislature could trim the number of committees and the accompanying procedural rules, making it easier for the public to watch what was going on and harder for legislators and lobbyists to manipulate policy discussions. The idea had been raised before: one important reason the 1913 legislative study group had recommended a small, unicameral body was to make government by the people direct and responsible. Norris preached the same message when he campaigned for the constitutional amendment.

But when Norris said "small legislature," he definitely meant small. The

senator originally proposed a body of only twenty-one or twenty-four legislators, but other unicameral promoters argued that that number was just
too small, even in a state with a relatively low population. Eventually, they
prevailed on Norris to set the minimum number at thirty and the maximum at
fifty. They believed any number in that range would be a fair representation
of a cross-section of the state's population and would reflect the interests of
urban and rural areas as well as diverse religious and ethnic groups.

Unicameral opponents said that was baloney. A small, one-house body,
they said, would mean larger districts and less representation for farmers. But
Senning argued that fewer legislators with larger districts would be a better
reflection of the reality of representation in the 1930s. The state legislature,
he said, should be made up "of forty-three arbiters of conflicting social and
economic interests, statewide in extent." Far from being a drawback, the
larger districts actually promoted better representation, giving the legislator
a wider perspective and letting him see statewide concerns telescoped in his
own district, the unicameralists believed.[27]

Trading Parties for Independence

Norris's ideas were generally accepted wholesale by the committee formed
in 1933 to write the proposed constitutional amendment to create the
unicameral—with one exception: nonpartisanship. Committee members worried that people would be confused if they had to choose a governor and other
state officers on a partisan ballot but their legislators on a nonpartisan basis.
They were afraid nonpartisanship would doom the amendment.

Norris would have none of it. He may have given in a bit on the size of the
body, but when it came to nonpartisanship, he refused to budge. He insisted
the nonpartisan feature remain in the proposal.

The committee members had reason to worry about the nonpartisan provision. It was nonpartisanship, more than any other part of the proposal, that
drew fire from the unicameral opponents. Some said nonpartisanship would
destroy legislative leadership, leaving only a batch of unorganized would-
be leaders. Others said it would allow special interests to get control of the
legislative process. According to that way of thinking—which has become
the norm in America—parties bring predictability to the political process;
absence of party structure and discipline opens the field to any individual or
group that can gather and sustain a coalition.

But Norris and other unicameral proponents argued just the reverse: that
the parties themselves were special interests that did not serve the will of the
citizenry. Those elected on a partisan platform are likely to follow the dictates
of party machines and bosses rather than the people whom they represent,

Norris said in his Model Legislature speech. Getting rid of parties would allow measures to be considered on their merit rather than on the basis of their political consequences. The nonpartisan unicameral, Senning wrote, would derive its power not from political dictators but from the people directly. Parties, to this way of thinking, are simply an obstacle separating the people from their elected representatives.

The unicameral supporters disliked parties for another reason: they believed parties were in cahoots with big business and questioned whether party leaders were "able or desire to distinguish between public and private interests in their political action."[28]

Furthermore, Norris said and wrote many times, "the business of the legislature of a state is in no sense partisan. . . . If politics were eliminated, members would be elected according to their qualifications for the state legislature and would give their best for the welfare of the state."[29] Parties stood in the way of that welfare.

Taking Care of Business

Instead of relying on parties or lobbyists, Norris and the other unicameral promoters wanted to see the legislature rely on experts and specialists for information that would help the body act like a "business administration." That meant every member could participate in every decision and each member would help to shape the body's shared interests. Where partisanship predominates in government, Norris said, economy and efficiency disappear.[30] And Norris and his friends were convinced the people wanted their government to be efficient and economical.

It was a notion typical of the progressive creed and one that the first unicameral enthusiastically adopted. The 1937 legislature expanded the services of the bill drafter into the Legislative Reference Bureau and hired three attorneys to advise on the constitutionality of all bills before they were passed. The legislature also expanded the Clerk of the Legislature's position into a year-round job.

In addition to hiring experts, though, the unicameral tried to develop more expertise among its members by creating the Legislative Council. The fifteen-member council was designed to meet between the biennial sessions and direct the study of various matters before the legislature in order to make the sessions run more smoothly. To assure it would have a dependable supply of scientific data, the council hired University of Nebraska political science professor Roger Shumate as director of research and put him in charge of its reference bureau. The unicameral was on its way to building a staff of experts to help legislators identify the will of the people and put it into policy.

The unicameralists wanted the legislature to discover and do the will of the people quickly and efficiently. But some critics said a nonpartisan, one-house body would move too fast, would pass hasty, ill-considered legislation—and way too much of it. Even many proponents thought that that was a legitimate concern, but they were equally interested in avoiding the deadlocks that had bottled up progressive legislation in the bicameral.

Norris had pointed out that special interests, corporations, and monopolies were "almost universally interested in preventing legislation—legislation which in one way or another regulates their activities and prevents injustice by means of monopolistic control." Preventing legislation and maintaining the status quo in a two-house body was relatively simple, Norris said.[31]

Between 1929 and 1935, Nebraska had enacted only 15 percent to 20 percent of the bills introduced; up to 70 percent of the legislation introduced was never even examined by the other house. One house might pass a bill and then urge the other to defeat it. Or a small group in one house was able to block legislation in the other until its demands were met.

Governor Charles Bryan said the two-house system had often deprived the people of their right to self-government. Two houses and a cumbersome organization had made it impossible to pass legislation the people wanted.[32]

By 1933, Senning said, people had developed "a sense of utter futility in respect to securing progressive legislation."[33] The unicameral promoters promised to change that.

Better Legislators, Less Money

Norris had also promised in his *New York Times* piece and frequently thereafter that the unicameral legislature would draw better men to its membership. One way he proposed to make that a reality was to provide higher salaries for legislators but keep the total cost under control by decreasing the number of members. In 1933 members of the Nebraska legislature were paid eight hundred dollars per two-year session, not high enough to enable most people to serve.

Of course, the unicameralists had to balance the proposition that higher salaries would attract better people with the fact that Nebraskans would not be likely to approve a big increase in the legislature's budget, particularly in the midst of the Great Depression. The committee eventually decided to set a dollar figure of $37,500 per year, to be divided among the total number of members, whatever that turned out to be.

Norris had originally hoped for more. He would have liked to pay an annual salary of twenty-four hundred dollars per member so that legislators could devote a full-time schedule to their duties, becoming "experts in legislation" and, as such, "more valuable to the state."[34]

Norris also hoped that a smaller body would attract better members—not just for the higher salaries but because each legislator would have more say in the body's deliberations and decisions. In a large body, he said, even the ablest and most conscientious members often had trouble getting involved in the body's procedures or decisions. In the smaller legislature, each member would have the opportunity to be fully involved in policy making. And the fact that no one would be beholden to a party structure or boss would give each member more freedom to influence policy as he saw fit.

Perhaps the least high-minded of the proponents' arguments in favor of a unicameral was the proposition that the proposed body would be cheaper to operate. But the supporters knew it was a proposition likely to appeal to voters, and they pushed it hard. Senning pointed out that criticism of the legislature's expenditures had actually been directed more at the number of employees and cost of supplies and printing than at legislators' salaries. The associated costs would fall with the elimination of one house and the decrease in number of legislators. Openness would help to prevent waste.

Filled with the Spirit
Armed with their belief in the perfectibility of human institutions and their faith in "the people," Norris, Senning, and the other proponents of the new legislative structure set out to make believers out of their fellow Nebraskans. Inspired by the progressive ideal, they were convinced the new system would better meet both the practical and the philosophical needs of the citizens. But first they had to overcome people's natural tendency to stick with what they know. And what the people of Nebraska knew as their government in 1934 was a two-house, partisan model. It had been that way for more than six decades.

2 / Power to the People

How Nebraska Made the Switch to a One-House, Nonpartisan Legislature

On the surface, it looks as if Nebraska made the shift from the traditional two-house, partisan legislature to a one-house nonpartisan body in 1934 for three simple reasons: money, a spillover boost from the other measures on the ballot that year, and reputation by association. The one-house body would be cheaper for the state to operate; the unicameral amendment was swept to victory along with amendments to repeal prohibition and legalize pari-mutuel betting in the state; and George Norris, Nebraska's highly respected U.S. senator, was one of the most visible promoters of the plan.

It seems like an open-and-shut case. Yet, the conventional wisdom doesn't reach below the surface to examine the influences of political thought and theory on the state's decision to change the form of its legislature. Average Nebraskans of the 1930s did not necessarily sit around their supper tables discussing the theoretical advantages of the unicameral over the bicameral legislative form. But the actions taken by the leaders in the pro-unicameral movement imply an inherent, although largely unarticulated, political philosophy about how the people should be the government and that government should serve the people's will.

Although the unicameral promoters may not have called their proposals "populist," much about the campaign to adopt a new legislative structure seems to indicate that they believed that the people were a homogeneous entity. Furthermore, those people were capable of making up their own minds and of governing themselves through representation that was as direct as possible, and they deserved a legislature that would facilitate that self-governance.[1]

But regardless of its philosophical underpinnings, the idea for a one-house legislature didn't spring full-blown from the dust of the Great Depression in 1934. It had its roots in the state's history, both economic and political.

The Frontier Foundations

The desire for a transcontinental railroad lay behind the Nebraska Territory's organization as part of the United States in 1854, and that same railroad and its brethren were later to play a major role, for better and for worse, in Nebraskans' economic and political development.

U.S. representative Stephen A. Douglas, of Illinois, most often remembered as Abraham Lincoln's debate opponent, had a hand in Nebraska's journey toward statehood. As early as the 1840s, Americans had begun agitating for a transcontinental railroad. Douglas favored a route roughly paralleling the Platte River so that Chicago, part of his constituency, could become the railroad hub of the nation. But if the route were to run across the Great Plains, the territory west of the Missouri River needed to be organized as part of the United States.

Douglas introduced a bill in the 1844 U.S. House of Representatives to organize the Nebraska Territory. When that bill failed to progress, Douglas tried again in 1845; again he was unsuccessful. After he was elected to the U.S. Senate in 1847, he kept at it. But slavery had become the central issue in the expansion of the nation, and it was not until May 1854 that the Kansas-Nebraska Act was passed, leaving the "slave or free" decision to vote by the people. President Franklin Pierce signed the bill into law on May 30, 1854, and Nebraska became officially a territory of the United States.

By the time the act was official, Native American titles had already been wiped out in most of the area, and the way was clear for the railroad to lay its track as Douglas had hoped. The act opened to white settlers what was left of the Louisiana Purchase. And settle they did.

The territorial population exploded, growing from 2,732 in 1854 to about 50,000 by 1867 as settlers claimed the land, broke the sod, and began producing corn and wheat. The first Nebraska territorial legislature met in January 1855 and granted charters to seventeen towns. By 1862 the territory was exporting enough agricultural produce to more than balance the value of goods imported.

The territory was governed by law that had its origins in the Northwest Ordinance of 1787 and was modeled on the three-branch structure that had become the standard in the United States. Executive and judicial officers were appointed by the U.S. president, and the legislature was popularly elected. It was a bicameral body made up of a thirteen-member council and a twenty-six-member house of representatives.

Thomas B. Cuming, who had been appointed secretary of state, became acting governor when Governor Francis Burt died two days after taking the oath of office in October 1855. Cuming ordered that a census be taken to determine legislative representation, but the undertaking had its problems. The line between Kansas and Nebraska was not clearly delineated, military personnel were not included in the count, and the territory's inhabitants were generally scattered and transient. But the seven deputy marshals assigned to the census project reported 1,818 inhabitants south of the Platte River and 914 north of the Platte.

The Platte was too wide and shallow for ferries, and it was difficult to ford. In the days before bridges, the Platte River was considered a natural dividing point that split Nebraska into two sections. As acting governor, Cuming intensified the natural sectional division, siding with Omaha—on the north side of the Platte—and against Bellevue, which was just south of the river and considered itself capital of the territory.

Even though twice as many people lived south of the Platte as north of it, Cuming assigned seven councilmen and fourteen representatives to areas north of the Platte, and six councilmen and twelve representatives to the south. On top of that, Cuming and the legislature declared the state capital moved from Bellevue to Omaha, where a capitol building was already under construction. People living south of the Platte were furious about what they saw as a great injustice and, under the leadership of J. Sterling Morton of Nebraska City, threatened to leave the Nebraska Territory and join Kansas. The dissenters held mass meetings, vilifying Cuming. Much of the first legislative session was spent trying to undo Cuming's high-handed decision to name Omaha the capital.

Eventually, the capital was moved to Lincoln in an apparent attempt to mollify Morton and his compatriots. But the argument over apportionment and the location of the capitol building intensified a north-south animosity that remained strong during the territorial years and continued in subtler ways for more than a hundred years thereafter.

It wasn't long before Nebraska residents became unhappy with the officials appointed by Democratic president James Buchanan, known for his pro-South, pro-slavery attitude. That discontent boosted Republican strength in the territory, but Nebraskans were slow to make any partisan political commitment. In fact, the Democratic Party's opponents in 1859 organized in Nebraska as the People's Party, not the Republican Party. In 1860, though, the People's Party aligned with the Republicans and supported Abraham Lincoln. Passage of the Homestead Act in 1862 boosted the Republicans' strength even further.

Settlers flocked to Nebraska to claim the land promised by the Homestead Act. But another measure passed in 1862 also had far-reaching effects on Nebraska. On July 1, Congress granted a charter to the Union Pacific Railroad to cross the Plains and gave the railroads seven million acres of Nebraska land. A multitude of railroad towns sprang up across the territory.

As the population grew, so did interest in Nebraska's becoming a state. But not everyone was convinced. When the matter was put to a vote in 1860, the referendum failed, and the issue went dormant until 1864, when the territorial legislature asked Congress to pass legislation making statehood possible—which it did on April 19. Nebraska convened a constitutional convention on July 4 that year, but the citizens were still not excited about making Nebraska a state; the group adjourned immediately and without any attempt to form a constitution.

In 1866 the Republicans pushed statehood through the territorial legislature via some unorthodox procedures: the constitution was prepared and moved through the legislature so fast that members never even saw a copy. That first state constitution included few provisions for a functioning government. Its primary goals seemed to be to simply to make statehood a quick reality and to make government as cheap as possible.[2] It was narrowly approved by the voters, 3,938 to 3,838, on June 2, 1866.

When the constitution was forwarded to the federal government for approval, Congress discovered that the document included a provision saying that only free white males could vote. After nine months of wrangling, Congress approved a revised version that allowed all males except Native Americans to vote. President Andrew Johnson vetoed the bill, but Congress overrode the veto. The state and territorial legislatures met in joint session on February 20 and 21, 1867, to organize the state government, and on March 1, President Johnson gave in to the inevitable and signed a proclamation admitting Nebraska as the thirty-seventh state.

In November of that year, the Union Pacific Railroad completed its rail line across the entire state.

Nebraska was both blessed and cursed by the fact that the state developed at the same time as the growth of mechanized commercial farming. Farming became increasingly more profitable thanks to rail transportation, mass production of steel, the invention of barbed wire, and the availability of steam power to dig wells. But the farmers who dominated the Nebraska population and economy were at the mercy of fluctuating agricultural production and prices.

The state's heavy dependence on agriculture combined with the nearly useless 1866 constitution made state government a difficult proposition. Problems were aggravated by an apparently common practice among public officials of playing fast and loose with public funds, a practice that led to Governor David Butler's impeachment in 1871 on eleven counts of fraud and corruption. He was convicted on one count, appropriating school funds from the federal government for his own use, and was removed from office. Praising the work of the senate during the impeachment trial, Addison Sheldon said the vote showed "no evidence of partisan or sectional prejudice." Instead, each senator voted conscientiously, according to his own opinion.[3]

Despite the state's political woes, the population continued to grow thanks, primarily, to two factors. First, the railroad had been given twenty sections of land for each mile of road constructed; it sold its land at prices that would produce as much immediate revenue as possible but would also encourage settlement along the right of way, providing a customer base and market for the railroad's services. As businessmen offering short-term credit rushed to exploit the new trading possibilities, the population in Nebraska quadrupled in a decade, growing from 250,000 in 1870 to one million in 1880.

Second, federal land policy—embodied in the Homestead Act—offered a quarter section of land to anyone who would cultivate it for five years. The policy encouraged settlers but included a loophole that allowed a great deal of land to fall into hands of the unscrupulous. Settlers could file their homestead claims and after six months commute the claim and purchase the land for a minimum of $1.25 per acre. Some speculators hired people to file the claims, then paid the commutation fees and took title to the land. The result was an ownership pattern that put more acres in fewer hands than the Homestead Act had ever intended. The practice produced a condition that would haunt the state's economy and politics well into the next century.

Along with the settlers, capital also moved west. The settlers were almost all potential borrowers, receiving their loans from easterners who earned high interest on the money loaned. The abundance of credit tempted the new residents of the Plains to overinvest and speculate. On speculation, farmers bought more land than they could cultivate, and land values boomed. As a result, many farmers relied more for their economic welfare on the appreciation of their land than on the sale of their crops. New towns sprang up across Nebraska and the other Plains states, and bonds were approved by the score to provide public buildings, schools, utilities, and streets—and, often, public assistance for the ever-present railroads.

The state had grown dramatically by 1875, but much of the land occupied was submarginal and did not produce enough to pay for the cost of farming it. In addition, people across the state, except in the sandhills, tried to practice the same humid-region diversified agricultural practices that had been successful farther east, believing the theory that the "rain follows the plow." Unfortunately, farmers found that those farming techniques didn't work in approximately the western two-thirds of Nebraska.

Things went well as long as rainfall was plentiful. In fact, the economy boomed during wet-years cycles, resulting in overexpansion. When rainfall dwindled or depression set in, people pulled back. Rather than blame bad weather or poor farming practices for their problems, Nebraskans tended to cast railroads and mortgage lenders as villains in the piece.

The farmer's relative economic position steadily worsened because commodities prices and land prices fell while freight rates and the prices of machinery rose. Many believed that their struggle to survive locusts, drought, and falling prices was only made worse by apparent collusion between politicians and groups to which the farmers were in debt: railroads, banks, and the commercial classes. Farmers were increasingly willing to listen to those denouncing government, railroads, bankers, and "middlemen" as the source of their troubles. By the 1870s, farmers were increasingly wary of powerful business and political interests.

A constitutional convention convened on June 13, 1871, two weeks after Governor Butler had been impeached, to write a desperately needed constitution that would make state government more effective. After two months of hard work, the convention presented a document modeled on the Illinois constitution of 1870. The constitution included measures to regulate railroads and business corporations, both of which fought the new document tooth and nail. And they succeeded; voters rejected all five sections submitted to them.

By 1875 the state government was in near chaos. Central and western Nebraska, which had been "naked prairie" in 1866, were now home to more than a hundred thousand people, people who had no adequate representation in the legislature. In addition, the state's revenue system had broken down, and many Nebraskans simply refused to pay their taxes.

Furthermore, Nebraskans were frustrated by the national economic instability of the mid-1870s, the state's political instability growing out of the Butler administration scandals, and the inadequacy of the constitution to deal with the problems.

State leaders tried again, calling another constitutional convention in 1875. The document created there eased some of the provisions the railroads had opposed in the 1871 constitution but retained the legislative power to regulate railroads. The new constitution enlarged the legislature to eighty-four members in the lower house and thirty-three in the senate with the provision that, after 1880, the numbers in the lower house could increase to a hundred. The document also added the offices of lieutenant governor and attorney general, set a limit on state debt, and separated the supreme court from the district courts. Once again the railroads bitterly opposed the constitution, but this time the people adopted it by a six-to-one margin.

The 1875 document was progressive for its time, but it was built on the undiversified economic and social force that dominated Nebraska in its early years: agriculture. And the document included provisions that would make it very difficult to amend the constitution, a problem that would come back to haunt the state.

In many ways, though, the 1880s were good years for Nebraska. Population grew, rain was plentiful, railroad track mileage almost tripled—and farming continued to dominate the state's economy. A land boom was sparked by the railroad boom that had begun in the 1870s and achieved epidemic proportions by the mid-1880s. Railroad officials visited the communities they planned to serve, promoting the sale of railroad bonds to help finance construction. Few communities turned them down; many took enormous risks that the railroads would bring them prosperity.

By 1890 settlement had pushed across the entire state, the population reached more than a million, and Nebraska had become a major food producing area. Encouraged by the good times, counties and towns floated bonds to help railroads and other enterprises. Corporations issued stock; individuals assumed mortgages. Companies in the East almost pushed loans on Nebraskans, and a fever of speculation in real estate developed. The result was the creation of fictitious wealth and the destruction of true value, a recipe for future trouble.

The boom exploded when deflation began in 1887 and when heat and drought that persisted for most of the next decade turned crops to dust. Eastern investment and credit dried up with the crops, and bankers, mortgage vendors, and railroad promoters went out of business. Many settlers gave up and went back East, handing over their farms to loan companies or simply abandoning them. The railroads that had lured farmers to the West backed down on their promises, sometimes withholding land for speculation, watering their stock, or setting startlingly high rates and installing convoluted regulations for transporting agricultural products.

Residents of countless towns in Nebraska, Kansas, and the Dakotas fled the failing economy, and the population in up to half of the counties of those states began to decrease. The great majority of farmers in the Plains stayed, though, and suffered through a decade of no crops and low prices, forming a discontented class "prepared for the doctrines of political and economic revolt."[4] Many believed the nation's ills were caused by interests that were trying to destroy the revered Protestant work ethic on which the settlement of the Plains was founded. Many believed those interests had taken over the government and were wieldingpower for their private benefit.

Even during the good years, farmers simply were not sharing in the prosperity they saw around them. Land was available, crops were good, and loans had been easy to come by, but prices stayed low. Many farmers didn't believe that the overproduction theory being preached by politicians and businessmen was enough to account for the price drop in a time when consumption was increasing and middlemen were making big profits. The wolf seemed always to be just outside the farmer's door, and many farmers were sure the wolf wore monopolist clothing.[5]

They suspected that high freight rates were caused by railroad monopolies, and they also complained about the stranglehold that grain elevators, bankers, and mortgage holders had over farmers. But the railroad was the biggest villain in the piece. Railroads were politically aggressive, lobbying public officials and providing free passes to each of them. Officers of the Union Pacific and Burlington railroads were rumored to wield undue influence in the election of U.S. senators from Nebraska, actually dictating the choice of one of the state's two senators. The legislature, given the authority in the 1875 constitution to regulate the railroads, seemed unwilling to do so, and the farmers suspected collusion. That fact, combined with growing discontent over economic conditions, fueled a spirit of political rebellion among the state's farmers.

Both major political parties appeared to be dominated by business interests and entrepreneurs. The Republicans wanted government to stimulate the economy by subsidizing railroads and regulating commerce, mostly through tariff legislation. The Democrats preached laissez-faire principles and personal liberty, the idea that the best government was the least government. Neither point of view appealed much to ordinary Nebraskans, and their discontent with government and politics continued to grow. That discontent found an effective voice in the Farmers' Alliance.

The movement began in the southeastern United States but spread to the Plains in the 1870s and 1880s. In fact, Sheldon wrote that the "storm center of the revolution of 1890 was the region between the Mississippi and the Rockies," including Nebraska.[6] The first local chapter of the Farmers' Alliance was born in the town of Filley, Nebraska. The first state alliance organized in Lincoln in 1881, primarily as a citizen lobby. Its first order of business: urging the legislature to pass laws enforcing the constitutional provision to regulate railroads.

By 1887, with economic conditions worsening, the alliance went on the offensive and organized twelve hundred local chapters in Nebraska during 1890 alone. Its stated objectives were education and philanthropy, but Olsen says it "could not have avoided political action if it had wanted to."[7] And, in reality, it didn't want to. As early as 1889, some county groups had run independent slates of candidates with some success. But that was just the beginning.

Farmers grew even angrier with the political system when their 1889 crop was a bin-buster but prices dropped lower than ever. Farmers were producing more than they could sell, and overproduction, combined with new competition from other countries in world markets, lowered commodity prices. Then deflation struck: as the U.S. population grew, the supply of money in circulation remained constant, and the value of a dollar increased. Farmers received relatively fewer dollars for their crops and could not pay off their pre-deflation debts.

By this time, many farmers were ready to believe alliance orators who said the root of their problem was man-made barriers between the producer and the consumer. The suffering "common people" had begun to realize that the American ideal of rugged individualism was not serving them well. They began to doubt the theory that people should be free enough to pave their own way to success and that America's bountiful space and resources guaranteed success to everyone who worked hard enough. They began to question and then reject the gospel of wealth, the doctrine that individuals had the right to acquire as much wealth as they could and to use it as they saw fit. They began to protest the manner in which the privileged few exploited the struggling masses, and they railed against the business monopolies they believed undermined the economic independence of farmers and laborers.

Farmers suspected a conspiracy was at work against them, and that suspicion deepened as they considered their place in a society that seemed to look down on them and their work. Young people left the farm in droves in the late nineteenth century, and those who remained began to understand they were losing status and respect in comparison to urbanites. The chasm between social classes was as big in the 1880s as it had ever been in Nebraska—or ever would be again.

Some scholars think the farmers' rank in society was at the heart of their discontent. Farmers knew, they say, that American society was actually composed of a number of loosely defined classes, but they wanted to believe in social dualism: monopolies and money power versus the farmers and laborers who produced wealth; the people versus the special interests; the public versus the plutocrats. Populists came to believe that the moneyed interests were deliberately oppressing the producers, and they had seen enough examples of bribery and corruption to indicate that their suspicions were not unfounded.

Furthermore, they began to believe that big business interests had control of government, that businessmen were using their wealth to secure privileges, erect defenses against regulation, and maintain their monopolistic positions. Populist farmers discovered that privileged business corrupted politics and began to see private interests as a danger to the public's interests, to believe that individualism alone was not enough to secure democracy in an industrial era. These "radicals" wanted government to restrain individualism, to return authority to the people, in whom they had complete faith and trust. They wanted to increase the state's authority over public goods.

Almost inevitably, the farmers and the alliance turned to politics as a recourse for their ongoing problems. A May 1890 meeting of the Lincoln alliance issued a call for a people's convention, and more than eight hundred delegates representing seventy-nine counties gathered at Bohanan's Hall in Lincoln on July 29. Strongest electoral support for the People's Party created that day came from a band of counties running from the southwestern corner of the state to the northeastern corner, the area where traditional farming practices most drastically fell victim to the arid climate.

The new party's platform rallied the people to demand change and reform from the interests they saw as their nemesis. The platform included calls for increasing the amount of currency in circulation; laws to set freight rates no higher than those in Iowa; a liberal service pension for old soldiers; adoption of the Australian ballot, a single ballot provided by the government rather than separate ballots provided by the parties—thus making "secret" voting actually secret; an eight-hour workday except for agricultural laborers. In addition to hammering out a populist platform, the delegates nominated their own candidate for governor.

When the People's Party organized, leaders of the established parties knew they were in trouble. The Republican convention actually included many of the populists' goals in the GOP's platform. But the populist orators drew huge crowds with their message that farmers were being persecuted in the battle for human rights.

Swept along by hot winds and drought that destroyed farmers' crops, the populists' campaign during the summer of 1890 "approached the sublime energy of the human tornado." On the campaign trail, one speaker said, "We farmers raised no crops, so we'll just raise hell."[8]

The People's Party took clear control of the state senate that fall, garnering eighteen seats to the Democrats' eight and Republicans' seven. The People's Party also took fifty-four seats in the house to the Democrats' twenty-five and the Republicans' twenty-one. At last, the populists must have thought, government would be made to work in their favor.

They must have been miserably disappointed with the next legislative session. Fred Newberry's bill to fix maximum railroad rates, one of the People's Party's primary goals, passed easily in the house, seventy-eight to seventeen, and, after three days and nights of debate, passed in the senate, twenty-three to seven. But James Boyd, the newly elected Democratic governor, vetoed the bill. A majority in both houses voted to override the veto, but neither house achieved the three-fifths majority needed, and the veto stood. The railroad reform bill was dead.

But the People's Party, inexperienced and politically inept as it may have been, was not entirely unsuccessful. The legislature did pass provision for the Australian ballot, a free textbook law, a public fund deposit law, a bill creating mutual insurance courts, a law for an eight-hour workday except on farms, and a decrease in state expenditures. The railroads, however, remained relatively untouched.

In 1892 the People's Party included in its platform a clear, emphatic statement of its belief in the role of government: "We believe that the powers of government—in other words, of the people—should be expanded . . . as rapidly and as far as the good sense of an intelligent people and the teachings of experience shall justify, to the end that oppression, injustice, and poverty shall eventually cease in the land."[9] And the party's national platform was scathing in its indictment of existing social conditions in America.

The party's convention nominated Senator Charles Van Wyck, an experienced politician, for governor. But Van Wyck lost to the Republican candidate, and no party had a majority in the 1893 legislature. The populists did have one victory: they elected William V. Allen to the U.S. Senate. Allen was one of about fifty members of Congress who were populists or owed their seats to the split the People's Party had caused in the Republican vote in their states.

Despite their burst of political success, the populists were unable to form a long-term organization. They could not count on consistent support from any social group. It wasn't that they polarized people along ethno-cultural lines; in fact, it seems they did appeal to "the people" as a unit. But ironically the resulting diversity and lack of clearly defined "we-they" group structure may help to explain why the People's Party was unable to maintain itself in the long term as a political institution. Once the party realized it could not make reform happen on its own, leaders negotiated to join forces with existing parties in what became known as "fusion."

The Nebraska People's Party fused with the Democrats in 1894, nominated Silas Holcomb for governor, and nominated an entirely populist state ticket. Many mainstream Democrats bolted the fused party and nominated their own ticket. Holcomb was elected governor, but Republicans took all the other state offices and regained complete control of the legislature thanks, some said, to significant financial backing from the Union Pacific Railroad, which expected the legislature to continue its hands-off policy.

The People's Party had given Nebraska's common people some voice in state government but had not been able to change farmers' economic position, which only got worse in the 1890s. And William Jennings Bryan displaced the People's Party as the voice of agrarian discontent. Bryan led the transformation of the Democratic Party in Nebraska and the nation from an organization of conservatives, horrified by an expanding government, into a progressive organization that wanted government to play a bigger role in people's lives.

As dissident Republicans returned to the GOP from their temporary membership in the People's Party, they also insisted that the government must help the farmer and laborer, prompting the growth of progressivism in the Republican ranks, too. But it wasn't enough to save the Nebraska GOP in 1896. That year, with Bryan running for president as the fusionist candidate, was the first time in history that the Republicans lost all the Nebraska state offices. Furthermore, the populists held seventeen of thirty-three seats in the state senate and forty-nine of a hundred in the house.

The fusionist legislature of 1897 passed a number of reform measures but, once again, failed to deal effectively with the railroads; bills to abolish free passes and reduce passenger rates were sidetracked or defeated. However, the legislature did adopt a measure authorizing the initiative and referendum at the local level, making Nebraska the first state in the nation to adopt this "peculiarly Progressive-inspired governmental reform."[10] The populists were educating the public about the excesses of conservatism in business and government, laying the foundation for what was to come under other political auspices.

By 1900 it was obvious the People's Party had been irreparably damaged by its fusion with the Democrats. The Republicans swept the state election. By 1908 the People's Party ceased to exist, although many of its ideas lived on in both of the traditional parties. In fact, the Republicans and Democrats of the first decade of the new century seemed to be competing to implement the populist assumption that government should be truly representative of the people and that the long-established tradition that allowed control of politics and economics by the few should end. Both parties began to see the need for government regulation of industry in the interest of the common man, both in Nebraska and in the Plains, and throughout the nation.

Populists may not have been successful at the polls, but much of their program eventually was adopted. Women got the right to vote, U.S. senators were elected by the people instead of the state legislatures, and states gave their citizens the right to "make" law by means of the initiative and to "unmake" law by the referendum and recall—all after the People's Party itself was virtually or actually defunct. As one scholar says, "[If] they lost the battle, the populists won the war."[11]

Ultimately, while populism cannot be considered triumphant, it should be considered to have had democratic promise. The agrarian revolt showed how the people of a society could generate their own democratic culture to challenge the traditional hierarchical culture. The idea—the philosophy—behind the movement represents the real populist achievement.

Nebraska and other Plains states, which had been the main strength of the populist crusade, lent significant support to its descendant: progressivism. The People's Party may have disappeared, but many populist reforms were championed by the progressives who followed.

Progressivism, a national movement for political reform that was born with the new century, picked up on many populist themes. By the summer of 1906, progressivism was sweeping Nebraska. Leaders called for societal control and regulation of businesses, especially of private utilities engaged in public service. Progressives seemed to agree that government should organize the common interest against special interests, that private interests posed a danger to the public's interest, and that government benefits for some "special" groups—business and industry—hurt other groups.

In Nebraska, Republican progressives saw they had to break the railroad's domination of their affairs. The Union Pacific and Burlington railroads' unseemly struggle to control the election of both of Nebraska's U.S. senators in 1901—instead of being content to select one each, as they had in the past—infuriated the citizens and laid the groundwork for the breakup of the railroad machine.

George Sheldon was elected governor in 1906 after campaigning on a strong antirailroad and anticorporation platform. His election wrested control of the state GOP away from ultraconservative, business-oriented leaders and turned the party in a new direction.

The progressive Republican majority of 1907 passed laws making permanent changes in the state's political structure. They crafted the machinery for a statewide compulsory primary election that put the power of nomination in the hands of the voters rather than the party elites. They passed the Child Labor Act, halting or, at least, limiting industry's exploitation of children. They finally succeeded in banning free railroad passes to politicians and government officials, a perk beloved by officials and loathed by the common people. They created a state railroad commission to regulate the mode of transportation that held such power over commerce and the common person's economic well-being.

At Governor George Sheldon's urging, the legislature also "went right to work admonishing lobbyists." Lobbyists employed by the railroads and other corporations had had unlimited access to the floor of the legislature; the new regulations banned lobbyists from the floor and provided that if any lobbyist violated the rules, the sergeant at arms "shall eject him."[12] The highly visible move to control special interests as well as the other reform legislation of 1907 brought to fruition the revolution in public thought begun in 1890.

The candidates campaigned on reform issues again in 1908, and the 1909 legislature passed a bank guarantee law and changed the primary from a closed to an open election. It also enacted more railroad regulations and made election of the state's judges nonpartisan. Nationally, Nebraska's George Norris became prominent for leading the insurgent progressives in their battle against the regulars for control of the Republican Party, first in the U.S. House and then in the Senate.

By 1910, although no frontier remained in Nebraska and growth had shifted to the cities, Nebraska remained mostly an agricultural state. And it remained largely homogeneous with regard to race, religion, ethnicity, occupation, and wealth. Politically, the progressives continued their reforms. From 1890 to 1910 state and local government grew dramatically. Eight new state institutions were created and twenty-three new state activities authorized. In addition, government became far more democratized, reflecting the progressives' agenda of getting more power directly to the voters.

Between 1901 and 1919, seventeen constitutional amendments were proposed; ten were approved. They included the Board of Railroad Commissioners, with regulatory powers, in 1906; the initiative and referendum procedure at the state level in 1912; woman suffrage in 1918. Those measures, along with progressive legislative steps like those discussed above made Nebraska a leader in government reform in the early 1900s.

During World War I, as the nation endured the trauma of the first modern, widespread war, the influence of populism and agrarian reform continued to be felt. Remnants of the old People's Party formed the Non-Partisan League in Nebraska, patterned on a similar organization in North Dakota. The league aimed to create state-owned stockyards, packing houses, cold storage plants, elevators, and creameries, attracting the wrath of the state's Council of Defense, which condemned the league's plan as too socialist, especially since many members of the league lived in communities with heavily German heritage.

Nebraska's primary contribution to the war was food production for the Allies, and the state prospered as farm prices increased spectacularly. However, instead of using their profits to pay off existing debt, many farmers bought more land, and mortgage debt hit new highs. When prices fell after the war, Nebraska agriculture went into a freefall from which it had not recovered when the stock market crashed in 1929.

In addition, the state's—and the nation's—conservative reaction to the aftermath of World War I slowed dramatic progressive advances. When Governor Samuel McKelvie called for a constitutional convention in 1919, some were concerned that radicals might take control and try to eliminate all foreign "influences" from the state. However, the members of the convention that met from December 1, 1919, to March 25, 1920, proved to be moderates who worked sincerely to remedy procedural defects of the 1875 constitution.

McKelvie believed the constitution no longer met the needs of a state facing changing social and economic conditions. He favored a new constitution that would institutionalize progressive reforms. Delegates were unwilling to go quite that far, though. Instead of a new constitution, the convention produced forty-one separate amendments to the old document, and the voters approved every one. One notable item the delegates considered was a proposal for a one-house legislature, which failed on a tie vote.

The nation entered the 1920s disillusioned with Woodrow Wilson and the progressivism he preached. Citizens wanted simply to be let alone to enjoy the postwar boom. Public hatred and distrust of wealth seemed to have subsided, and by the time Calvin Coolidge was elected president in 1924, many seemed willing to accept his notion that "the business of America is business." [13]

The country's intellectual leaders lost faith in "the people" and often cynically repudiated progressivism's ideals. And the progressives who remained in government often could not agree among themselves on the problems facing society, much less what should be done to address them. In fact, some scholars argue that the so-called Congressional Progressives of the 1920s gave only lip service to the progressive philosophy, with the exception of George Norris, who remained true to his progressive ideals throughout his decades in Congress.

State politics in the postwar period centered on taxes, state expenditures, and exercise of regulatory powers already granted to state government. National issues had some impact, but Nebraskans proved to be independent voters. They frequently crossed party lines and voted on state issues as if those issues had nothing to do with national issues, implicitly endorsing Norris's assertion that the business of state government is not partisan and lending credence to scholars' assertion that Nebraskans have a long history of weak partisanship. [14]

Throughout the 1920s Nebraskans continued to vote primarily Republican in national elections. But Sheldon said the "returns of the 1922 election exhibited the spirit of political independence which had developed since the initial farmers' uprising of 1890." For instance, Gilbert Hitchcock, a Democrat, was defeated for the U.S. Senate, but Charles Bryan, another Democrat, was elected governor. A separate Progressive Party was not much of a force, but the two mainline parties were dividing into progressive and conservative factions, and party labels no longer controlled elections.

Nebraskans demonstrated their political independence by electing Democrats in three of six congressional districts in 1924, supporting progressive Robert LaFollette for president and reelecting Norris, still registered as a Republican, to the Senate. Norris supported Roosevelt for president in 1932, and many progressive Nebraska Republicans did, too. They also elected a full slate of Democrats to the Legislature that year.

Many heard in FDR's inaugural address remnants of the old populist tradition. The president talked, in Jeffersonian idiom, of common folk being exploited by special interests and about the virtues of farming and country life. Like the populist and progressive movements, the New Deal's goal was to reform capitalism, not to dump the economic system in favor of something else. The aim was to control government for the common good; economic justice, the New Dealers believed, would naturally follow.

The populists and progressives may have lost their identity as political movements, but their ideas and goals lived on.

Nebraska Takes the Plunge

In Nebraska, as in many other states, Progressives of the 1930s concentrated their efforts on legislative reform. State government had come in for plenty of criticism over the years, partly because state legislatures were stuck in a pattern designed for a self-sufficient economy and couldn't cope with the social and economic problems of an industrial society.

The populist movement had built on farmers' discontent with their place in that changing society, and one result was the persistent belief among many that state government was unresponsive to the common person. Progressives especially condemned legislatures' inefficient methods and frequent subservience to special interests, most notably the railroads. Unhappy Nebraskans said the procedural intricacies and divided responsibility of the legislature meant the people did not know whom to blame or praise, or how to make the legislature responsive to their problems.

The progressive movement in Nebraska as early as 1911 had gotten people excited about social reform and about adapting the machinery of state government to social and economic change. Some suggested revising the structure of state government in order to change the substance of government policy, understanding, at least instinctively, that "the rules of the political game, as defined by the structure of institutions, cannot be divorced from the stakes for which the game is played."[15]

One of those suggested structural changes was unicameralism, an idea that had arisen in fifteen states in the early years of the twentieth century. Bicameralism, according to this view, simply complicated government and added to confusion, resulting in a waste of effort and in frustration.

John Norton was behind the first attempt to establish a unicameral legislature in Nebraska. In 1913 the state senator from Polk said Nebraska's legislative machinery was antiquated, expensive, inefficient, and in need of an update. He suggested that the existing legislature establish a study commission made up of members of both its houses to see what could be done to improve the body. The commission reported to the 1915 session of the legislature, recommending a one-house body with a membership somewhere between the thirty-three members then serving in the senate and the hundred in the house. Commission members said they saw "no need to retain a second house to represent the wealthy class or the aristocracy in a democratic state."[16]

Furthermore, they said one body could more directly represent the public will of a democratic people and would be more representative and responsible, eliminating the opportunity for vote trading and buck-passing between houses. As rousing as the proposals may have been, the legislature declined to put the necessary constitutional amendment on the ballot in 1915 and again in 1917, so the citizenry didn't get a chance to voice its opinion.

The next attempt came when Norton introduced a proposal for a one-house body in the 1919–1920 constitutional convention. The delegates almost added the unicameral to their list of forty-one recommended constitutional amendments, but in the end the proposal was defeated on a forty-three to forty-three tie. A 1923 petition drive tried to place the idea before the voters, but promoters couldn't get enough signatures to put the proposition on the ballot.

But the idea had begun to catch on and got continuing nationwide publicity. The National Municipal League model state constitution of 1920 advocated a one-house legislature, and the January 28, 1923, *New York Times* published a piece by Senator Norris promoting a one-house nonpartisan state legislature. Norris denounced party politics and conference committees, which progressive politicians frequently criticized as the place where reform legislation either died or was emasculated. And Norris praised nonpartisanship in no uncertain terms. Caught up in the spirit of reform, the Farmers Cooperative and Educational Union resolved at its 1924 convention that Nebraska should establish such a body.

The legislature tried, and failed, to put the question on ballot in 1925, and the idea may have died from sheer exhaustion had not the Great Depression "awakened the people to an interest in remaking the legislative body which had ceased to function with any degree of effectiveness."[17] The Depression bred discontent with institutions and willingness to try new ideas. People who had developed "a familiar attitude of disrespect for the legislature and a sense of utter futility with respect to securing progressive legislation" were ready for change.[18] As Nebraska experienced a period of drought and depression similar to that of the 1890s, its citizens seemed interested in new ways of doing political business.[19]

It fell to George Norris to take the lead. A devout Republican when he was elected to the U.S. House of Representatives in 1903, Norris had gradually moved away from Republican orthodoxy and toward politics on his own terms. Nebraskans sent him back to the House four more times and then elected him to the Senate in 1912. After backing the progressive Robert LaFollette for president in 1924 and the Democrat Al Smith in 1928, Norris finally left the GOP and declared himself an independent. And Nebraskans kept on electing him into the 1940s.

In a foreword to a 1960s reprint of Norris's autobiography, Arthur M. Schlesinger Jr. wrote that Norris believed the greatest danger the American system had faced was "consuming ambitions, both for power and for wealth; the greed and avarice of individuals and groups for wealth; the injection of privilege, favoritism and discrimination in national policy." Norris saw government as one means to combat the forces of entrenched, organized greed, Schlesinger wrote, and had faith in the people and their capacity to govern themselves prudently and wisely.[20] Norris believed in the populist/progressive ideal: that "the people" should be in charge of their own government.

And Norris saw the state legislature as a primary arena in which the people should assert their will. Norris never abandoned his crusade for a better legislature. In fact, he had expressed some interest in 1931 in being governor of Nebraska so that he could lead in reforming a state government "now utterly outworn in form, governed by Lilliputian politicians for private or party advantage."[21] In Nebraska, Norris's voice was one to be reckoned with.

The 1933 legislature, dominated by newly elected Democrats swept in on FDR's coattails, may have provided the straw that broke the bicameral's back. The legislators of 1933 had said they would pass few laws, talk little, and get home for spring plowing. But they passed almost two hundred measures, argued a lot, and had the longest session on record.

They fought frequently and publicly and fumbled badly on tax legislation, liquor regulations, and reapportionment. To top things off, they didn't even pass an appropriations bill and had to be called back to a special session to provide the state the wherewithal to continue to function. They were, Senning said with some understatement, unprepared to cope with the "staggering questions" surrounding the Depression.[22]

In the midst of the disastrous session, Senator John Boelts of Merrick County took one more stab at reform. He proposed that the legislature be reorganized as a "house of representatives only." The bill reached final reading in the senate but did not pass.

But the 1933 senate did pass a resolution to establish a nonpartisan commission made up of members of both chambers. The commission would make a systematic study of the cost of state government and recommend improvements. The house of representatives, though, refused to pass the resolution authorizing the study. That kind of thumb-your-nose attitude sent a signal to the public that the legislature wasn't really interested in reforming itself.

Public disgust with the 1933 legislature contributed to the public's willingness to consider a new system. Norris thought the time was ripe to bring the power of his influence and popularity to bear on Nebraska's struggling legislature. He said he had received requests from all over the state, urging him to head a movement toward a unicameral body. "People trusted his judgment and integrity," Senning said.[23]

Norris wanted to return the state's legislature to the people. He wanted to simplify law so that Nebraska could have "a real democracy" and a legislature so open that the ordinary person could easily understand and observe it in action. Then every Nebraskan could "clearly see whether his or her representative in the legislature was carrying out his promises and working for the betterment of mankind and for the improvement of our system, or whether he was covering up his tracks while serving special interests."[24]

On December 21, 1933, Norris wrote a draft of a constitutional amendment to remake the Nebraska legislature. He presented his proposal to a crowd of eight hundred in Lincoln on February 22, 1934, and a group of prominent men and women from across Nebraska formed the Model Legislature Committee to revise and promote the amendment.

After some debate, the committee decided to make the amendment general and short, covering only the essentials of the new institutional structure. The amendment left the lieutenant governor in place as presiding officer, set a total dollar figure for salaries (seventy-five thousand dollars for the biennium), and continued the practice of biennial sessions.

Negotiation was more difficult on some of the other points, though. Norris had wanted to designate twenty-one members for the new body but compromised to a number between thirty and fifty, to be set by the last bicameral body. He also would have preferred that legislators serve four-year terms but ultimately went along with the familiar two-year term.

On nonpartisanship, however, Norris would not compromise. Norris had consistently said he would like to abolish party responsibility and establish personal responsibility to the citizens in its stead. Even his fellow committee members' fear that including nonpartisanship might doom the amendment was not enough to change the senator's mind. In fact, Norris told his compatriots that the nonpartisan aspect of the proposed amendment "would be one of its strongest appeals."[25]

In his February kick-off speech, Norris tied the reform proposal to his long-held progressive philosophy. He traced the origins of the democratic ideal in America, asserting that the history of U.S. civilization had been basically a contest between rulers and ruled. Norris said the U.S. Constitution, with its liberal democracy model, reflected the theory that "common people . . . were not sufficiently civilized and sufficiently educated to govern themselves" but added that history had seen inevitable advances toward the achievement of real democracy.[26]

Once the idea was introduced to the state's citizens, the committee took advantage of Nebraska's initiative process and started a petition drive for the fifty-seven thousand signatures needed to place the proposed unicameral legislature on the ballot. The first problem was to find enough people to circulate the petitions, and the committee concluded at one point that it would need to pay circulators five cents per signature. Norris himself donated a thousand dollars to the cause and rounded up some friends to do the same. As it turned out, enough people volunteered to circulate petitions that the fund was never used. Once the drive got going, "support grew like a snowball rolling downhill," Norris said.[27] Eventually, ninety-five thousand people signed the petitions.

Supporters of the amendment campaigned all over the state, led by the seventy-three-year-old Norris, who spoke on the radio or in person once or twice a day about the amendment during the month before the election, driving all over Nebraska, nearly wearing out his car and paying his own expenses.

The proposal had plenty of opponents, including nearly all the newspapers in the state. Only the *Lincoln Star* and the *Hastings Tribune* editorialized in favor of the plan. The rest of the more than four hundred papers then publishing in Nebraska—mostly weeklies—either ignored the amendment or opposed it, preferring to maintain the status quo. They cited Alexander Hamilton and others, whose arguments in favor of bicameralism in the early days of the nation rested on a defense of property rights. And they said a legislature needed two houses in order to check sectional interests. Many disliked the small number of members proposed for the unicameral, warning that lobbyists would be able to "buy a few men cheap" in such a body.[28]

An *Omaha World-Herald* editorial on October 30, 1934, urged readers to pay attention to the amendment's potential threat to democracy. The paper said a unicameral "would be an about-face from the democratic plan of making laws by the people into the unexplored realm of making laws by a bloc or oligarchy." An aspiring dictator, the paper opined, would be able to shortcut his way through legislative checks and balances and have his way with the law.

Furthermore, the editorialist wrote, by doing away with the two houses and their 133 members from all geographical sections and substituting the exclusive one-house plan with its maximum of 50 members from large districts, "Sen. Norris proposes, in effect, to take representation away from the farmer and the worker." Those were "red flag" words in a Nebraska economically and psychologically committed to the farmer.

Other groups who did not want Nebraska to change its system included leaders of both political parties, bankers, and businessmen. Some said a unicameral legislature would put too much power into the hands of only a few people; others said without the checks of two houses, too many laws would be passed. The political parties opposed the amendment's nonpartisan feature and the small size, and they, too, played the rural card. The parties said farmers would not be adequately represented in the new system.

Agricultural leaders picked up on that theme. The editors of the *Nebraska Farmer* produced a brochure opposing the amendment. Norris admitted the farm vote was divided; for instance, many farmers believed the legislature should be composed of at least a hundred members in order to assure better representation for the agricultural sector.

But it was, apparently, the measure to make the legislature nonpartisan that drew the greatest criticism, just as the Model Legislature Committee members had predicted. Some critics said nonpartisanship would deprive the voters of an important basis on which to make their voting choices. Other warned that absence of party discipline would give special interests a huge advantage. However, the average citizen apparently wasn't worried about the nonpartisan provision. Nonpartisanship was popular in the Midwest during the progressive era, and Nebraska's political culture gives evidence of being traditionally nonpartisan.[29] Apparently, many voters believed Norris's argument that institutional reforms like the nonpartisan unicameral would result in efficient, democratic government where decisions would be made by responsible individuals following their consciences, judging issues on their merits and without the influence of party.

The critics thought they would be able to preserve the status quo. On the eve of the November 6, 1934, election, Norris wrote, many of the state's politicians were certain the proposal would be defeated. On the contrary, the amendment passed handily, approved by 59.6 percent of those voting on the measure, a three-to-two margin. Two other amendments on the ballot also passed, repealing prohibition and legalizing pari-mutuel betting. Rumor had it that supporters of the other two measures had urged people to vote "yes" on all three, sweeping the unicameral along in the tide.[30] But the unicameral amendment passed with the highest margin of approval. It was rejected in only a scattered nine of ninety-three counties and only 73 of 2,029 precincts.

Nebraskans had made history, important history. "Both from an institutional and a political point of view [the creation of the unicameral legislature] probably represents the most radical innovation in the history of American state government."[31] Senning, the political scientist, provided the big-picture explanation. The common people of the late nineteenth and early twentieth centuries, he said, felt less reverence for their so-called betters, and that leveling of the social structure helped break down the two-house system. He listed indications of a rise in the nation's democratic—as opposed to "republican"— spirit: the universal voting franchise (as of 1919); the election of U.S. senators by popular vote rather than by state legislatures (as of 1913); the common people's increased access to political information via cheap newspapers and radio.[32] The passage of the unicameral amendment demonstrated that a large majority of voters had become convinced that a one-house legislature would be more responsive to their needs.

At the fundamental level, Norris's support was probably the factor that put the amendment over the top. Other states in the Plains and South also had strong populist and progressive roots, although it can be argued Nebraska's roots were deeper, stronger, and longer lasting than those in most other states. Many other states had considered but not adopted a unicameral system. But none of them had a George Norris to evangelize on behalf of the reform. Nebraskans knew Norris, knew his reputation for honesty and integrity. They believed him when he said he was fighting for the common man and against special interests. "No one doubts him; his record backs him up at every point."[33]

The record pointed to an independent and progressive spirit. Norris may officially have been a Republican from his first election to the Congress in 1902 until he registered as an independent before his 1936 reelection to the Senate, but he was associated from the start with the progressive philosophy and a devotion to the common people. In 1910 Norris led a group of reformers from both parties in passing a resolution limiting the autocratic powers of the Speaker of the U.S. House of Representatives. In 1917 because he believed big business was stirring up pro-war sentiment, he voted against the United States's entry into World War I. "Patriots" vilified him for his act of conscience, and Norris felt compelled to return to Nebraska and explain his vote to his fellow citizens. "I have come home to tell you the truth," he said. Nebraskans believed his explanation, respected his honesty, and returned him to the Senate for another term.

That wasn't all. Norris was the father of two major federal policy initiatives: the Tennessee Valley Authority, which built dams to control flooding and generate electricity, and the Rural Electrification Association, which brought electricity to rural areas throughout the nation. Both projects were criticized by some as too "socialistic," but Norris defended them as innovations that would benefit the common folk of America.

Senator Norris's reputation as someone willing to fight for what he believed in and as someone who believed in the rights of the common people undoubt-edly led Nebraskans to trust him when he said a nonpartisan unicameral would serve them well. And, thanks to his nearly frantic campaigning on behalf of the plan, pretty much everybody in the state had had an opportunity to hear or see the venerable senator's political and personal dedication to the cause. Norris should definitely get the bulk of the credit for Nebraska's adoption of the unicameral.

The amendment's way was probably also eased by the fact that, in the midst of the Depression, a one-house body would be cheaper to operate. People were desperate to save money, both individually and collectively. Further-more, the memory of the pathetic 1933 legislature and its failure to make needed public policy may also have prompted people to vote for change.[34] In addition, voters may have been influenced by the progressive New Deal philosophies taking hold in America: a renewed spirit of liberalism and ex-perimentalism sweeping the nation, a spirit George Norris endorsed and embodied.

In other words, the timing was exactly right.

The amendment's promoters were elated by their success. On the day after the unicameral amendment was approved by the voters, C. A. Sorensen of Lincoln, chairman of the Model Legislature Committee, called the victory "the beginning of a New Deal in legislative efficiency and responsibility."[35]

The amendment left it up to the 1935 legislature—the last bicameral, par-tisan group—to work out many of the provisions for the new unicameral. That included exactly how often the body should meet—the legislators retained biennial sessions—and how many members the unicameral would have. The amendment required between thirty and fifty, and it required that the state be reapportioned to provide for districts as nearly equal in population as possible but with the stipulation that counties could not be divided among districts.

John Senning brought in map after map of potential districts. After some negotiating, the number of districts was set at forty-three. It became obvious that a legislature of fifty members would mean the eastern one-third of the state would have eighteen more legislators than the western one-third. With forty-three members, the difference between the two regions was only thirteen. With fewer than forty-three, the balance again tipped toward the east.

Responding to critics who said even fifty legislators was not enough to be representative, Senning said the new, small legislature would actually provide better representation for the people of Nebraska. The old idea that a legislator, elected from a specific area, was chiefly responsible for promoting the interests of his geographic district, Senning said, had "given way to the modern idea of representing social and economic interests." People of similar ideas combined with like groups throughout the state, he said. As a result, every state legislator was "one of forty-three arbiters of conflicting social and economic interests, statewide in extent." Far from being a detriment, the larger districts actually promoted better representation, giving the legislator a wider perspective and letting him see statewide concerns telescoped in his own district.[36]

After plenty of discussion, redistricting was accomplished, and the stage was set for a legislative experiment not seen in the United States since Vermont abandoned its unicameral form almost exactly a century earlier—in 1836.

3 / Let the Sun Shine In

The Unicameral's Wide-Open Processes and Institutions

George Norris had faith in the wisdom of the common people and, thus, an abiding faith in the possibilities of democracy. As a good progressive, he believed a fundamental requirement for a democratic system was that it be open and accessible to the citizenry. Openness was one of the primary goals he and others like John Senning, then chairman of the political science department at the University of Nebraska, set for the unicameral. They came up with a variety of ways to reach that goal.

Unified Responsibility

The two houses in a bicameral legislature, Norris said, frequently did battle with each other. As a result, lots of important legislation got lost in the political shuffle, and it was hard to change the status quo. The common people were the losers, Norris said. Even more important, the two-house structure automatically required conference committees, which Norris called a "third branch" of the legislature and an evil one at that. And of course, one house would just be easier for citizens to understand and follow. Legislators' actions would be clear-cut and open, and each member would have to stand or fall on his own record.

When a 1913 joint committee of the Nebraska legislature had proposed a one-house body, the committee members had made the same points. Two houses, the committee's report said, let members off the hook when, for instance, one house would pass a bill and then some members who voted in its favor would privately urge the other house to defeat it. Or a small group in one house might easily hold up legislation from the other house until members "extort from it what they demand."[1] In other words, the two-house structure provided all kinds of opportunities for legislators to hide their true motives and actions from the people who elected them.

"Responsibility for failure is thus divided, enabling participants in the fraudulent procedure to conceal their own records and to cover up their own tracks," Norris wrote.[2] In a one-house body, the unicameralists asserted, members would have far fewer places to hide.

The conference committee, a necessity in a bicameral legislature, was the source of the most dastardly legislative evil, Norris believed. Norris particularly hated the fact that conference committees met behind closed doors.

"Thus, we see that in vital legislation, in which the people are deeply interested, laws are defeated in secret, without a record vote, and without a roll call vote, by two members of this powerful third house," Norris said. "In this way, all kinds of jokers get into our laws, and the people are not able to place the responsibility upon the shoulders of those who are responsible for these jokers."[3] Very often what emerged from the conference committee was an entirely different product from what had been passed, more or less in the open, in either house. And citizens were deprived of any opportunity to pass a just and fair judgment upon the result, Norris said.

The senator repeatedly explained that the concept of a two-branch state legislature was carried over from America's mother country, Great Britain, where one branch represented the common people and the other the aristocracy. In this country, Norris said, "we have no such classes" and the constitutions of the states reflect the rock-bottom American belief that "there is but one class." So it made no sense to elect two groups of people on the same basis and with the same jurisdiction. The only result was to make the proceedings in both the houses harder to follow and more open to manipulation.

And finally, Norris had no sympathy for those who believed removing one house would eliminate the checks and balances so much a part of the traditional American democratic system. "[A]fter these checks and balances are posted," Norris said, "it will be found that the politicians have the checks, and the special interests have the balance."[4]

Participation for All
Plenty of critics thought reducing the size of the Nebraska legislature from 133 members to fewer than 50 would be a big mistake. But Norris argued that a smaller body would be more open to public inspection. Besides that, he said, a large membership was detrimental to real representation. In a large body, many members seldom had the chance even to offer amendments on important pieces of legislation. They often had to vote for bills containing items they didn't like in order to get things they did like. Or they may have had to vote against some bills because the bad outweighed the good. If every member had the right and opportunity to debate and offer amendments, better legislation would result, Norris believed.

Proponents of the unicameral believed a small body would mean individual members would debate freely and be able to amend bills to make them better. They said all points of view would be represented and each member

would feel more responsible for studying and weighing the merits of proposed legislation. They said a small body wouldn't have to delegate power
to committees, shifting and dividing responsibility. And, with all members
participating in the discussion and debate, every member's record on every
bill "would clearly appear."[5]

Norris wanted a body small enough to insure that every member would
be involved in deliberation and discussion, that no member could avoid his
responsibilities, and that his constituents could watch him at work and hold
him accountable. Norris eventually agreed to set the membership of the new
unicameral at between thirty and fifty. The members of the 1935 bicameral
drew the legislative districts and determined the final number. They settled
on forty-three.

No Party Skirts to Hide Behind

Norris's enthusiasm for a nonpartisan legislature was another point of conflict among the unicameral's promoters. Many on the committee thought
Nebraskans might buy the idea of one house but vote against the proposed
amendment because of the nonpartisan provision. On this point, though,
Norris would not give in. He had been preaching for more than a decade
that the business of the state is in no way partisan, and he was not going
to back off from that position when the new legislative structure was ready
to go before the voters. In fact, he told the others on the committee that
he believed the voters would like the nonpartisan feature of the new body as
much as or more than any other part of the proposal. In that regard, Norris was
probably well in tune with Nebraskans and their tradition of independence
and nonpartisanship.[6]

Norris had complained that men were often elected to the legislature
because they happened to be candidates on one party ticket or another. But
he said legislators' duties had nothing to do with the national administration or
the success of any political party. And anyway, he said, eliminating party labels
from campaigns and ballots would result in members' being elected on the
basis of their qualifications, not what he saw as a superfluous party affiliation.
Actually, Norris said, a citizen who voted a straight party ticket that included
state legislators often ended up voting for someone "who disagrees with him
entirely upon all matters over which he will have jurisdiction if he is elected."
The result was a legislature out of harmony with the state's people on state
issues, he said.

But it wasn't only in elections that nonpartisanship was to be significant.
Within the body itself, organization would be done without the usual reliance
on party structure—no majority and minority leaders, no party whips, no

party discipline. And that would lead to independent thinking on the part of the legislators, Norris said in his Model Legislature speech. "Those elected on a partisan platform are inclined to follow the bidding and dictates of party machines and bosses," and the likely result is privilege for the few at the expense of the many: "The good of all the people is sacrificed for the personal gain of a part of the people."[7]

Opponents of nonpartisanship charged that absence of party leadership and discipline would result in chaos at worst or confusion at best. But proponents said freedom from party and the rewards and punishments party could dish out would allow legislators to use their own judgment and decide issues on the merits rather than on the basis of the dictates of party leaders or party platforms. They said nonpartisanship would end political bickering and rivalry among members and that each member would "assume a position of responsibility rather than that of a cog in a political machine."[8]

In other words, eliminating party discipline and party pressure would, like the one-house structure and the small size of the legislature, set every senator squarely in the spotlight of public attention. Rather than being beholden to party bosses, the legislators would be beholden only to the people. Rather than being able to blame party leaders for some vote or position, the legislator would have to bear for himself the responsibility for his actions and votes. There would be no party to run to and nowhere to hide.

The senators in the first unicameral session proclaimed their loyalty to the principle of nonpartisanship and their commitment to represent "the people." Speaker Charles Warner told the *Lincoln Star* on the unicameral's opening day, January 5, 1937, "We owe no allegiance to any party or to any group. Our responsibility is to the whole people of Nebraska." Earlier, looking ahead to the first session, the newspaper had made much the same point: the legislators would answer not to parties but "only to the people."[9] After the session, the *St. Louis Post-Dispatch* agreed: "Under the unicameral, the people are the driver."[10]

Keep It Simple

Norris and his fellow unicameralists like John Norton were determined the body would be open to public scrutiny. Norton was elected to the first unicameral and served as chair of its Rules Committee, giving him an excellent opportunity to shape the legislature's rules to accomplish that goal.

The rules that first session included the requirement that every standing committee hold a public hearing on every bill referred to it and that the hearing be preceded by at least five calendar days' notice (Rule VII). It was a radical idea.

Neither house in the old bicameral legislature had been governed by any rule requiring public hearings. The unicameral amendment's innovative procedure was "one step in abolishing the relic of secret sessions," soliciting public comment and input and helping to make the public aware of the issues before the legislature, and it was met with "widespread enthusiasm" from the public.[11] No longer could committee members discuss a bill among themselves with little or no input from the public or other members of the legislature.

Besides that, the rules required that each standing committee keep a record of its proceedings and that any two committee members could call for a roll call vote on any bill or amendment. That roll call was to be made part of the committee report and was to be entered in the daily journal (Rule VII.9).

Perhaps even more important was the legislature's decision that, while the general public could be excluded from a committee's executive sessions "for purpose of deliberative acceleration," reporters should be allowed to remain and to report on what they observed.[12] That meant committees could hide little or nothing from the public—or from the legislature as a whole.

Furthermore, the rules stipulated that a committee could take final action on bills only at regularly scheduled meetings (VII.10), another attempt to assure visibility and accountability to the public—and perhaps also to the legislature as a body. All these measures meant that "a legislative thicket has, indeed, been cleared for the cultivation of representative democracy."[13] Keeping procedures open allowed the legislature to delegate authority to committees and increase the efficiency of the entire body while at the same time keeping the clamps on potential committee elitism and privilege.

The constitutional amendment itself was also forthright about exactly how open the unicameral was expected to be. It stated that "the doors of the Legislature and of the Committee of the Whole shall be open, unless when the business shall be such as ought to be kept secret." The reference to open sessions was a clear contrast to the rules of the 1935 senate, which included special provisions for secret sessions and confidentiality, and punishment for those who disclosed secrets.

Some other specific rules also were laid out in the language of the amendment itself. For instance, the amended constitution's Article III, Section 14 went into detail about just how a bill should progress through the legislative process: It was to be read by title when introduced. Each member was to have a printed copy of the bill. No final votes could be taken until at least five legislative days after a bill was introduced or until it had been on file for final reading at least one legislative day. No bill was to contain more than one subject. And the bill and all amendments were to be printed and "read at large" in the legislative chamber before a vote on final passage.

The idea behind most of these specific provisions was to insure that bills would be considered as fully by one house as they would have been by two. The unicameral promoters were sensitive to critics' fears that a unicameral body would rush legislation along so fast that the average citizen would have no time to figure out what was going on and that many a legislator could be stampeded into inept policy making. The unicameralists wanted to be sure each bill would get two thorough considerations on the floor and that both citizens and legislators would have time to digest just what was in a bill before a final vote was allowed.

Openness and accountability were also facilitated by other rules the 1937 unicameral adopted in the early weeks of its existence. Although Norris was not involved in shaping the rules, he had advised the new body that all proceedings be kept completely open, and the legislature made a point to follow that advice. Procedures were kept simple but included enough restrictions to make action deliberate and slow enough that a watchful public could understand and, if it wished, intervene.

For instance, the rules mandated that legislators introduce only bills they were willing personally to support (Rule XII.2), a requirement intended to keep legislative processes straightforward and prevent manipulation of the system. Each bill was to contain only one subject, and that subject was to be clearly expressed in the title (Rule XII.15). Omnibus bills were not allowed, preventing the possibility that a group of legislators could take control of the agenda by grouping measures together and shepherding them through the legislature as a package.

Under the watchful eyes of and with significant input from the public, each legislator was expected to maintain his independence and do the people's bidding. The rules were framed so that any voter could see how the legislator from his district stood on every issue.

The number of standing committees was slashed in the switch to one house. The 1935 legislature boasted twenty-eight standing committees in the senate and thirty-one in the house, probably because each of the 133 members of the legislature demanded a seat on at least one committee.[14] Before the new unicameral met for the first time, Senning suggested that the spirit of unicameralism would best be served by reducing the number of committees to six and the membership on each to no more than six. Of course, even in the small, forty-three-member body, that arrangement would have left some legislators with no committee assignment at all, not exactly an idea most legislators were likely to embrace.

John Norton, senator-elect from Polk, had also begun to plan for the new unicameral's structure and rules; he suggested fifteen committees. Once the session began, Norton and the Rules Committee eventually settled on a total of sixteen standing committees—plus their own select committee—a configuration the unicameral adopted.

Committees were organized around major fields of legislation instead of individual subjects. The rules assured no overlapping in committee assignments (Rule VI.4) so that members had no more than one committee hearing or meeting on any given afternoon and no legitimate excuse to miss a hearing. Each member was expected to participate in the work of his committees and to be accountable for his own and the committee's actions.

A reporter for the *Christian Science Monitor Magazine*, writing about the first session of the unicameral, said it had devised a set of rules "to create an internal machinery and procedure to facilitate accuracy, clarity and reasonably speedy enactment."[15]

The ultimate goal of an open legislature was better government, government more responsive to the citizens. Keeping government's workings open to public view would mean legislators could not "without exposure, indulge in practices which will result in legislation contrary to the public good."[16] Instead, as Norris wrote in his 1945 autobiography, the simplified procedures of the unicameral legislature made it impossible for members to evade their duty and easy for ordinary citizens to place responsibility for the passage or defeat of legislation "where it belongs."[17]

Going on Faith

George Norris was first elected to public office in 1890 as a Republican and served in the U.S. House of Representatives and later the U.S. Senate until his defeat in 1942, most of those years as a maverick and independent. He was a politician, a statesman, and a thinker, a man who left his mark on the Congress and on his constituents.

When Norris met with Colonel John Maher, John Senning, and about eight hundred men and women from across Nebraska on February 22, 1934, to lay out his plans for a one-house, nonpartisan legislature, it was the culmination of years of thinking and speaking about and planning for this revolutionary new body. While a number of early American colonies had adopted unicameral legislatures, only three states had kept the structure. Vermont was the last to revert to the two-house system, and it did so in 1836, almost a century before Norris began proposing that Nebraskans adopt the unicameral structure.

Norris and the other proponents for change had their goals firmly in mind and thought the system they were proposing would get the state where they thought it should go. But the fact remains that, despite careful thought and planning, they were, to an extent, going on faith—faith that the structure and system and rules of the unicameral would be specific enough to accomplish their goals and broad enough to adapt to changing times and changing needs.

Openness and accountability were at the heart of the plans for a one-house, small, nonpartisan legislature with simple rules and procedures. Norris and his fellow unicameralists intended that the institution they created would serve the people indefinitely, despite changing times that were bound to come.

Mixed Reviews

Nebraskans appear to have wholeheartedly embraced the notion that a one-house legislature is more open and accountable. Almost no serious attempts have been mounted to revert to a two-house structure.

Having observed the first session of the unicameral in 1937, Curtis Betts, a reporter for the *St. Louis Post-Dispatch*, declared it far superior to a bicameral system. He said the new structure made it impossible for members to pass the buck the way they had been able to do in the bicameral. "Every individual member is constantly in the public spotlight, with his every official action open to public view," he wrote.[18] Governor Robert Cochran, who had not been an enthusiastic supporter of the unicameral, told the Annual Conference of Governors in September 1937 that he did see some advantages to the new system. Especially, he said, "It comes more nearly to fixing legislative responsibility on each individual member."[19]

In fact, the opposition raised against the unicameral before the 1934 election faded rapidly once the new system began to function. A one-house legislature had become a fact of life for Nebraskans by the 1970s. Probably the only serious challenge was a 1954 petition drive that would not only have restored two houses but also would have increased membership to eighty-six and restored partisanship. It did not reach the ballot.

The nonpartisan feature has been embraced less wholeheartedly. Although plenty of newspapers editorialized in 1934 against making the legislature nonpartisan, neither major political party took a stand on the question in their platforms that year, when the constitutional amendment was on the ballot. Within the legislature itself, nonpartisanship seemed to take hold from the start. The 1937 body, in which a majority of members were registered Democrats, elected a Republican, Charles Warner, as speaker.

However, not all the members were satisfied that the arrangement was ideal. In 1939 a proposal to restore the partisan feature by placing a constitutional amendment on the ballot reached general file before being defeated. Similar measures were introduced in 1951, 1957, 1963, 1967, 1971, 1972,

1973, 1974, 1977, 1978, 1980, 1982, and 1984 but none had enough support to be advanced from committee.

Perhaps the closest call for nonpartisanship came in 1973, when a proposal made it through committee, onto the floor, and all the way to final reading, where it received a solid majority of twenty-eight votes in favor to nineteen against with two senators not voting. However, a proposal for a constitutional amendment requires a three-fifths majority—thirty votes—and the bill appeared to be dead. But then senators approved a motion to reconsider the measure, allowing the legislature to vote on it again. This time four senators sat out, and the votes in favor numbered twenty-six, still further from the three-fifths majority required.

In 1963 and 1984 similar proposals were killed in committee, but in both cases senators tried to rally enough votes on the floor to pull the bill out of committee for consideration by the entire legislature. In both years, the attempt didn't even come close. In 1963 it failed thirty-four to eight with one senator not voting, and in 1984 it failed twenty-six to seventeen with six members not voting. Since then, the Legislative Journals indicate, no resolutions have been introduced to return partisanship to the unicameral.

But plenty of attempts to revert to partisanship have been made outside the legislature itself. From the beginning, Governor Cochran was no fan of nonpartisanship. In the same speech in which he praised the one-house feature of the legislature, the governor complained about the nonpartisan feature. He was particularly unhappy that, with the departure of party structure in the unicameral, "all formal lines of communication between the legislative and executive branches have been removed."[20] The governor also had some complaints about the effect nonpartisanship had on legislative leadership, complaints that will be examined in the next chapter.

Cochran was not the only party activist dissatisfied with the nonpartisan arrangement. In the ensuing years, the two major political parties, Democrats and Republicans, frequently endorsed a return to a partisan legislature.

For many years, the Republican Party's election-year platform has included a plank calling for such a move. In 1964 the state GOP platform endorsed a petition drive, ultimately unsuccessful, to place the question of a partisan legislature on the ballot. The 1974 platform called the nonpartisan unicameral a noble experiment that had not lived up to its promise. The Democratic Party platforms through the decades almost paralleled the Republicans' in their advocacy of a return to partisanship.

Norris had promised that nonpartisanship would make the unicameral more open and, thus, make senators more accountable in the sense that individual members would listen to their constituents rather than to parties as they made their policy decisions. They would be open to public scrutiny and unable to hide behind party skirts. He argued state business did not deal with the kinds of partisan issues found on the national level, so voting for a state official because of his party was irrational. Furthermore, he believed party structure and party discipline in the legislature itself made it harder for a legislator to act sincerely on behalf of the people of the state and to be accountable to them. Norris defined accountability somewhat differently from the way scholars today define it, as explained below. Nebraskans, however, seem to have bought into Norris's point of view.

Despite the agitation among some to make Nebraska's legislature partisan once again, it is significant that no constitutional amendment to that effect has ever actually made it to the ballot. It is impossible to say what its fate might be were the matter put to a vote of the people, but the fact that neither the legislative nor the initiative process has managed to put nonpartisanship to the test seems to indicate a general contentment with nonpartisanship among the general populace. It has survived for sixty-five years.

The relatively small size of the unicameral was promoted as another way to keep the body open and accountable, and the numbers have changed very little since the 1937 session.

In 1957 legislators gave approval to place a constitutional amendment on the ballot that would have increased the maximum size of the body, but it was defeated at the polls in 1958, possibly because it was linked with a salary increase for legislators and a provision allowing the senators to set their own salaries rather than submitting proposals for increases to the voters.

At the 1962 election, however, the voters did approve reapportionment, and the legislature in 1963 increased its number from the original forty-three up to the current forty-nine. But the desire for reapportionment involved more than just concern that districts would grow too populous for one senator to handle. It was also a reflection of the tension between Nebraska's rural and urban interests.

Between 1937 and 1962 the state's population had gradually shifted from the rural areas to the urban areas, but the urban areas had no more votes in the legislature than they had had in 1937. Feeling cheated, the urban areas tried repeatedly to get the state to redistrict and reflect the population shift.

But rural interests weren't about to give up without a struggle. The plan approved by the voters in 1962 and put into action by the legislature in 1963 was based on a formula that included area as well as population, an effort to allow the geographically dominant rural parts of the state to maintain some of their influence.

It may have been a good plan politically in a state whose psyche, at the very least, was still dominated by agriculture. But it was not a good plan constitutionally, according to standards enunciated by the U.S. Supreme Court in *Baker v. Carr* and *Reynolds v. Sims* in the early 1960s. The Court said apportionment had to be done on the basis of population alone, so the legislature went back to the drawing board and configured its forty-nine districts according to the court's mandate.

Interestingly, the state's population had actually increased very little from the time the voters passed the amendment creating a unicameral of between thirty and fifty members. Population was 1.38 million in the 1930 census and 1.41 million in the 1960 census. When the 1935 legislature drew the forty-three districts for the unicameral, each legislator represented about thirty-two thousand people. When the legislature expanded to the forty-nine districts that took effect in 1965, each senator represented just under twenty-nine thousand people.

By the time the legislature reapportioned in response to the 2000 census, each of the forty-nine districts included almost thirty-five thousand constituents, more than ever before in the unicameral's history but not a huge departure from the 1937 figures. However, Nebraska's population continues to shift to the eastern third of the state, which means some districts in the Lincoln and Omaha areas are relatively small geographically, and some in the more sparsely populated western part of the state cover more than fifteen thousand square miles.

Figuring that more legislative districts would be smaller legislative districts, Senator Jim Jones of Eddyville proposed in 1998 that the constitution be changed to allow more than fifty members. He introduced an amendment to increase the maximum number of members to fifty-five by adding two members each time the legislature goes through redistricting—every ten years. The proposal got support from the unicameral's Executive Board, which designated the resolution as one of its priorities. The amendment made it out of committee and advanced to general file but died on the vine at the end of the session. Jones introduced the same measure on January 14, 2002. It met the same fate.

Jones said he knew that increasing the number of seats in the legislature would add more representatives from the populous eastern part of the state, but he hoped the increase would also help the western part of the state at least maintain its proportion of members and not increase the geographic size of its legislative districts.

"I could see the number of senators disappearing in rural Nebraska," Jones said. "My district is sixteen thousand square miles," an area bigger than that of four states in the Union and encompassing thirteen different counties. "I can't even do it justice now," Jones said. For instance, when the legislature starts talking about taxes, he said, "I can get thirteen calls from thirteen different courthouses."[21]

Nebraska's forty-nine-member legislature is the smallest in the nation. The only states that come close are Alaska with sixty members and 10,500 people per district; Delaware with sixty-two and 12,638 people per district; and Nevada with sixty-three members and 31,718 people per district. Considering the ratio of representatives to constituents, it is probably about as easy for Nebraskans today to keep track of their senator in a body of forty-nine as it was for Nebraskans of 1937 to watch the body of forty-three. But the population's shift to the east has exacerbated a problem of disparity in districts' geographic size that has existed at least since the 1930s. That fact may continue to put pressure on the state to increase the total size of its legislature.

High Marks for Simplicity

A little more than thirty years after it was created, the unicameral was evaluated along with the legislatures of the other forty-nine states by the Citizens' Conference on State Legislatures. Publishing its findings in 1971, the conference ranked Nebraska's legislature number one in the nation for openness and accountability, largely on the basis of its one-house nature and small size. But the internal processes and rules also contributed to the ranking, and both have remained relatively constant during the unicameral's history. The processes have had some ups and downs, but at the end of the story, openness and simplicity remain the heroes of the piece.

Writing after the 1937 session, Saylor said, "It is clear that the rules are designed to help fix responsibility and to make the record of every member known to the public." As a result, Saylor said, citizens were becoming more watchful, were subjecting their legislators' actions to close public scrutiny.[22]

Citizens who may have felt shut out from the bicameral legislature's workings were welcomed into the fold by the 1937 rule stating that each bill must have a public hearing and that committee meetings and hearings must be regularly scheduled and publicized. The first unicameral devoted every afternoon to committee meetings and hearings, a practice that also exists today. But in 1965, pressed to shorten its sessions and do business with greater dispatch, the legislature changed the rules to allow noncontroversial bills to go directly to the legislative floor, bypassing a hearing in committee. However, if, during the following five days, even one senator objected to the bill's being referred directly to the floor, the bill would be rerouted to a committee for a hearing.

Senator Richard Proud said the change raised the danger that important bills could be acted upon without public hearing and destroyed "one of the fine things about our Unicameral."[23] But another measure passed the same day indicated that the unicameral didn't intend to abandon public hearings. That motion mandated that any committee chair deciding not to hold a hearing on a bill on the assigned day must get permission from the Reference Committee. The 1997 legislature somewhat streamlined the process by requiring that such changes must simply be reported to the clerk of the legislature.

But very few such changes are requested. Patrick O'Donnell, the legislative clerk in 2002, said the only bills that don't get a public hearing are those designed to clean up archaic language or make minor adjustments to keep laws compatible and consistent.[24]

The 1937 rules kept close watch on committees by mandating that each committee report should include a statement of a bill's purpose and the reason a committee decided to advance or kill a measure. The rule was designed to prevent committees from working behind the back of the full legislature—and the citizens.

In 1961 some members proposed dropping the requirement that a statement of purpose be required when a bill was reported from committee, but the motion failed early in the session. However, the Rules Committee in 1971 asked that the rules be amended to say that legislative staff should be allowed to help prepare the statement of purpose. That proposal, which was adopted, seems to be a way out of a growing dilemma: the desire to keep committees honest but the realization that legislation was becoming increasingly complex, too complex for committees to handle without some help from professional staff. The good progressives of the 1930s would have approved of the decision to make use of expert help.

The legislature also took steps to assure that citizens would be able to have their say on prospective legislation when it resisted an attempt to set tighter limits on the amount of time allowed for testimony at committee hearings. A 1969 proposal to limit each individual's testimony to five minutes was rejected.

A 1987 proposal would have turned things upside down, eliminating the mandate for a public hearing on every bill and leaving the decision to hold a hearing or not up to standing committees, by a vote of three or more members. That idea got nowhere; it was defeated twenty-six to five with eighteen senators not voting. The proposed change was designed to save time, and while it has been rejected in various forms through the years, O'Donnell said it may eventually pass if the limit on legislative days in a session remains in place. In other words, the legislature has a tough time meeting its mandatory adjournment deadline and, at the same time, allowing all interested citizens to have their full say in committee hearings.

Compared to other states, Nebraska's legislature is nicely accessible to the citizens. Most state legislatures do open their committee meetings to the public, although Nebraska is one of twenty that permit some executive sessions.

But if the legislature is really to be open to public input, the public has to know when to show up. In twenty-one states, at least one legislative house does not require any advance notice of committee meetings or hearings. In the remaining thirty-nine states, sixteen require notice of three days or less; some require twenty-four-hours' notice or less. Only two besides Nebraska, which moved from a five-day notice to a seven-day notice in the 1960s, require notice of a week or more for public hearings. That appears to be sufficient time for interested parties to know just when they must show up to testify.

But the time problem remains. The unicameral founders were torn by competing goals: that the unicameral be open to the citizens and to all the legislators and that the unicameral be efficient. Being open and inviting everyone to get involved necessarily requires taking time to consider a multitude of ideas. Being efficient means narrowing the field so that some ideas take precedence over others. Since its first session, the unicameral has struggled with that inherent conflict.

Before the first unicameral met in 1937, John Senning had outlined a number of important things he thought the rules should do. One of those was setting a limit on the number of bills each legislator could introduce in an effort to keep the amount of legislation down and make the new unicameral more streamlined. But the 1937 legislature declined to adopt that closed rule, and the forty-three members introduced 581 bills, some through committees. The volume of measures to be considered was only natural, Senning said later: as long as legislation was looked at as a cure for social and economic ills, "the stream of suggestions will come forth to improve the common lot of men."[25] In other words, Senning concluded that allowing each senator to introduce an unlimited number of bills made the legislative process more accessible to the citizens.

The practice continued for more than thirty years until the legislature changed its mind on the matter in 1971. Perhaps it was because the body made the switch to annual sessions that year and sensed that it could suddenly be dealing with twice as many bills as it had in the past. Or, more probably, it was because approval of annual sessions was accompanied by a limit on session length—ninety days in odd-numbered years and sixty days in even-numbered years. At any rate, the senators amended Rule V on May 19 that year to say that each member would be limited as introducer or co-introducer to a total of ten bills each session except for bills introduced by an interim study of the Legislative Council or by the Executive Committee.

But the mechanism quickly broke down. A 1975 *Lincoln Evening Journal* editorial agreed with Senator John Cavanaugh of Omaha that the limit was a fraud. Senators who reached their limit of ten bills simply shopped around for a committee to sponsor further legislation. The Executive Board alone introduced eighteen bills that year. What may have started as an attempt to decrease the workload was subverted—as was the norm of openness. "Senators can mask a good deal of their private enterprise behind a committee screen," the editorial writer said. [26]

That same year, several proposals were made to remove the limitation on bill introductions. Similar proposals were made in 1977, but instead, the limit was tightened further when the unicameral approved a seventeen-bill limit for each two-year legislative term.

In 1981, after discussing several options, the senators dropped the restriction on bill introductions by individuals but limited committees to eight bills per session. Proposals to reinstate limits on individual senators were introduced in 1984, 1987, and 1995, but the amendments never made it to a floor vote, and the 1981 arrangement was still in place in 2002.

O'Donnell, clerk of the legislature, said the decision to remove bill introduction limits on individual senators in 1981 was designed to keep legislative machinations on the up-and-up. Senators were doing exactly what Cavanaugh complained about, and committees were introducing bills on behalf of individual senators late in the session. And bills introduced under those circumstances often didn't have time for public hearings.

In 1999 the legislature adopted a measure limiting individual senators to introducing eight resolutions per session, not including resolutions proposing a constitutional amendment or proposing an interim study. Many resolutions are ceremonial—congratulating a winning high school basketball team, for instance—and *pro forma*. Constitutional amendments and interim studies, of course, are substantive in nature, and it is significant that no limit has been placed on their numbers. Nor has the limit on bill introductions been reinstated, allowing individual senators a great deal of freedom to address whatever matters both they and their constituents may believe are important.

The unicameral's original embrace of the press as a way to keep legislators in touch with citizens became less ardent in the early 1950s, and the body adopted measures that tightened media access and made legislative activity less open to the public for several decades. On March 12, 1953, the Rules Committee proposed and the legislature adopted a new paragraph for Rule XVI, ordering the press to report responsibly on legislative actions and threatening that any journalist who "flagrantly or persistently violates the ethics of news reporting by assuming the facts without regard for accuracy" could be barred from the chamber after a hearing on the alleged infraction.[27] The proposal didn't mention how the senators planned to reconcile that demand with the First Amendment to the U.S. Constitution. Perhaps the threat was intended to be more symbolic than substantive.

More significant, another rule change that year said reporters would be allowed to remain in executive sessions but "shall respect the confidentiality of discussions," including how individual members voted. Another part of the proposal, which said committee votes would be recorded and open to the press, was defeated.[28] So reporters were allowed to give a vague synopsis of proceedings and a final vote tally but no particulars about who said what or how any individual senator voted.

In 1959 the legislature approved another Rules Committee proposal regarding the press, this one to amend Rule VI. The resolution, adopted January 21, said the press would be allowed to remain in closed committee sessions but would be required to keep the proceedings confidential. That was a real departure from Norris's intention that every aspect of legislative activity be disclosed. A rules change proposed by a motion from the floor that year would have required that members not divulge the proceedings and votes of standing committees in executive session and, in fact, that all votes in those sessions be by secret ballot. That motion was referred to the Rules Committee but did not resurface during the session.

Perhaps the legislature's desire for secrecy reflected the spirit of the times in the 1950s, the era of McCarthyism and fear. But things gradually began to change in the 1960s, beginning in 1963 when the Rules Committee recommended that reports from standing committees include the voting records of members but that those votes not be made public until a committee's recommendation was sent to the floor. The motion failed.

Relations with the press warmed up again when a 1969 motion to strike from the rules the paragraph about a "responsible" press was adopted. And press and public access got a boost in 1971 when reporters were given permission to identify which way committee members voted in executive sessions, although they were still expected to keep discussion confidential. That decision was not without controversy, however. Some senators believed having a committee's voting records made public would inhibit committee discussion. But, during debate, Senator Ernie Chambers asked, "Is your objection to having your constituents know how you vote?"[29] It was a question George Norris himself might have asked.

The following year, a Rules Committee proposal would have further amended Rule III to state that all accredited reporters would be admitted to executive sessions of all standing committees and would be allowed to report on all discussion and all votes of individual members. But that was apparently too much for the senators to swallow; the proposal failed.

It was not until 1980 that the legislature returned fully to its original goal of keeping all its activities open to the public and press. During that session, Rule III was amended again, this time to say that all executive sessions would be open to the media and that the press may report on action taken in executive session but could be asked to leave under "extraordinary circumstances." The 1981 legislature took one more step in the same direction, amending Rule III to add that the media could report not just on action taken in executive session but also on all discussions in those sessions.

When Senator Don Wesely proposed the change to Rule III, he met with some argument from Senator Dave Newell. Newell said it wasn't necessary to add language to the rule because the press had always had the right to report on executive sessions except in extraordinary circumstances, when a committee could vote to bar the press from its deliberations.

Wesely said the proposal would correct an omission in the previous year's rule change regarding executive sessions, an omission that essentially took away some of the rights the press had previously had. Wesely cited the unicameral's ideals and traditions. "The Legislature has been founded on openness," he said. "We have been recognized nationally . . . for our willingness to open ourselves to the media. . . . this is just further recognition of that outstanding quality that we have displayed in Nebraska, the open and accessible."[30] The amendment making it clear that the press could report on anything said in executive sessions passed twenty-six to one with twelve senators not voting.

Another big step to guarantee that legislative proceedings would be open to public view came in 1998 when the legislature placed on the primary election ballot a constitutional amendment that required legislative committees to hold open meetings and required the recording and publishing of many of the votes in those meetings. Nebraska's voters approved the amendment by a resounding five-to-one majority.

That action placed Nebraska among the majority of states that require roll call votes on committees' decisions to advance or kill a bill. In eighteen states, at least one house in the legislature does not require committees to record roll call votes on final action. In the other thirty-two states, both houses must report a roll call on final votes; some indicate they require a roll call record for every vote taken in committee. The requirement increases accountability and assures that bills will not simply be introduced to appease constituent groups and then conveniently swept under the rug and abandoned in committee.

And officially allowing the press to remain in and report on even executive sessions of committees returned the unicameral to one of the traits for which it was admired in its early years. The *Christian Science Monitor*, commenting on the Nebraska experiment's first decade, praised the legislature for settling its problems in full public view with no secret sessions or closed hearings. The *Monitor* noted that even when committees went into executive session, the press was allowed to remain.[31]

While the legislature over the years has struggled to keep its committee proceedings open to the public, the committee structure has changed little since 1937. Standing committees have been renamed; some have been dropped and others added in response to changing needs. For example, the original Drainage Committee and the Highways and Bridges Committee were combined in 1939 into the Public Works Committee. Miscellaneous Appropriations and Claims became Miscellaneous Subjects in 1957. What was originally called the Appropriations Committee, charged with deciding where and how to spend the state's money, became the Budget Committee in 1949 but reverted to Appropriations in 1971. Study committees in 1957 and 1965 recommended changing a number of committee names, and names continued to fluctuate in succeeding sessions.

Throughout the decades, however, the number of committees remained nearly the same. The 1937 session adopted fifteen substantive committees plus the Rules Committee. In the late 1940s the number was thirteen; after some fluctuations up and down, the number was thirteen again in 1977. A reorganization in 2000 revised some committee jurisdictions but resulted in fourteen substantive standing committees.

Because all other states have bicameral legislatures, all other legislatures have a higher number of standing committees than Nebraska has. But even given that factor, Nebraska stands out. Seventeen state senates have fourteen committees or fewer, but only eight state houses of representatives do. Aided dramatically by its one-house nature and small size, the unicameral has resisted the temptation to allow committees—and, thus, committee chairmanships—to proliferate wildly. The changes the legislature has made have been almost entirely attempts to streamline and better coordinate committee jurisdictions and to be sure committee names accurately reflect those jurisdictions.

Some other parts of the unicameral's simplified procedure have remained stable despite challenges. A proposal in the 1965 session would have eliminated the rule that said members were to introduce only bills they were willing to support. The motion was referred to the Rules Committee, where it disappeared. Killing the rule would have made it easier for members to hide their true motivations and positions on policy matters and would have cast doubt on the legislature's dedication to openness. Of course, it always has been possible for a senator to introduce a bill for which he or she has little or no enthusiasm, but under the current requirements that all votes be on the record, constituents can easily see whether their senator exhibits that kind of two-faced habit.

The orderly, open process for bill deliberation that Senning, Norton, and the other fathers of the unicameral were so proud of—three stages of floor debate and reading "at large" at the final stage—has remained pretty much intact. But a change to one procedure mandated by the amendment that created the unicameral did, after repeated attempts, pass muster with the voters and become part of the constitution. It typifies, again, the struggle between openness and efficiency.

The noble idea of reading all bills aloud on final reading so that legislators and citizens alike might have one last, deliberate opportunity to hear exactly what was being proposed began to seem burdensome as the volume of legislative work grew. Bills got longer, too, and final reading gradually morphed from a careful enunciation of a bill's provisions into a speed-reading mumble by the clerk or his assistant. Legislators began to look for a way to remedy the situation.

In 1962 the Rules Committee recommended allowing the presiding officer to designate only parts of a bill to be read aloud unless one member would object, in which case the entire bill would be read. But the legislature wasn't ready for the idea yet, and the proposal was defeated twenty-one to nine with thirteen not voting.

By 1969, though, things were different. The unicameral approved a constitutional amendment for the 1970 ballot that would have eliminated entirely the "at large" reading on final consideration, but when the measure reached the people a year later, 60 percent voted against it. Voters turned down a similar measure in 1976, again by a 60 to 40 percent margin. The *Lincoln Evening Journal* editorialized against the change, saying reading bills aloud on final reading allowed legislators to catch things that might otherwise fall through the cracks.[32]

In 1980 legislators returned to the 1962 approach and proposed amending the constitution to eliminate reading at large unless a senator requested the reading. The governor let the amendment proceed to the ballot without his signature, but once again the voters turned it down, this time by a slightly smaller margin: 55 percent to 45 percent.

Despite three defeats in a little more than a decade, the senators were not ready to give up the fight against this well-meant but time-consuming practice. A measure proposing that a summary of a bill be read on final reading was introduced in 1985 but made it no further than general file—the first of three considerations. It was carried over to 1986 but died at the end of the session.

The legislature tried again in 1992 with a bill that would have provided for final reading by title only unless one-fifth of the members present request full reading. That proposal, too, died at the end of the session. The idea returned in 1993, and Speaker Dennis Baack set it as a priority bill. The proposal went no further than general file that year but moved to select file January 20, 1994.

In the ensuing debate, the senators seemed to be searching for a compromise that would allow them to maintain the spirit of openness and thoroughness intended in the 1934 amendment but still save them some time and make their procedures more efficient. Senator Doug Kristensen proposed amending the bill to say that final reading may be suspended by a three-fifths vote of all members. When the measure reached the primary election ballot that spring, voters bought the new approach and approved the constitutional amendment by almost a two-to-one margin.

When the senators met in 1997 to amend their rules to reflect the change in the constitution, they agreed that if three-fifths of the members agreed to dispense with reading at large, the bill would be read by title only and voting would remain open for three minutes. O'Donnell said legislators today vote to waive final reading on most bills, particularly those that are fifteen pages or more in length. Nebraskans had finally been persuaded to allow their legislators more efficiency in the face of what seems clearly to be a larger and more complex volume of business than the unicameral's founders had anticipated.

The legislature has had a similar identity crisis involving the practice of adding unrelated amendments to bills until the originals are decorated like Christmas trees. The 1934 amendment's requirement that each bill contain only one subject remained largely unchallenged over the years. Unlike the U.S. House and many state legislatures, the Nebraska unicameral did not allow so-called Christmas tree bills—bills to which numerous unrelated amendments may be attached. All amendments had to be germane to the subject matter in the bill to which they were attached. In fact, the first unicameral was so concerned about keeping the subjects of bills clear and to the point that the 1937 rules provided that when standing committees combined the provisions of several related bills into one measure, the "substitute bill" had to be introduced as a brand new bill.

By 1996 that had changed, at least in practice. And after some argument, the legislature chose to change the rules to meet the practice. Senator Ron Withem said committees were being allowed to gut a bill and substitute other measures "as they see fit," then ask the entire legislature to approve the new content as an amendment.[33] Withem proposed that the legislature make it official that any material a committee added to a bill would be considered germane as long as it was under the subject matter jurisdiction of the committee—whether or not it was specifically associated with the material in the original bill. Withem said, and Senator Ernie Chambers agreed, that the practice would provide a way to handle emergency situations.

But the "new" bill created by the amendment process would not necessarily be required to have a public hearing, and Senator Lavonne Crosby didn't like it. She said that could shut the public out of the hearing process. Furthermore, she objected to the idea that amendments coming from committees should be automatically considered germane without debate on the legislative floor. "That's what we're here for, to be really sure that all of those things are germane," she said.[34]

On the other hand, Senator Doug Kristensen said he supported the rule change because it would lead to more logical and cohesive legislation. He pointed out that the entire legislature could still tell a committee to restructure an amended bill or to go back and hold a hearing on it. Furthermore, if the senator who introduced the original bill didn't like what had been done to it by the committee, he or she could ask that it be withdrawn from floor consideration.

When another senator questioned whether the new bill produced by amendments would be required to have a hearing, Withem said no, it would not. He said the legislature passed proposals via amendment each year, proposals that had not had a public hearing. He added he was sure most committee chairs would want the public hearing to take place if a bill had been significantly changed by amendment. "We all want to see public hearings take place, and we only do these sorts of things in . . . what we consider to be extreme circumstances," Withem said.[35]

Withem's proposal was adopted twenty-eight to seven with fourteen not voting. The debate over the rule change illustrates again the conflict between openness and efficiency. As legislative business becomes more abundant and more complex, legislators look for ways to change their procedures to meet changing circumstances. But the debate also illustrates that unicameral members are still concerned that their business be done in the open and with plenty of access for citizens, true to the populist/progressive promises on which the institution was founded.

Openness and accountability were at the top of the list of George Norris's goals for the Nebraska unicameral, and the structure he and his friends recommended was designed to meet those goals. Aware of the expectations placed on them, the members of the first unicameral wrote rules to facilitate the unicameral's the goals. Observers of the early unicameral praised it for being open and accountable. Surveying the performance of the first unicameral, *News-Week* reported in its May 22, 1937, issue that "the result was something near the ideal of democracy." Nearly sixty-five years later, unicameral fans say the legislature has lived up to Norris's promises.

"Naked to Public View"

No Citizens' Conference on State Legislatures has done a comparative rating of legislatures for more than thirty years, so an assessment of how open and accountable the Nebraska legislature is today must rely on other measurements and observations.

The structure of the institution has remained unchanged since its founding. If a one-house, small, nonpartisanship institution does, indeed, foster openness and accountability, as the unicameral's proponents said it would, then the institution remains open to public scrutiny. The rules, of course, have changed to adapt to changing needs and circumstances, but to a large extent, as noted above, they have maintained or even expanded the public's access to its legislators and their proceedings.

Nebraska's newspapers, originally mostly opposed to the concept of a one-house, nonpartisan legislature, now find reasons to editorialize about its virtues. "It's more open," the *Lincoln Journal Star* said in an August 11, 1995, editorial. "Single house means it is easier to track legislation and find out what's going on. Nonpartisan means state senators are accessible and accountable to constituents, not parties."

Bill Barrett, then speaker of the unicameral, told the *Lincoln Journal* in 1987 that "no other state legislature is more naked to public view, more responsive to the consent of the governed or freer from the influence of political machines than Nebraska's. Every step in the legislative process, from the introduction of bills to their debate and disposal, is open to public participation and scrutiny."[36]

Another legislative observer, former lieutenant governor Kim Robak, made the same point: "All decisions and votes are made in full public view."[37]

Current and former state senators said many of the same things about the unicameral's openness. And they attributed that effect to the structure and rules.

The small number of senators is a plus, according to Jim Pappas, who served in the unicameral from 1982 to 1987: it makes it easy for people to see what their senators are doing and makes the legislators accessible to the average citizen.[38]

It leads to more accountability, Don Wesely said. Wesely, who was a member of the legislature from 1978 to 1999, said a body with 120 to 200 people would make it harder for citizens to track their legislator's actions.[39]

Dennis Baack put it the other way around: the small unicameral means ordinary citizens are "not overwhelmed by hundreds of representatives."[40]

Peter Hoagland agreed. Hoagland served in the unicameral from 1970 to 1986 and in the U.S. House of Representatives from 1988 to 1994. Generally speaking, he said, the smaller the body the more accountable it is "because each person's vote counts for more, and people watch more carefully."[41]

DiAnna Schimek, in her fourth term in the unicameral in 2001, pointed out the unicameral's accessibility: a citizen who wants to have a voice on an issue can actually contact all forty-nine members of the legislature if he or she pleases.[42] Many other senators said the same thing, either in personal interviews or in response to a 2001 survey of current and former legislators.

Vard Johnson, senator from 1979 to 1989, said, "I got lots of calls. So did all my colleagues."[43] Arlene Nelson, senator from 1985 to 1993, said, "With only forty-nine members it is easy to track a senator's record."[44]

But Scott Moore wasn't so sure the legislature's size was the big factor keeping the institution accessible. Instead, he believes it is the one-house structure that makes Nebraska's unicameral open and accountable. "Even if you had 133, [if they were] all in one house it would still be easier to follow," said Moore, a state senator from 1987 to 1995.[45]

"In a unicameral there's no place to hide," Moore said. "You can't pawn it off on the house or the senate. When you vote, it's your vote."[46]

And that vote is easy to follow, said Doug Kristensen, who completed his fourth legislative term in 2002. Nebraska state senators are very recognizable. People know who their legislators are. Kristensen said he thought the legislature would be even better if it were even smaller—about forty-four members instead of forty-nine. He said the decrease in the number of districts would increase the number of constituents per district and the diversity in each of those districts.[47] That sounds like the proposal George Norris and John Senning recommended as they promoted the small unicameral body in 1934.

Doug Bereuter took a different point of view. Bereuter, one of Nebraska's representatives in the U.S. Congress from 1979 to 2004 and a member of the unicameral from 1975 to 1979, said he thought a small increase in membership and the resulting decrease in constituents per senator would make the body more accessible. It would also provide more input for increasingly complex issues, he said. "Given the issues we deal with today, you wouldn't want it smaller than it is."[48]

Several senators praised the absence of conference committees. Pappas agreed with Norris's negative view of conference committees. "You can vote for a piece of legislation, then it goes to a conference committee and it comes out completely different," Pappas said.

Lowell Johnson feels the same way. Johnson, who served from 1981 to 1993, said he couldn't think of a legislative structure that would allow a body to be more open to the people. In a two-house body with conference committees—which don't hold public hearings—the legislators "really lose contact with the public," he said.[49]

Not only that, but in a bicameral, neither house is completely in control. Therefore, citizens can't be sure which house to watch. David Landis, in his sixth term in 2001, said things were different in Nebraska. "We have *all* the lawmakers in one room. You can be *in* the room where we're making law. In other states, there's always another room where they're doing it, too. . . . You can't see the whole frame [in other states]."[50]

Bereuter agreed. "If people want to understand who's doing what to them, they have a pretty good chance here."[51]

The vast majority—about 83 percent—of current and former senators responding to a 2001 survey favored keeping the Nebraska legislature a unicameral. That sentiment held true no matter the decade in which the respondents served (see appendix 1, table 1).

Nebraska citizens surveyed in 2000 agreed almost as strongly. Fifty-eight percent of the survey respondents disagreed with the statement that Nebraska should return to a two-house legislature; only 27 percent agreed strongly or somewhat with the statement[52] (see appendix 1, table 2).

But unicameralism isn't the only factor involved. Nonpartisanship also contributes to keeping things open, Pappas said. If the legislature were partisan, "the party would call them (senators) up and tell them how to vote. It takes away the involvement of citizens."[53] Moore agreed that Nebraska senators were accountable to the people rather than to party bosses.[54]

Bob Wickersham elaborated. "We're accountable only to the persons who elect us," said the senator who had served in the unicameral ten years as of 2001. "Party structure could claim they elected us . . . or could claim they will un-elect you." That decision, he said, should be up to the voters alone.[55]

Schimek said she, too, liked the nonpartisan feature of the unicameral, but she also implied that party labels could be helpful in keeping senators accountable to the voters. "Maybe we should put party labels on the ballot" next to a senator's name, she said, although the unicameral's organizational structure would remain nonpartisan.

In fact, such a resolution to amend the constitution was introduced in the 1995 session of the legislature by Senator Kate Witek. The resolution said senators would continue to be nominated and elected in a nonpartisan manner but that the ballot for nomination and election would include an indication of each candidate's registered political party. The Government Committee killed the measure March 16 of that year.

Despite Witek's and Schimek's belief that identifying senators by party might make senators more accountable, Schimek said there were no guarantees. "Party labels are not absolutely foolproof."[56]

But not everyone who has served in the Nebraska legislature thinks its nonpartisan nature is a good thing. Vard Johnson, for instance, believes nonpartisanship makes the unicameral less accountable in the traditional sense. Without party labels, Johnson said, "You can't pinpoint collective responsibility for what has occurred." He said he believed senators would be more accountable at election time if citizens were looking at parties instead of just "forty-nine nice people."[57]

Peter Hoagland also took the more traditional point of view: that party labels would give citizens useful information when they go to the polls. Voters have less information about someone's philosophical underpinnings in a nonpartisan race, Hoagland said.[58]

In survey responses, Bill Swanson, senator from 1968 to 1974, remarked that party affiliation would make the public more aware of what his or her senator stood for, and John DeCamp, senator from 1970 to 1986, said a partisan body would be more accountable.

Bereuter supported that view. In a partisan body, citizens could more easily decide whom to blame if something did not get done according to their liking. "Here, responsibility is diffused," he said.[59]

The senators were expressing the view some scholars take: party identification helps voters know what to expect from candidates and offers voters a way to hold their representatives accountable. A candidate who aligns herself with a particular party announces she will be part of a voting bloc, giving citizens information on her probable behavior if they elect her to office. A legislator who professes membership in and loyalty to a party signals a general outline of his political values and ideals and ideas for governance. Once the legislator has served a term, voters can compare those signals to the legislator's performance and draw their own conclusions about whether to return the representative to office.

According to this argument, if voters are to make their choices on some rational basis, they must know how a representative is likely to behave or has behaved in office. Evaluation of a candidate is possible only if the voter knows something about where the candidate stands on an issue. Parties provide a shortcut for the "reasoning voter" to make that decision[60] and participate in the governing process at the polls. In a nonpartisan election, the voters have a harder time predicting how a candidate would vote on policy issues if elected.

But a majority of Nebraska citizens and senators surveyed at the turn of the twenty-first century apparently saw no problem with nonpartisan legislative elections. Of the senators surveyed in 2001, only 19 percent agreed with the statement that "voters have difficulty making voting decisions without knowing the candidates' party labels." Fifty-seven percent of the respondents agreed with Norris's argument that "partisanship is unnecessary in state politics."

Citizens surveyed in 2000 appeared to hold the same point of view, albeit in somewhat smaller numbers. Sixty-five percent of citizens responding to the survey said absence of party labels was not a problem at the polls, while just 30 percent said they agreed strongly or somewhat that it was hard to make voting decisions without knowing the candidate's party label (see appendix 1, table 3).

Former senator Tim Hall praised the unicameral's size and structure for making it easy for citizens to keep an eye on their representatives: "There's one person to call and hold accountable on Election Day," said Hall, who served from 1984 to 1995.[61] Carol Hudkins, serving her third term in 2001, said, "We are answerable to the people and not dictated to by political parties."[62]

But scholars say nonpartisanship can be a problem in another way, too. Instead of increasing citizens' participation in the electoral process, it may actually lead to a decline. Without party labels to help guide their choices, more than one-fourth of citizens who voted in the partisan contests—for president and governor, for instance—simply didn't vote in the nonpartisan legislative races in the early 1980s.

However, that trend apparently did not continue. In the 1988 election, 88 percent of Nebraskans who voted for president also voted for a legislative candidate. In 2000 the figure was 86 percent. Perhaps citizens should be concerned about even a 14 percent differential between the votes for president and those for legislator, but the figures don't seem high enough to be cause for real alarm. Nor is it possible to know for sure that it is absence of party labels that prevents people from casting a vote in the legislative races.

Despite the nonpartisan nature of legislative campaigns and ballots in Nebraska, many new senators arrive in the unicameral with their partisan instincts intact, Senator Roger Wehrbein said. But that doesn't last long. "They adjust to this as best for all the people."[63]

Ardyce Bohlke, a legislator from 1991 to 2001, said some people had a good reason for disliking the legislature's nonpartisan feature. "If you're the executive director of the Democratic or Republican party, you'd rather have it be more partisan." But she, too, said nonpartisanship makes the legislature more accessible to the average citizen.[64]

The vast majority of those who serve or have served in the legislature appear to favor keeping the body nonpartisan. Of the 198 current and former senators responding to a 2001 survey, only 17 percent said the unicameral should return to partisanship while more than 76 percent opposed such a change, although those serving in recent decades seem to feel less strongly about the matter (see appendix 1, table 4).

Reading the citizens' pulse quite accurately, Wehrbein said he believed that the people of Nebraska overwhelmingly favored the nonpartisan nature of their legislature.[65] In fact, citizen responses to the Bureau of Sociological Research (NASIS) survey almost paralleled legislators' response to their survey. Sixty-eight percent of the Nebraskans surveyed disagreed with the proposal that the state should return to a partisan legislature; about 22 percent took the other point of view[66] (see appendix 1, table 5).

When they were preaching the unicameral gospel in 1934, Norris and company were depending on the institution's structure to increase and maintain its openness and accountability. But they also expected the unicameral's rules and procedures to contribute to those goals. Many contemporary senators believe that's just what has happened.

In the 2001 survey, 86 percent of the legislators responding agreed that the legislature's procedures were simple enough that citizens could clearly see how their representatives were behaving (see appendix 1, table 6). In addition, 79 percent agreed that the body's procedures and decision-making processes are open and understandable to the citizens.

In comments included in survey responses, many senators said the legislature provided an open, accessible form of passing legislation into law. Several used the word "transparent" and "accountable" to describe its processes.

Holding a public hearing on every bill is still a good idea, senators said, and one of the primary ways the unicameral offers citizens access and input. Some observers question whether the hearings are more than just a formality, but senators say what they learn at hearings can make more than a symbolic difference.[67] Sometimes what senators hear at those sessions helps them make decisions on bills, Dave Landis said. "People who come [to testify] have a good shot at persuasion."

If the issue is high-profile, senators have probably heard a lot about it from lobbyists and individual constituents before the bill comes to hearing. But for many bills that is not the case. "I've had my mind changed" because of testimony at hearings, Landis said.[68]

The hearings take time, Moore said, "but it's a good tradeoff" to keep the process open and citizens involved. Former senator Don Dworak said he loved the committee system's openness: "Your dirty laundry hangs out," he said, "but it's okay. People should know" what their representatives are doing.[69]

Gerald Matzke, a senator from 1993 to 2000, remarked that "it is unique that anyone can walk into a committee hearing out of the hallway in the State Capitol and testify on any bill without any prior appointment or scheduling . . . this is the most open legislative procedure that can be designed."[70]

The 2001 survey of current and former senators supports those individual comments. Asked whether requiring a hearing on every bill takes too much time, only 20 percent of the 198 respondents agreed even "somewhat."

In comments included on the survey responses, many senators praised the required public hearings as enormously important in keeping the body close to the people. Jessie Rasmussen, who served in the unicameral from 1990 to 1994, said the "public hearing requirement is a treasure" that gives Nebraskans great access to their legislature. Barry Reutzel, who served from 1976 to 1990, said, "Public input is sought on every bill and citizen participation encouraged."

Public hearings—accompanied by ample notice of time and place—were the subject of several items in the 1969 survey conducted by the Citizens' Conference on State Legislatures. The unicameral gained points for requiring a public hearing on every bill, a situation that is still true for all but the most routine legislation—bills that clean up language in statutory code, for instance.

Nebraska's one-week notice continues to exceed the conference survey's standard, and the method for giving notice also ranks high. The unicameral schedules its meetings and hearings at regular times and sends notice of hearings to people who request them, announces hearings in the newspaper and posts notice in the capitol and on the legislature's Web site. That combination of ingredients earned the unicameral sixteen out of a possible nineteen points on that measure of accountability and remains in place today.[71] Closely connected to the open committee process is the absence of a limit on number of bills each senator may introduce. Pappas said if the legislature were to try again to impose a limit—as it had done during the 1970s—it would probably also have to eliminate the rule that all amendments must be germane to the main bill in order to give senators enough leeway to introduce everything they believe is important to their constituents. Then "stuff will pop up that nobody knows about," Pappas said, and some proposals will not receive a public hearing anywhere along the way.[72]

Of course, about ten years after Pappas left the legislature, the 1996 body changed its rules to weaken the germaneness provision a bit. Amendments still have to be germane to the committee's jurisdiction but would not necessarily require a hearing unless senators specifically requested it. O'Donnell, clerk of the legislature, said the germaneness rule was usually interpreted liberally. The rule and its interpretation are a trade-off, once again, between maintaining openness and achieving enough efficiency to deal with an increasing volume of legislation.

At least one former senator thinks weakening the germaneness rule was a mistake. He said too many bills were changed drastically on the floor of the legislature, well after the hearings at which citizens testify. Sometimes, he said, entirely new bills were substituted in place of original content. "I am sure this is not what George W. Norris would have approved," the anonymous senator said. [73]

On the other hand, Norris probably would have been happy about some measures the unicameral has taken to keep its processes open. Although he could not have anticipated what new communications technology would make possible, Norris would undoubtedly have been delighted that it has become ever easier for citizens who want to watch the legislative process in action to do so. "There's accountability everywhere," Wickersham said, "and in fashions Norris and his contemporaries couldn't have contemplated."

Wickersham—and others—cited the gavel-to-gavel cable television coverage of floor sessions, available since 1971, as well as the unicameral's Web site, which has been steadily growing since 1997, providing Internet access to legislative bills and notes on their progress as well as other information about the legislature. That kind of direct citizen access is even better than lots of coverage by the press," Wickersham said. "The processes we have in place, the effort we make to make information available makes us extremely accountable." [74]

Of course, that kind of exposure can sometimes cause a flap, Moore said. Because reporters and the public can be in on even the very early stages of debate, before many facts have been unearthed and explored, "the legislature's propensity to think out loud often gets it into trouble with the citizenry." [75] But Moore also cited the unicameral's openness as one of its strengths.

Senators responding to the 2001 survey overwhelmingly expressed support for keeping sessions open to all; 94 percent disagreed somewhat or disagreed strongly with the statement that some sessions should be closed to press and public.

However, not only are nearly all committee and floor sessions open to the public, but records of committee reports and votes—as well as floor discussion and votes—are made available. O'Donnell said that the practice, laid down in the 1937 rules, had always been followed, but a 1998 constitutional amendment simply set it in cement, affirming the spirit of openness.[76] All those practices assure that the unicameral would still rate high on the accountability scale set by the Citizens' Conference survey.[77]

Consensus from senators who were interviewed or who responded to the 2001 survey is that the Nebraska legislature has lived up to its promise to be open, accountable, and accessible. Of course, that doesn't mean senators never talk business in the halls of the capitol or at restaurants or at parties. But the system itself demands that state business be done in the open and that legislators be accessible and accountable to the citizens they serve.

Dennis Baack was a senator from 1984 to 1991, the last few years as speaker. In his leadership role, he had a lot of contact with and learned a lot about other states' legislatures. "I never discovered a more open system with as good access for the ordinary citizen as Nebraska," Baack said.[78]

Don Wesely said the best thing about the unicameral was "the inability to place blame for the institution's failures on another legislative body or political party. Failure to address issues is borne by all members. Thus, there is a mutual advantage to succeed."[79]

While citizens were not specifically asked whether they consider their legislature to be open, accountable, and accessible, those surveyed did appear to approve, resoundingly, its one-house, nonpartisan nature. It apparently meets Nebraskans' needs—or, at least, has become entrenched in the Nebraska political culture.

Bill Barrett, who has served in both the two-house, partisan U.S. Congress and the unicameral, had high praise for the state's system. He called Nebraska's legislature a shining jewel.[80]

Doug Bereuter, who has also served in both legislative bodies, said the unicameral had lived up to its billing as an open, accessible, and accountable institution.[81] "George Norris would not be disappointed," Bereuter said.

4 / Forty-nine Independent Contractors

How Power Is Decentralized in the Unicameral

When Thomas Jefferson wrote in the Declaration of Independence that "all men are created equal," he was expressing a populist notion. When George Norris wrote that a large legislature could not be trusted because it "must of necessity surrender many of the individual rights and prerogatives of its members," he was doing the same thing.[1]

Populists believe political power is rooted in the people, that the voice of the people—not a few elites—should be the guiding force in government. In Norris's interpretation, that meant that a legislature should be small and simple and nonhierarchical enough that members would represent their constituents in every decision the body made. Populists fear the tyranny of the ruling elite, not of the majority—"the people." They believe *more* democracy is the cure for corruption and seek *more* involvement of the people in order to protect the individual from the arbitrary power of nongovernmental elites. Populists assume what Jefferson declared: that the common people are capable of good judgment in their own governance.[2]

As George Norris and his compatriots set out to propose a new legislative design for Nebraska, they translated that big-picture populist/progressive ideology into a specific legislative structure and the procedures they believed would grow from that structure.

Norris promised his fellow Nebraskans their new legislature would offer not only openness and accountability but also the closely related virtues of equality and efficiency. Norris decried any system that delegated powers for introducing, routing, considering, deliberating, and dispatching legislation to just a few of the legislature's members, both because such a system made it too easy for members to hide their activities and also because it seemed elitist. But he also promised that the new system, with participation by all, would be more efficient than the old bicameral. His plan for the legislature's new structure and his recommendations for its rules and procedures reflect those promises.

Letting Everyone Play

As noted, Norris wanted an exceptionally small legislature so that every member could be involved in every aspect of legislative decision-making. With a small body, authority would not have to be delegated to a subset of members, nor would privileges be granted to a few. Only in such a small group, he believed, would the state be able to avoid a return to control by a handful of elites.

In a large body, Norris said, legislators have to surrender to committees the right to determine procedure. Rules often prohibit members from thoroughly debating matters on the floor or from offering amendments to legislation reported out of committees. Those procedures may be necessary to keep things moving in a large body, but they are not likely to produce good legislation, Norris said. A smaller group would let everyone be involved in discussion and deliberation and result in the application of the "highest wisdom" in lawmaking.[3] And, the unicameralists hoped, the smaller size would put a stop to endless bickering by representatives concerned only about their own relatively small districts.

Furthermore, a large legislature usually means more committees, which can actually slow work because of their sheer numbers, the unicameralists believed. Not only that, they charged, but the committee system also allows an assembly to be dominated by leaders or lobbyists and enables the speaker to become a virtual dictator if he is allowed to appoint committee members or chairmen. Those same points about committees and leadership apply to the unicameralists' argument in favor of nonpartisanship.

Stamp Out Conference Committees

The traditional two-house legislature, Norris said, grew out of a belief that society consists of different classes and that each must be represented—and be able to check the other—in the legislature. Officially, those class distinctions had never existed in the United States nor in the individual states, Norris said. And by the early twentieth century, the populist/progressive philosophy had reinforced the idea that all American citizens were assumed to be on an equal level. So, Norris said, it seemed silly to perpetuate a system that had lost its reason for being.

Even worse, Norris said, a two-house legislature makes conference committees inevitable. These groups, made up of a handful of members from each house and usually appointed by the party leadership, meet to resolve differences between bills passed in the separate houses. The results of their negotiations are taken back to the parent houses, where they must be approved or rejected but cannot be amended. The legislation that comes out the conference committee is often very different from what the members of either house originally had passed, Norris said.[4] The conference committees and the leaders who appointed them became, in essence, a third house, wielding tremendous power.

This is a far cry from what Norris and his fellow reformers promised that the unicameral would do: give each representative a greater sphere of independent action, preclude centralization of authority, and eliminate the danger of control by minorities—by which they meant elites. They embraced the populist ideal of equality and loathed the idea that a few legislators might be allowed to exercise the authority that comes with strong leadership.

The Business of the State Is Not Partisan

The same rationale applies to political parties. Norris is remembered for his assertion that the business of the states had little or nothing to do with national issues and that electing people without national party labels would allow them to address state issues more freely. But an equally important aspect of nonpartisanship, in his mind, was the fact that members of the legislature would be free from the influence and control of party machines and party bosses within the institution itself. Just as small size preserves equality and independence of members, so does elimination of political structure and party discipline.

The ideal legislature, according to the populist way of thinking, should have "such outward structure and such internal organization to render it an effective and responsible agency of the public will. Both the internal organization and the rules governing proceedings should be free from unnecessary complications in order to give every bill a fair hearing and to ensure full publicity for all discussions, committee work and legislative decisions."[5] Partisanship, then, was nothing but an unnecessary and undesirable complication.

Many of the reasons cited in favor of nonpartisanship apply to the principle of equality as well as to openness. Eliminating parties from the equation eliminated majority and minority leaders, party whips, party programs, and party discipline. It eliminated the privileges of authority and prestige that went along with party leadership, and left the legislators on a more equal footing.

Norris also believed that a nonpartisan body would be more efficient because it would apply business principles, rather than party ideology, to policy making. "Take partisanship out of the government and you have at once put more business in the government," he wrote.[6] The state should be thought of as a gigantic corporation and the legislators as members of the board of directors whose duties would be mainly of a business nature. Presumably, if the state were run as a business, all members of the "board of directors" would work together, on an equal footing, for the benefit of the stockholders—the people. Norris never suggested the board would have a "chairman" who would command disproportionate influence over his fellow legislators.

Legislative scholars agree that Norris's approach would give more voice to all representatives and, implicitly, to all the citizens. Populist demands receive more weight in a body with weak leadership, and that's exactly what Norris wanted. Newspapers carped that nonpartisanship would result in lack of leadership, but Norris and his colleagues believed placing responsibility on all members of the legislature would develop truly responsible leadership based on experience and ability rather than party fiat. Leadership would be a meritocracy, and it would necessarily be informal, not set out by structure or rules.

Assessing the first two sessions of the unicameral, John Senning, one of the theorists behind the body, said it had manifested that goal. Legislative leadership, he said, did not rest in the hands of one man or several men, dictated by party, but in the power of reason and common sense.[7]

That sounds wonderfully high-minded and noble, but the idea is not without its dangers. The Nebraska State Teachers Association report on the 1937 legislative session was blunt about the matter: "It is generally recognized that there was a dearth of leadership in the first unicameral."[8] Abolishing political parties left an institutional vacuum, the report said, but despite the drawbacks, the NSTA thought the situation was not all bad: "Nebraska does not want the type of leadership that comes from cracking the party whip over the heads of recalcitrant members or the type which secures support of a measure because it is good party strategy."[9]

A Texas newspaper story about the first session noted that, in the absence of party discipline, members had more freedom to exercise individual judgment than ever before and showed a striking spirit of independence, exactly what the unicameralists had hoped for.[10] But newspapers closer to home pointed out the down side. A letter to the editor of the *Lincoln Star* said the new unicameral "developed no outstanding leadership but did develop about 43 would-be leaders."[11] An opinion piece in the *Omaha Morning Bee News* on May 9, 1937, attributed the dearth of leadership to absence of parties, which had previously been able to get members into decisive alignments.

Thirty-five years later, one scholar noted that nonpartisanship had a far-reaching effect on the leadership structure in the early unicameral. In the absence of political parties, he said, leadership selection could be a free-for-all, sometimes resulting in a breakdown in the system of friendly relations needed to get legislative work done. The nonpartisan body guarded against that danger by making the official leadership posts so weak that it made no difference who held them. The result was diffused power and greater reliance on individuals taking informal, ad hoc leadership roles.[12] The NSTA report published in 1937, after the first unicameral session, had predicted that was exactly the kind of leadership that would develop.[13]

Putting the Clamps on Power

Thirty years after Nebraska's legislature took on its new form, one scholar declared that "institutionally, there is no provision for legislative leadership in the Unicameral."[14] Removing political parties from the election process also removed them from the legislative process and from any potential leadership structure. And, purposely, neither the Nebraska constitution nor the unicameral's rules provided for strong leadership positions. In fact, the original rules provided for a legislature that was as unstructured as possible.

The constitutional amendment that created the unicameral and decreed that the lieutenant governor would be its presiding officer did not necessarily grant him authority and influence. That would be up to the legislature itself as it laid out its rules of procedure. And the unicameral's rules were stingy with that authority and influence.

Beyond that, the precise legislative structure was left up to the members of the first unicameral when they gathered in 1937. What they created was largely as egalitarian and nonhierarchical as Norris had urged—with all the benefits and costs that the approach entailed.

One criticism of the bicameral legislature had been that it put too much power in the hands of too few members. The presiding officers were able to appoint standing committees and their chairs, select the committee to which to refer each bill, and appoint members of the conference committees that worked out differing versions of bills passed by the two houses. All that gave those leaders the chance to exercise enormous control over legislation.

Probably in a reaction to what was perceived as undue influence, the unicameral put the clamps on its presiding officers' authority. Although the lieutenant governor was elected on a partisan ballot, he had no political clout because the legislature had no party structure. He could not vote on a regular basis because the constitutional amendment mandated that he should vote only to break ties.

Nor did the lieutenant governor have power over the calendar—the order in which legislative bills would be considered—a prerogative that would have given him an effective role in coordinating varied interests. Bills came up for consideration as committees reported them to the floor, and only a majority vote by the legislators could change that order (Rule XII.3). Essentially, then, the legislature did not have a calendar. The presiding officer could not promote his own or the governor's agenda by arranging the order in which bills were taken up on the floor.

Furthermore, the constitutional amendment and the rules laid out a detailed series of steps and a time frame by which bills were to be acted on: first reading, second reading and reference to a committee, report by the committee and reference to general file, debate by the legislature, reference to the Committee on Enrollment and Review, another round of debate on the floor, re-reference to the Committee on Enrollment and Review, reference to third reading, vote on final passage at least five days after its first reference for enrollment and review and at least two legislative days after reference to third reading file and at least one legislative day after being printed and made available to members (Rule XIII). It was cut and dried. The lieutenant governor was given no discretion to hurry a bill to passage.

The lieutenant governor did have one power: he referred bills to standing or select committees. If the unicameral had adopted a plethora of committees, this prerogative may have been of considerable use to the lieutenant governor, allowing him to refer particular measures to a committee he thought would dispose of the legislation according to his own preferences. But the unicameral had streamlined its system to include only fourteen substantive standing committees. Theoretically, the lieutenant governor could refer what he deemed important measures to committees controlled by people whose opinions he favored. But in the unicameral, even that power was circumscribed by the caveat that a majority of the legislators could vote to re-refer a bill to a different committee (Rule XX.1). Thus, the lieutenant governor's options were limited. Furthermore, the absence of party structure in the unicameral meant there was no predicting just who would be in charge in any given committee. And, by definition in the nonpartisan legislature, a lieutenant governor could not choose to refer a bill to a committee controlled by his own party.

The speaker was even worse off. He was simply the president pro tem, presiding when the lieutenant governor was absent. The December 30 and 31, 1936, editions of the *Lincoln Journal* cited Senator L. C. Nuernberger's and Senator O. Edwin Schultz's opinions that the speaker should be chairman of the Committee on Committees as he had been in the old house of representatives. As it turned out, the speaker was not even a member of the Committee on Committees, the group that appointed standing committee members. Instead, the committee was made up of two senators from each of the five congressional districts in Nebraska in 1937.

Some observers suggested that taking appointment power away from the speaker guarded against his being used as a tool of lobbyists, who knew full well the value of controlling committees, and had eliminated the possibility that members would pledge their votes for a speaker in return for his promises of desirable committee assignments. That seems a logical suggestion, given the populist and reformist nature of the new body.

For both theoretical and practical reasons, the speaker was left with largely an administrative function; the position was little more than honorary. Unlike the speaker in the former house of representatives, the speaker of the nonpartisan unicameral had no political clout—partisan or nonpartisan.

In short, both of the legislature's presiding officers were expected primarily to "preserve order and decorum" (Rule I.4), the kind of carefully circumscribed role one would expect for leaders in a legislature that intended to be egalitarian and populist.

With the presiding officers' positions cut down to size and party slots nonexistent, perhaps the only remaining area in which leadership could be exercised was through membership on and leadership of standing committees. Some scholars say committees are likely to perform better and have more influence on the final legislative product when they are less dependent on formal leaders for direction. Without political parties to undergird the appointment process and with the speaker stripped of such power, committees were strengthened by default, if nothing else.

Legislators were able to request particular committee assignments, and some committees were more popular than others and were perceived to carry more prestige. The Committee on Committees tried to grant as many members' committee requests as possible, concerned that if they ignored too many people's preferences, their recommendation might be rejected and they would be sent back to the drawing board.

The *Lincoln Journal* reported on January 8, 1937, that the Committee on Committees's recommendations for committee membership were ratified without debate or dissent and added that a "rumored attempt to upset the cart" by moving to allow each committee to select its own chairman did not happen. The story went on implicitly to recognize the influence of both the Committee on Committees and the chairmen of the standing committees: "[T]he chairmanship plums, as usual, were (to be) distributed by the daddy committee."

Those chairmanship positions were, indeed, perceived to be influential. The committee chairmen presided over their committees' public hearings and their deliberations, where they had some opportunity to shape the discussion. Furthermore, their names appeared at the end of the committees' written reports to the legislature, and they made the actual presentation on the floor. That gave chairmen a certain prominence and enabled them at least to frame a measure in a particular manner. It's no surprise that chairmanships were considered plum positions or that senators were not united about how those plums—among the most powerful prerogatives available to a legislator—should be dispensed.

Not everyone in the legislature liked the idea that one small group would have the power to bestow the legislature's few leadership positions. Some still believed committees should elect their own chairmen. A week after the newspaper story reporting that the Committee on Committees would select the chairmen, Senator John Comstock of Lincoln "took the lead in eliminating a relic of the bicameral days, one of the choicest morsels within the power of the party in power to dispense: standing committee chairmanships." Comstock first offered an amendment to strike the provision that the Committee on Committees should recommend one member of each committee to serve as chairman; the amendment was approved on a twenty-four to fourteen vote. Then Comstock proposed that the committees elect their own chairmen; that proposal was approved unanimously.

Comstock told the Lincoln paper he did not want the Committee on Committees to have power to appoint standing committee chairmen because, in the bicamerals of the past, "members would trade their shirts" in order to land a spot on the parent committee in the hope of plucking standing committee chairmanships for themselves or their friends.[15] Although the absence of parties in the unicameral made it officially impossible for the Committee on Committees to consider party identification when making assignments, the senators apparently wanted also to eliminate both the reality and perception of cronyism from the assignment process. And they were willing to flatten the hierarchy and to deny privileges to the members of the Committee on Committees, keeping the legislature more democratic and egalitarian than it might otherwise have been.

The legislature didn't seem quite sure how much authority to grant its committees nor how much deference to require from them. Although John Norton, chair of the 1937 Rules Committee, had recommended that standing committees set priorities on legislation and consider and report bills in order of importance, the rules didn't demand that kind of process. Instead, committees considered bills in whatever order they pleased, and bills reported to general file were considered in the order in which they were received.

The speaker of the 1935 house of representatives had pointed out the problems that could arise under such a system. "If the entire body has to pick out bills for consideration or consider all that are introduced, the legislature cannot make progress," he said. "Committees are essential to picking out important legislation."[16] But the 1937 unicameral was unwilling to give any subgroup authority to "sift" bills and narrow the entire body's choices to that extent.

Also, the legislature reserved the right to second-guess committees both on a grand scale, by resurrecting dead bills, and on a smaller scale, by amending and re-amending committee recommendations. Unquestionably, the legislative rules constrained committee power and tried to assure that policy would be made by the body as a whole.

Furthermore, the legislature could demand a report from a committee after ten legislative days, a safeguard against a small group's "sitting" on a bill, effectively killing it in committee.

The rules also said every bill must be reported out of committee, even if the committee's recommendation was to "indefinitely postpone" or kill the measure (Rule VII). That was an effort to stop a committee from doing its work behind closed doors and to increase members' accountability to both the legislature and to the public. But, of course, it also diluted the committees' authority.

In addition, every bill was to be accompanied by a written statement of the committee's reasons for its recommendation—and the minority view "if such there be" (Rule VII.6). The statements were mimeographed and placed on each member's desk when the bills were up for discussion, giving the entire body some idea what was said in committee hearings and the reasoning behind the committee's recommendations. That, too, made committees less independent and powerful.

But the biggest check on committee authority came with the requirement that a standing committee hold a public hearing on every bill referred to it and that the hearing be preceded by at least five calendar days' notice (Rule VII.3). While Norris highlighted the benefits of public hearings in terms of keeping the public informed about legislation, the requirement also had another purpose: to prevent a small group in committee from killing a bill that a majority of legislators favored. No longer could a committee control a bill's fate with little or no input from the legislature at large.

Some observers of the 1937 unicameral praised the committee design and rules for their democratic (actually "populist") nature. Making sure committees had plenty of contact with the public allowed the legislature to delegate some authority to committees and ease the workload for the entire body while at the same time decreasing the risk of a public outcry against committee elitism and privilege.

But others thought the unicameral hadn't gone far enough to avoid hierarchy. When the Nebraska State Teachers Association surveyed the members of the 1937 legislature, asking how they thought the restructured institution had worked, some respondents thought the committees had too much power. Some said the entire membership should participate in hearings on every bill. They didn't like the idea that a subgroup like a committee made the decision whether a bill would advance or die. At the very least, they recommended that the entire legislature together hold hearings on the most important pieces of legislation; ten of the twenty-two senators who responded to the survey favored that procedure. The populist spirit demanded that no one be left out of any part of the decision-making process.

It was a delicate balance. Although the legislature's workload in 1937 may look relatively light and simple compared with legislative business at the turn of the twenty-first century, it was, even then, too much for forty-three members to handle in open sessions on the floor. Senning, Norton, and their compatriots realized the committee system was necessary to provide members with a way to develop some expertise in specific areas, to sift through the mass of proposed legislation and to assist the body at large in making its decisions.

Solid information of the kind assembled by committees was important to the 1937 unicameral. "I have witnessed no legislative session which placed such open reliance upon data as does the Nebraska one . . . already there are a dozen men who refuse to advance a bill if they believe that insufficient data have been presented," Professor Cortez Ewing wrote at the end of the first session.[17] Senning noticed "the effort on the part of members to use factual information to determine the merit of a measure."[18] Much of that specific information was produced and provided via the committee system.

The committee system and the expertise it produced also fostered what leadership the unicameral allowed. Some observers noted that the most influential legislators in the new unicameral were "those who have mastered their subject, who have studied the proposal and present the facts in logical argument. . . . Aren't those the right kinds of leaders?"[19] Members' prominence depended not on their rank in their political party or on their seniority but "on their personal ability and initiative," others said. That was precisely the kind of leadership Norris had wanted to see develop in the one-house, nonpartisan body.

Making Some Legislators More Equal than Others

Perhaps the most significant step the 1937 unicameral took toward specialization and division of labor was its decision to establish the Legislative Council. It was an idea Senning began promoting even before the first session of the new body. He recommended that the legislature name some of its members to a council that would meet when the legislature was not in session and would investigate the state's problems, suggest solutions, and create a program to help organize the legislature's work when senators returned for the following session.

In March, Norton made his proposal to the Government Committee. He said the council would be a fact-finding group to give the parent body background data, which would eliminate spur-of-the-moment votes. The newspaper cited Senning's support for the council; he said it would act as a "board of directors" for the legislature, in keeping with the unicameralists' wish that the legislature function like a business.

A week later, the legislature created the council. It consisted of fifteen members, including the speaker, and no more than three members from any of the five congressional districts. The council would be expected to prepare a legislative program and to cooperate with the governor "to find ways to enforce the laws and improve the effectiveness of administrative methods."[20] Norton stressed that the council's authority would be advisory only and that all its recommendations would be subject to review by the legislature. The bill was approved on final reading April 21 by a thirty-one to eight vote and was signed by the governor three days later.

The Legislative Council was intended to be an important way to provide leadership for the unicameral, to allow members to specialize, and to divide the workload. The makeup of the first Legislative Council reflected the membership of the legislature as a whole: four attorneys, five farmers, six businessmen, and two professionals. But the council did include the chairmen of the Appropriations, Agriculture, and Public Highways committees, and some were suspicious that the council was really a covert way to allow a few leaders to develop additional expertise, making it likely they would be returned to their chairmanships if they returned to the legislature. After all, the unicameral met every other year, and legislators were elected for two-year terms. Allowing fifteen members to sit on a council in the off year may have given them an electoral advantage were they to run for another term.

In other words, the Legislative Council was going to make some legislators more "equal" than others. Senning, Norton, and others approved of that idea, but not everyone agreed. Some said the council would become too influential and that the small group of leaders would have power to decide the course of action for the state. The idea did not sit comfortably in the populist legislature.

Senator Allen Strong, a farmer/stockman from Gordon, was vehement in his opposition. The council, he said, would disrupt the harmony of the legislature by giving a small body of men the right to present a "cut and dried program to the succeeding Legislature." The council was a repudiation of the whole idea behind the unicameral, Strong said. "The hope of the proponents of the Unicameral was that each and every member should know what each item of legislation was all about." Thanks to the formation of the council, "only 15 out of 43 will be fully informed."[21]

Council members were not deaf to the criticism. When the Legislative Council assembled for its first meeting on September 13, 1937, even Norton, the legislative father of the council, warned that the group must not set itself up as a "super legislature" but should serve as just an interim committee. Furthermore, he recommended that the council create a committee system and appoint noncouncil legislators to the committees so all senators could be involved. "That will avoid making us a little better than the others and being a little legislature," he said.[22]

Eventually, the council members decided that their purpose was to gather information and present facts to their fellow legislators and to the public, not to prepare an agenda for the next legislature. "We should not form any conclusions," Senator Emil Von Seggern said. "Let the people do that." The purpose of the council should be to educate people, he continued. With a one-house, nonpartisan form of legislature, "it is necessary that the people know what is going on if it is to succeed."[23]

The commotion over the Legislative Council illustrates the philosophical conflict between egalitarianism and efficiency. The council was created because the legislature became aware that its structure constrained leadership and that lack of leadership made policy making difficult and relatively inefficient. The problem was exacerbated by the fact that legislators were elected for only two-year terms and, thus, were guaranteed participation in only one session, during the first year after their election. So it was very possible that many legislators at each session would be new members with no institutional memory.

It was possible that even members of the Legislative Council might not be reelected or might choose not to run for re-election. The short terms and the potential turnover would seem to make it all the more necessary for a group like the Legislative Council and its staff to develop a policy program to be considered by the next legislature. Surely it would have been a step toward preventing the need to reinvent the wheel at every session.

But, in the face of the sniping from those who resented any semblance of privilege or elitism, the council members had second thoughts. They backed away from the opportunity to enhance their own leadership and decided, instead, simply to be researchers and teachers.

Perhaps the small size of the unicameral fostered and intensified the senators' desire that all members consider every measure. In fact, Norris had encouraged that very situation in his campaign for the unicameral. By the time the legislature had one session under its belt, its members seemed convinced they should follow Norris's advice and assure that every legislator was involved in nearly every aspect of decision making. That conviction led to the emasculation of the Legislative Council. A practice shaped by the body's structure and rules had developed into a norm. Even those who were handed leadership on a legislature-produced platter were reluctant to accept it.

Undoubtedly, the information the council and its director gathered and presented to the next legislature was useful. One can assume it resulted in more informed legislators—both on and apart from the council—who may, as a result, have been better leaders. But the members of the council were better leaders because they had a slight advantage in expertise, not because the Legislative Council gave them additional institutional authority. What may have come naturally to previous Nebraska legislatures smacked too much of elitism to be acceptable in the 1937 Nebraska unicameral. In true populist fashion, the members of the Legislative Council cut themselves down to size. In true progressive fashion, they proposed to educate themselves, their colleagues, and the citizenry so that all parties would be better able to participate in making good public policy.

The unicameral's institutional structure as well as its rules and procedures were designed to further the populist notion of equality for all members. But an equality that eliminates nearly all formal leadership opportunities and relies on spontaneous leadership by the entire body may find itself in frequent conflict with a desire for efficiency, another of Norris's promises for the new system. It's likely that legislative bodies founded on the populist/progressive ideology would rather live with at least some chaos than grant disproportionate influence to any individual or group. But even they must find ways to make policy and to serve the needs of their constituents. In some cases, that may require tipping the balance a bit away from equality and toward measures that increase efficiency. That seems to be what has happened in Nebraska.

Finding Efficiency, Preserving Equality

Nebraska's legislature is still one house and still nonpartisan and has increased only slightly in size since 1937. No parties have been installed to provide leadership positions and leadership direction. All the criticisms about what nonpartisanship could do to leadership and, concurrently, efficiency are still valid. Nebraskans have consistently rebuffed efforts to change the basic structure of their legislative institution.

But within the framework of that institution, the unicameral senators themselves have been busy almost from day one, adjusting their rules and procedures to deal with the problems of making policy in a body that is purposely and determinedly nonhierarchical.

Decision Making without Benefit of Party

In the United States system of government, people are elected to legislatures as individuals, not as part of a group. Nowhere is that more true than in Nebraska with its nonpartisan system. And each of the individuals thus elected brings to the body his or her own specific goals and interests. Once individuals become part of the legislature, though, they must begin to look for places where their goals and interests overlap with those of other members so that, together, they can form a majority to make policy choices in accord with those shared goals and interests.

In the traditional American legislature, political parties are the dominant means by which goals and interests are coordinated and action is taken. Party discipline can facilitate the formation of coalitions within the party. Those coalitions, in turn, can negotiate handily with coalitions in the other party or parties, and shared interests will, ultimately, be coordinated. The variety of choices open to the legislators can be drastically narrowed to a manageable number and a simplified form that, theoretically, at least, can be better understood and acted on.

In the process, of course, party members limit their own choices and their own influence by submitting to party leaders, rules, and structures. Parties can bring coherence and consistency to the debate if they have formulated solid platforms to which members are expected to adhere. However, what the legislature gains in efficiency it loses in the representativeness of the body. In theory, every voice should have a chance to be heard via the party apparatus; in practice, some voices will be silenced or at least muted as the leadership sets direction for the party and enforces party discipline and loyalty.

The very traits that make parties useful in legislative procedure turned the populist stomachs of George Norris and his fellow unicameralists. They decried what they saw as artificial alliances, forced on legislators by party leaders. They wanted every legislator's voice to be heard on behalf of his or her constituents. Not only was the business of the state in no way partisan, but neither did the process of decision making require partisan control.

Officially, at least, the Nebraska legislature has held fast to Norris's philosophy throughout its sixty-seven years. Members are still elected without party labels, and the body functions without party discipline. The result, as assessed below, would probably sometimes please, sometimes baffle, and sometimes appall Senator Norris, but the absence of political parties in the legislature seems firmly entrenched in Nebraska.

Creating Leaders among Equals

The unicameral may have steadfastly refused to go partisan, but the legislators have found other ways to make it easier to coordinate their interests and set policy. At the top of the list is a slow but steady increase in leadership opportunities and prerogatives.

Perhaps most prominently, changes in both rules and norms have gradually increased the power and authority of the office of speaker during the unicameral's sixty-five years. Elected by the entire legislature—as he still is—the speaker had largely an administrative and ceremonial function in 1937. But that began to change in 1939, when the legislature decided it didn't like the idea of allowing the lieutenant governor, a member of the executive branch, to refer bills to committees. Never mind that the absence of parties automatically diluted whatever power bill reference offered the lieutenant governor. It was still too much for the senators.

As of the 1939 session, the lieutenant governor lost a bit and the speaker gained a bit when the legislature created a bill reference committee made up of the lieutenant governor, the speaker, and the chairman of the Committee on Committees. Membership on the Reference Committee did not exactly give the speaker extraordinary power, but it was a start.

In 1974 the Executive Board, of which the speaker is automatically a member, became the committee that refers bills to committee; that was still the case in 2002. The speaker's inclusion in the Reference Committee and Executive Board were significant steps toward making the office more substantive and less ceremonial. A 1998 attempt to change the makeup of the Reference Committee to one made up of the chairs of all standing committees and the chair of the Executive Board, eliminating the speaker from the process, failed.

The legislature decided in 1965 that the speaker was the appropriate person to help the body function more efficiently and added to his duties the coordination of chairs of the standing committees. That made him a facilitator, though, not a leader with real clout. The measure recognized the speaker as someone who might help the process go better, but it gave the speaker no authority to order the committee chairs to do anything at all.

The speaker's position did gain importance in 1967 when the legislature amended Rule V to remove the speaker from service on any standing committee. What may at first glance look like a demotion was actually a promotion, making the speaker unique among the members. The change implicitly recognized that the speaker should be allowed to devote his time to his duties as presiding officer, coordinator of committee chairs, and member of the Reference Committee and should not be required to serve in the committee trenches with the rest of the body.

The time the speaker actually spends presiding has also increased over the years. The lieutenant governor is still officially the legislature's presiding officer despite repeated attempts to amend the constitution to eliminate that designation. Amendments to remove the lieutenant governor from the presiding officer's chair were introduced in the legislature ten times between 1969 and 2000 and actually placed on the ballot in 1969, 1974, 1976, and 1998. Each time, the proposal was defeated by the voters. However, the lieutenant governor has, apparently, taken the hint and gradually chosen to absent himself or herself more and more from the legislature since the 1970s. By 2002 the lieutenant governor seldom presided. The speaker or another senator he designated presided over nearly all floor debate.

The position of speaker also got a boost in 1981 when Richard Marvel ran successfully for reelection to a second term in the office. Nothing in the unicameral's rules had ever put a one-term limit on the speaker's job, but legislative practice had done so. It makes sense that such a norm would have developed, considering that equality was one of the principles on which the unicameral was founded. Even though the position was largely ceremonial at first and grew in actual influence only gradually, election to speaker did single out one person as, at the least, the symbolic leader of the legislature.

It was something of a vicious circle, though. If a person served only one term in the position, he was unlikely to be able to develop much influence either through the formal responsibilities of the office or through the informal powers of persuasion and expertise that come with longer service. And that, in turn, meant the office offered few returns on the investment of time and effort and was likely to be handed off to someone else in the next session.

The absence of leadership made it harder for the unicameral to get its work done. In fact, the 1971 report from the Citizens' Conference on State Legislatures ranked Nebraska thirty-fifth in the nation in functionality. The report recommended that Nebraska discontinue its "rotating leadership," saying the practice of limiting the speaker to one two-year term disrupted the continuity of leadership within the body and had "profoundly adverse effects on many aspects of legislative performance."[24] Ever since Marvel broke the ice, each speaker has been reelected to at least one additional term, and Senator Doug Kristensen was elected speaker in 1998 (to fill the unexpired term of Ron Withem), 1999, and 2001. (Kristensen resigned from the legislature following the 2002 term.)

But it is probably the speaker's ability to influence the legislative calendar and order of debate that has offered the biggest boost to the position's power. In 1937, the legislature considered bills in the order they were reported to the floor. No one set a calendar, and that got the body into a tight spot late in its first session. On the seventy-seventh legislative day, eager to end the session but faced with a glut of pending legislation, the unicameral created a sifting committee to "sift" the bills and order them for consideration on the floor. Things haven't been the same since.

Although the concept of considering legislation in the order in which it appears on the floor and allowing no one to manipulate the calendar is certainly egalitarian, it also proved to be dramatically inefficient. Each session from 1939 through 1943 used an ad hoc sifting committee to order bills for consideration on the floor. In 1945 the Committee on Order and Arrangement—a calendar committee—was appointed to the do the job; its members were the chairs of the standing committees and the chair of the Committee on Committees, a total of about twenty people, nearly half the membership of the legislature. The speaker, however, had no part in the process.

In 1965 the unicameral changed the makeup of the calendar committee to include all the members of the Committee on Committees—eight people by that time—as well as the lieutenant governor and the speaker. That brought membership on the calendar committee down to about one-fourth of the total legislators, still a good-sized group.

In 1976, though, the legislature told the speaker he should set the calendar —with his decisions to be approved by the Executive Board. The rule allowed the body to override the speaker's calendar by a simple majority vote, which, apparently, turned out to be something the senators were all too happy to do.

By 1979 the Executive Board requested that the rule be changed to require a three-fifths, or thirty-vote, majority to override the speaker's decisions. In introducing the amendment, Senator Frank Lewis said the change would help "shore up our process here and particularly give the speaker the authority that he needs to carry out his functions."[25] That rule change passed on a thirty-one to six vote with little discussion, and accepting the speaker's ordering of bills for consideration seems to have become a norm of behavior in the ensuing years. Today the calendar is seldom challenged, according to Patrick O'Donnell, clerk of the legislature.

The speaker has also gained—and lost—some procedural powers since the 1970s. In 1977 an amendment to the rules declared that a majority of senators present, rather than a majority of total members, would be enough to sustain the chair's ruling on a challenged point of order. But a 1983 proposal that would have made it even harder for the body to override the chair's ruling on questions of germaneness failed.

During debate on the rule change, which would have required a three-fifths vote of the entire membership to override a germaneness ruling rather than a simple majority of those present, several senators argued that a three-fifths requirement would make it almost impossible for senators to overrule the chair when attendance was low. One said requiring only a majority of those present would be "much more democratic." Another said the hard-to-come-by three-fifths requirement would, by default, give the speaker total power to determine what is germane. The belief that the speaker's power should be limited in the populist unicameral prevailed.

In 1982 the speaker's power made a quantum leap forward on another front when he was granted authority to designate an unlimited number of priority bills, those that can leapfrog ahead of other legislation in order to have a better chance of being considered in full debate by the entire legislature. Priority bills were to be a mechanism to assure that legislation senators felt was particularly important would actually make it through the legislative process before the mandated end of the session. The 1982 change to Rule V gave each senator the option of designating one bill a priority bill. Each standing committee chair was allowed to designate two of the committee's bills as priorities, and the speaker was allowed to designate any additional number of bills for priority consideration, potentially allowing him to shape the legislative agenda dramatically.

The 1982 rule change also allowed the speaker to set the deadline by which senators needed to announce their priority designations, although the speaker's deadline had to be before the forty-fifth day in the ninety-day session and before the thirtieth day in the sixty-day session. Priority bills were to be scheduled for committee hearings before nonpriority bills and, once reported out of committee, could be moved to the head of the line for floor consideration.

However, the following year the senators had had second thoughts about how much power they had given the speaker with the priority bill rule and decided to pull back a bit. Instead of being able to designate an unlimited number of priority bills, which could have allowed him to pretty much dominate the decision as to which legislation would actually be considered by the body, the speaker was now to be limited to twenty-five priority bills. "[R]eally there is not a need for more than that," said Don Wesely, chairman of the Rules Committee, in presenting the change.[26] In 1985 a measure was introduced to let the Executive Board rather than the speaker designate twenty-five priority bills, but that idea never came to a vote.

By 1996 the legislature was feeling more and more frustrated by its inability, within the constitutional time limits on the sessions, to get at some legislation many senators and citizens thought was vitally important. Rules

Committee chair Eric Will noted that the Rules Committee had tried for several years, without a lot of success, to streamline debate and to prevent "dilatory actions" by individual senators.

Now the committee was ready to try a new approach, one that would increase the speaker's power again. The ensuing debate, which stretched over three legislative days, raised all the major arguments on both sides of the equality versus efficiency dilemma.

The original proposal would have allowed the speaker, before the twentieth legislative day—ten days after the deadline for bill introduction—to designate up to ten bills or resolutions as "major proposals," or super-priorities, as they came to be called. The speaker's designations would have to be discussed with and approved by the Executive Board.

Once the designations were final, the speaker could require the committees to which the ten super-priority measures had been referred to hold a public hearing by a specific date agreed to by the speaker and committee chair. After the committee hearing, the speaker could force the committee to take action, positive or negative, on the bill. If the committee reported the bill to the floor, the speaker could place the bill at the top of the agenda for consideration on the floor.

Perhaps even more important, this proposal would, for the first time, allow the speaker to determine the order of amendments and motions filed during debate; to that point, amendments and motions during floor debate (other than those from the committee or from the bill's introducer) were simply taken up in the order in which they were filed, causing "a race to the clerk's desk," one senator said.[27]

Speaking to a reporter later, Speaker Ron Withem said the race often resulted in thirty to forty amendments being filed on major legislation. Some of those amendments raised only minor issues, and others were specifically intended to cause delay, he said, and a few were of significant importance to the issue at hand. If those important amendments happened to lose the race to the clerk's desk, the legislature might never have a chance even to consider them.

When Withem addressed the proposal during debate, he said he had not sought additional power for his office but would not shrink from exercising such power if the rule change were passed. He pointed out that it was "a major enhancement of authority that the speaker would have" and that the legislature should consider not whether it wanted to grant more power to him personally but whether making the office of the speaker more powerful would benefit the body in the long run.

Withem asked the senators whether they would like to amend the proposal so that the speaker's super-priorities would be chosen only from among bills already named as priority bills by the members, limiting the speaker's authority a little. But he commended the recommendation's provision that allowed the speaker to require committee action, a power no one in the legislature had at the time. The new rule would let the speaker "hold a committee chair's feet to the fire" and require that major proposals be considered in a timely manner.[28]

Withem also commented on the other major change the proposal made: granting the speaker authority to determine the order in which amendments and motions would be considered on the floor. If the senators wanted to give an individual authority to "take actions to break log jams," the proposal would be a step toward doing that, he said.

Without giving specific examples, Withem said that during the years he had been speaker he had seen a number of major issues that "ought to be debated, ought to be kicked around, that the legislature ought to massage considerably" get bogged down under a pile of amendments that had to be considered in order of filing. Some of those amendments were filed for the sole purpose of delaying action, Withem said, although he acknowledged that such a tactic was, indeed, legitimate. But other amendments that actually got to the heart of measures and needed to be debated in order to assure the best legislation fell too far down on the list and often never saw the light of floor debate. As a result, Withem said, the legislature sometimes "put forth proposals that are less than our best product."[29]

The other part of the 1996 proposal was less important, Withem said. The speaker already had some power over the calendar, power to order matters for floor debate with concurrence from the Executive Board. The January 9 proposal only reinforced and codified what already existed in fact.

Then Withem addressed the underlying philosophical issue: "This Legislature in comparison with other legislatures around the country has a comparatively weak speaker system." And he praised that system. "We are a unicameral Legislature. We are a nonpartisan Legislature. We don't have the check of the other house or the discipline of party membership to organize things, and we don't want to invest too much power in one individual."[30]

George Norris, John Senning, and John Norton must have been cheering from the heavens to hear a speaker, sixty years after their plan went into action, still preaching the populist goal of equality among legislators. Withem said he didn't want Nebraska to switch to a system in which the speaker would set the rules for debate, refer bills to committee, and choose the committee chairs. But, he added, "I do, from time to time, get requests verging on demands when we hit a log jam that say, 'You, the speaker, have to do something about this.'" The rules change being considered January 9 would be a good start at enabling speakers present and future to do something, Withem said.

In response, Senator David Bernard-Stevens said that was exactly the trouble with the proposal. He said giving the speaker power to demand committee action by a certain date would violate the integrity of the committee process. Bernard-Stevens said Nebraska had a weak speaker—and weak committee chairs—for good reason. The only real power committee chairs had, he said, was to put bills they didn't like at the very end of the hearing schedule. Even that authority could be overruled if a senator named a bill one of his or her priorities, and it would be further eroded if the speaker had a say in how a committee chair scheduled hearings.

Bernard-Stevens also objected to the speaker's being able to order amendments during floor debate because the speaker could prevent some amendments from ever even coming up for debate. "That is not only tremendous power, that is setting policy," he said. Then Bernard-Stevens got to the heart of the philosophical matter, addressing the nature of the institution: "It is a decentralized system. It is difficult because of that, but I think it protects the rights of members far, far more."[31]

But the proposal was not removing all the checks on the speaker, Senator Curt Bromm said. The Executive Board, representative of the whole body and, specifically, all the geographic areas of the state, would still have to approve the super-priorities set by the speaker. And the legislature itself could overrule the speaker's designations if it wished. At the same time, increasing the speaker's authority could increase the quality of debate on important measures, Bromm said. The original nonhierarchical system was a good one, he said, but "I don't think when our one-house system was created that we probably envisioned the complexity and the volume of measures that we would face in a given session."[32]

Senator Chris Beutler agreed. The danger the unicameral was facing, he said, was not the investment of too much power in a few leaders but the absence of any power to coordinate the body "to get a reasonable program of legislation through in a reasonable way."[33]

When the legislature returned to the subject the following day, Senator Ernie Chambers laid into the proposal on philosophical grounds. "This is one of the worst usurpations of authority and power in the Legislature that has been attempted since I've been here," he said. Chambers was particularly unhappy with the provision that would allow the speaker to order amendments for floor debate and called it "a blueprint for disaster."[34]

Senator Bromm, however, said the change would simply allow the leadership of the legislature—the speaker and the Executive Board—to get important issues before the body in a timely manner. He added that he was sure speakers would want to use their ability to special-order legislation very sparingly, making the assumption that the unicameral's norms of weak leadership would continue.

Senator Beutler acknowledged Chambers's fears about allowing the speaker to order amendments for debate. In fact, he said, speakers in the past had done exactly that, even though the rules authorized no such action. When he was elected to the legislature in 1978, Beutler said, "We had a very powerful Speaker with a couple of very powerful lieutenants, and they'd put any damn thing they wanted right on top of the agenda every time, and you didn't know it was coming until the morning it was there because they didn't distribute agendas the day before." The priority system restored to individual senators and committees more control over the agenda, Beutler said. But the rule change under consideration in 1996 would assure a "participatory process, a way by which we all could know what the important bills are."[35]

Chambers returned to the egalitarian theory underlying the unicameral's system. "Elitism should not be what the Unicameral is about," he said. George Norris did not intend for agendas to be set by a few individuals and foisted on the body, not even for the sake of efficiency.[36] Later in the debate, he said, "I don't believe in anything that's going to take away the basic rights of the weakest senator in here."[37]

But Beutler countered that orderly procedure was "an absolute prerequisite to orderly democratic government." The unicameral's rules, he said were "so liberal and so loose" that one or two individuals could bring the whole legislature to a halt. The proposed rule change, he said, would be "one small step a little more on the side of order."[38]

Senator Dave Maurstad added it would give the speaker "tools necessary to be able to administer our work as effectively as possible."[39]

Senator Dave Landis, though, was not so sure the proposal would really be effective. "We've written our rules to promote discussion," he said. The only way to cut off what the majority may consider dilatory discussion would be to grant unfettered discretion to the speaker: to rule something dilatory, to rule a senator out of order, to change the orders of amendments as they were raised, to be "arbitrary." That kind of discretion would not be granted, Landis said, because it "is actually unpalatable to us" and offered power the legislature simply was not about to give to any one member.[40]

At that point, the legislature approved a Maurstad amendment to change the number of super-priority bills in the amended rule from ten to five. And then Chambers spoke to the "Lola" amendment he had introduced the day before.

" 'Whatever Lola wants, Lola gets.' Lola shall mean whoever is the speaker," Chambers said, quoting from the musical *Damn Yankees*.

"That's what you're doing with this kind of thing. You're giving everything away, and I will not agree to it." But, he added, if the legislature were determined to do that, then it should be done in a clear, straightforward manner the public could understand "and that is to say the speaker is to be given a type of power that no single individual in the Legislature should have or wield based on what the rules authorize."[41]

Senator Jerome Warner responded, saying he planned to support increasing the speaker's authority. He said he appreciated Senator Chambers's concern that the rules allow every voice to be heard. But as long as legislative sessions were limited to a certain number of days, Warner said, the body would need a mechanism "to be sure things that need to be done can be done."[42]

Chambers's "Lola" amendment failed on a thirty-eight to two vote. Then Bernard-Stevens proposed an amendment that would have stricken the portion of the rules change that allowed the speaker to order amendments and motions during floor debate. Beutler said striking that part of the proposal would kill the whole thing. A speaker could still designate five super-priority bills, "but why would they be important? Why would anybody listen?" If the speaker had no control over the order in which amendments were considered, his super-priority designation really wouldn't matter. "There's no way to bring order out of this chaos of amendments," Beutler said. "This amendment is about orderly process," a process that would assure that substantive issues were dealt with.[43] Bernard-Stevens's amendment also failed.

Then Maurstad proposed one more amendment. This one removed the twenty-day limit for the speaker to set super-priority bills but inserted language requiring that the super-priorities be selected from among bills already designated by senators as priorities. Chambers said that language would, at least, assure that the speaker could not go entirely outside the wishes of the senators when designating super-priorities. In a one-house, nonpartisan legislature like the unicameral, he added, "the worst thing is to concentrate power in the hands of one individual rather than having a legislature which is responsive to the people, as this one is supposed to be."[44]

Maurstad said he believed his amendment would make the rule change a more cautious approach than the original proposal; the amendment passed on a twenty-five to zero vote.

But the matter was not settled yet. Chambers proposed another amendment, this one requiring unanimous approval by the Executive Board of each of the speaker's super-priority designations. After some discussion in which several senators pointed out that such a measure could allow one member of the Executive Board, by veto, to control all super-priority designations— simply replacing the speaker in that process—Chambers withdrew that amendment and proposed, instead, that two-thirds of the Executive Board be required to approve the speaker's designations. That proposal was adopted on a twenty-eight to three vote.

Nearly a week later, on January 17, the legislature approved the amended rules, mightily increasing the speaker's authority over what it had been. But the Nebraska speaker still has far fewer prerogatives than his counterparts in other states or in the U.S. Congress. The debate over rules and subsections of rules clearly illustrates the senators' understanding of the tension between equality and efficiency and the philosophical points of view underlying that tension.

To Filibuster or Not to Filibuster

Various measures to limit or cut off legislative discussion have run on something of a parallel track with increasing the speaker's power to control the calendar and the order of debate. Of course, any limit heads away from the original unicameralists' goals of unfettered debate among all members of the legislature, but the fact that the matter has come up regularly indicates the problems that can arise from even such a lofty ideal.

The rules adopted by the 1937 legislature limited each senator to speaking no more than twice upon any one question in debate on any given day without specific permission of the legislature unless the senator was the sponsor of the matter in question. Then he would be allowed to reply after everyone else who wanted to speak to the question had done so (Rule V.2). The rule set no time limit on the senator's two turns to speak.

That changed in 1959, when the legislature adopted a Rules Committee proposal continuing the "no more than twice" provision but setting a 10-minute limit on each turn (Rule IV.10). Several attempts to change the number of times and length of time a member could speak failed during the 1976 session. However, in 1977, the legislature amended the rule to allow each member to speak three times in any one day on a particular question but for only five minutes at a time; the sponsor of the bill or motion was allowed ten minutes to present the bill and five minutes to respond at the end of the debate (Rule II.10).

In 1978 the legislature tried another way to limit debate, this time making it easier for a senator to call for cloture—to end all debate on a bill and any pending amendments at that stage of consideration. Although the rule limiting members to three five-minute presentations on each question was still in effect, senators had found a way around the limit. By introducing numerous amendments and motions during floor debate, they were able to multiply the number of times they could speak and, thus, were able to extend the debate for hours—to filibuster, in other words.

The 1978 legislature attempted to add a new section to Rule VII. It said that at any stage of consideration, the bill's introducer—an individual senator or the chair of a committee—could move for cloture. After thirty more minutes of debate, the presiding officer would end the discussion and allow the bill's sponsor to wrap up his or her argument. The motion for cloture would not be debatable and would need a three-fifths majority—thirty votes—to pass. But the proposal failed.

The 1981 Rules Committee took on the filibuster problem again, recommending the cloture rule be changed so that a motion would be in order after two-and-a-half hours of debate on a priority bill or after one hour of debate on any other bill. That proposal failed, too.

In 1989 the legislature tried to change Rule VII again, this time adding the provision that, after a full eight hours of debate at each of the three stages of consideration on the floor—twelve hours for an appropriations bill—the individual or the chair of the committee that sponsored the measure could move for cloture. That motion, which would be nondebatable, would require a two-thirds majority, or thirty-three votes, for passage. If it was successful, the body would vote immediately on the matter under debate. The legislators were still not ready for this kind of limit on their right to speak, and they defeated the proposal thirty to thirteen. But two years later a nearly identical rule change was adopted on a twenty-nine to twelve vote.

The unicameral tried in 1994 to beef up its ability to bring an end to debate by proposing to amend Rule VII yet again. This time the proposal said if amendments or motions were offered "and it is obvious they are being used as the basis of obstruction," a member could move that the specific items were obstructive. A two-thirds vote would be required to pass such a motion; if it passed, all the "obstructive" matters would be declared out of order. The amendment was soundly defeated, twenty-eight to eight, but it returned the following year, couched in slightly different language.[45]

In 1995 the proposal to add a new section to Rule VII said motions and amendments "shall not be filed for dilatory purposes" and gave the speaker authority to temporarily remove an item from the agenda if he believed it to be dilatory, and to meet with the introducer to try to straighten things out before ruling the motion in order or out of order. The proposal provided no way to overrule the speaker's decision, a real departure from the unicameral's tendency to hold the speaker with a tight rein.

Before that rather radical proposal was even discussed, though, the Rules Committee offered a different version. This one allowed the amendment or motion's introducer to move to overrule the speaker if he or she wished and also removed the item in question from the agenda for only one legislative day. Senators Beutler and Chambers proposed adding that any amendment or motion ruled out of order by the speaker not be introduced again by any member in any form at the same stage of debate, and the revised version of the Rules Committee's amendment passed twenty-five to seven.

Even restrictions like that, though, failed to foil those who really wanted to filibuster, and in 1998 Senator Eric Will tried another approach. He proposed that no senator other than the primary introducer of a bill be allowed to offer more than three motions, amendments, or amendments to amendments at any one stage of debate unless the presiding officer thought the limit would preclude full and fair debate. Senator Chambers, one of the legislature's staunchest defenders of rules that preserve equality among senators, tried to change the limit from three to twenty and then to nineteen, but both attempts were defeated. Eventually, Will withdrew the proposal entirely.

But the frustrations remained. The unicameral tried to limit filibustering again in 2002 with another amendment to Rule VII. Under the previous wording, a bill's sponsor would have to wait until after eight hours of debate to move for cloture. Under the amended rule, the sponsor could ask for debate to cease at any time; the two-thirds, thirty-three-vote majority was still required to approve the motion. But the new rule also gave the legislature's presiding officer—often the speaker but sometimes another senator—unchallengeable authority to overrule a cloture motion if he or she believed the body had not given a matter "full and fair" debate.

Senators told the *Lincoln Journal Star* the rule change was directed specifically at Senator Chambers, known for his ability to use long debates and filibusters to prevent bills from coming to a final vote. Chambers had been the obvious if officially undesignated target of much of the previous antifilibuster legislation, too.

Despite their irritation with filibustering and its effect on policy making, not all senators favored the new cloture rule; eleven senators voted against it. "This new rule will not magically alter what we do," Senator Dave Landis told the newspaper. "It could lead to a presiding officer who wants to hear a full eight hours of debate one day and another presiding officer who thinks five minutes is enough."[46]

While various senators serve as presiding officer from time to time, the speaker usually takes over when questions about legislative rules are expected to arise. But the supermajority required to pass a cloture motion and cease debate meant that if the presiding officer allowed the motion to go to a vote, those wishing to cut off discussion would need the thirty-three-vote, two-thirds majority, which was far more difficult to come by than a simple majority of twenty-six votes.

The evolving rules to limit and cease debate are another example of the struggle between the legislature's desire that every legislator be able to debate every issue and proposal and its concern that individual senators not use the rules to stop the legislature from taking action. Once again, the conflict is between equality and efficiency. Once again, the answer is an uneasy compromise.

Committees on a Short Leash

From the beginning, the unicameral dealt with committees in the same egalitarian way it tried to deal with most everything. Rather than giving either of the official presiding officers authority to appoint standing committee members, it created the Committee on Committees to do that (Rule VI). In the absence of parties, geography became the guiding force for committee assignments.

The appointment practice has continued pretty much unchanged throughout the ensuing sixty-seven years. In the unicameral's early days, the groundwork for the Committee on Committees's appointments was laid by the senators from each of the districts who met in nonpartisan caucus to recommend who from their districts should be appointed to which standing committees. That same practice is followed today.

But the makeup of the caucuses and the Committee on Committees itself changed as Nebraska's population shifted and its congressional districts were redrawn. The 1937 committee was composed of two members from each of five congressional districts plus the chair, chosen at large. In 1941 the membership changed to three members from each of what had become four congressional districts plus the chairman, still selected at large by the entire legislature. The 1937 rules had provided that the members of the standing committees would elect their own chairmen (Rule VI, Rule VII), but that didn't last long. Already in 1939 the Committee on Committees was anointing the standing committee chairmen.

By 1961 Nebraska had dropped to only three congressional districts, and the legislature considered choosing its members of the Committee on Committees from each of the three districts. But the Rules Committee opposed it, and the body kept the old four-district configuration, apparently an effort to give the less populous western part of the state a little extra say in committee assignments.

A 1977 attempt to centralize power in the Executive Board at the expense of the Committee on Committees and the Rules Committee failed. The proposal suggested the Executive Board, then made up of two members from each of three groupings of legislative districts plus the speaker, should take on the duties of the other two committees. It was defeated twenty-two to fourteen.

It was not until 1992 that the legislature began selecting its Committee on Committees on the basis of the state's three congressional districts. Since then the thirteen-member committee has consisted of four members from each of the three districts plus the chairman, elected at large.

The Committee on Committees had been responsible all along for selecting the members of each standing committee, but in 1972 the group was sheared of some of its power when the legislature decided to elect chairmen and vice chairmen of committees by secret ballot on the floor, a change that took effect with the 1973 session. An attempt was made in 1995 to change the procedure to election by roll call vote, but it failed resoundingly, thirty-three to seven, with nine senators not voting.

Among the fifty states in 1999, only seventeen selected committee members and committee chairs by some group process, either a Committee on Committees, the Rules Committee or some select committee or by election. In the other thirty-three states, the committee members and chairs were appointed by the speaker of the house or president or president pro tem of the senate.

The unicameral's rules regarding committee selection have remained true to its founders' belief that legislative leadership should be developed on the basis of ability, not conferred as a matter of popularity, party loyalty, or even seniority. A 1985 proposal that would have given the most senior members of the legislature first pick of committee assignments, failed, also on a resounding vote: thirty-three to nine with seven not voting.

Nonetheless, electing committee chairs on the floor strengthened the committee system and has led to more chairs serving longer on a given committee, providing more stability for the system. But that does not necessarily mean committee members and chairs today have a lot of power. Even the early unicameralists recognized the need for committees to develop expertise in specific areas and to be able to sort and sift the total volume of legislation into a workable mass to be dealt with by the entire body on the floor of the legislature. While they may have wished that all business could be conducted by all legislators together on the floor, they understood that the sheer size of the workload would overwhelm policy making.

Standing committees in the new unicameral were inevitable, although their number was reduced and their activities were streamlined. But the unicameral kept its committees on a relatively short leash—and it still does.

For instance, the requirement that every bill have a public hearing has been in place during the unicameral's entire history. While that practice has been praised primarily for the way it keeps the legislature open and accountable, it also keeps the legislators on an equal footing. No committee can simply kill a bill without any public consideration. The committee chair can make it more or less likely that a bill will make it to floor debate simply by scheduling a hearing late in the session, but the senators' right to declare certain bills as priorities trumps that option in the case of at least some legislation.

And the legislature as a whole can still resurrect bills killed in committee, although the legislators have changed their minds several times about just how hard it should be to do that. The 1943 legislature amended the rules to allow the body to pull a killed bill from committee by majority vote within five days after the bill was reported. But in 1945 the senators changed the number of days from five to three and added that the vote required a two-thirds majority, making the process more difficult and tipping the balance a bit more toward the committees.

But those provisions didn't last long. In 1947 the legislature decided to allow a simple majority to demand a bill be pulled from committee and either placed on general file or returned to the committee for further action. In 1957 and 1959 the unicameral defeated proposals to return to a two-thirds or three-fifths majority, respectively.

The legislature flip-flopped on the question several times during the 1960s. In 1963 the body adopted a Rules Committee recommendation that a three-fifths majority be required to pull a killed bill from committee. In 1965 the senators returned to a simple majority. But ten years later, they settled on a three-fifths majority, which has remained relatively stable ever since. The 2002 rules indicated a three-fifths vote required to pull a bill from committee if the motion were made within three legislative days after the report or a two-thirds vote after more than three legislative days (Rule III.18).

All the second-guessing seems to indicate the legislature has had a hard time deciding to what extent the standing committees should be kept under the thumb of the entire body. If only a simple majority is needed to resurrect a dead bill from committee, the legislature can, relatively easily, second-guess a committee's decision. If a supermajority is required, the committee's decision is more likely to stand.

Of course, it is not only bills killed in committee that have been the subject of legislative oversight. The legislature has also reserved the right to ask for a report—positive or negative—from a committee after a specified number of days, preventing a committee from purposely postponing action on a piece of legislation until it would be too late to deal with it. The 1937 rules said the legislature could, by simple majority, demand a report any time after ten days (Rule VII.5). The 1959 rules changed the number of days to twenty and exempted the Appropriations Committee from the rule, allowing it almost unlimited time to develop the state's budget.

In 1997 the legislature amended the rule again to define the twenty-day deadline as the date by which committee debate on the measure must begin, not the date by which action must have been taken. That amendment seems to split the difference between what could be regular interference in a committee's business and a completely hands-off policy. The committee is still held responsible for timely action on bills referred to it, but being required to start debate by a certain date is less intrusive than being required to take action by that date.

The gradual move toward respecting the committee's authority on a number of fronts, justifiable in the name of efficiency, is compatible with other changes in the unicameral rules that have strengthened leadership and made the body more hierarchical in 2002 than it was in 1937. But the rules, and the debates over amending the rules, continue to reflect the senators' concern that the legislature avoid granting privileges to a few leaders at any level and to assure that all senators are involved in the policy making process.

Two Steps Forward, One Step Back

Both legislative scholars and interested observers as well as members themselves have noted that the structure of the unicameral does not promote power. That is the way it was designed, and that is what senators have struggled with as they have faced increasingly complex policy questions. No matter how strongly they may believe in the populist ideal of equal participation, legislators throughout the unicameral's history have taken steps—sometimes two steps forward and one step back—to strengthen leadership and streamline processes in order to become more efficient.

It Isn't Party; It's Ideology

Some folks find it hard to believe that members of the unicameral truly do form coalitions and make their vote choices on a nonpartisan basis. Yes, the legislature is officially nonpartisan, these critics say with a cynical smile, but everybody knows the senators actually vote along party lines.

Not so, say the senators. They admit that, on issues like congressional redistricting or other matters that make a difference in the partisan parts of government, the votes may be influenced by party affiliation.[47]

But beyond that, the voting is truly nonpartisan, the senators insist. It is true that some votes may look as if they reflect party loyalty, but they actually reflect ideological patterns. All but a handful of senators during the unicameral's sixty-seven-year history have been registered as either Republicans or Democrats. Their party affiliation is some indication of their political ideology, and political ideology may be one reason senators vote a particular way. The result may sometimes look like a party-line vote but actually reflects an ideological split.

The senators' response to the 2001 survey, though, indicates party may play more of a role in a senator's decisions than the senators like to admit on the record. About two-thirds of those who responded to this item agreed that party affiliation influences a senator's vote choice, although only about 10 percent agreed strongly. Republicans were more inclined to agree with the statement than were Democrats. Fewer than 9 percent asserted strong disagreement with the notion that party influences votes in the unicameral (see appendix 1, table 7).

It is impossible to say whether the senators responding to the survey item were considering party affiliation in the broader sense of ideological tendencies or in the more traditional sense of party loyalty. It is also impossible to know whether the senators were admitting that their own choices were influenced by party or whether they thought that was true only for other senators.

On the record, senators told the *Lincoln Journal Star* in 2001 that party affiliation really does not matter when it comes to forming coalitions and making policy in the legislature. In fact, many senators said they didn't even know their fellow senators' party affiliation. Senator Ernie Chambers, who had served in the legislature for thirty-one years, was one of those.

"I can't tell you more than ten or eleven people are from one party or another," Chambers said. Instead, the senators split most often along "supporting big business or not" or supporting rural or urban interests, he said. However, he, too, said party affiliation was more likely to show in matters like redistricting.

The *Journal Star* story also noted that a number of senators were elected from districts where the majority of voters were registered in the opposite political party. And the story quoted Republican governor Mike Johanns's opinion on the independence of the legislators: "I need 25 votes to pass legislations, and there are 29 senators who are registered Republican, but it

The Sower is readied for its perch atop the Nebraska capitol. *Photo courtesy of the Unicameral Information Office.*

The Nebraska capitol was constructed during the Great Depression. This picture, taken in 1932, looks northwest from the building's site on K Street. *Photo courtesy of the Unicameral Information Office.*

The last session of the bicameral legislature met in 1934. This photo of the 133 members of the two houses posing in joint session was taken in the west chamber of the new capitol. *Photo courtesy of the Unicameral Information Office.*

The Unicameral membership had grown from forty-two to forty-nine by the late 1980s, but the body continued to be one-house and nonpartisan. *Photo courtesy of the Unicameral Information Office.*

The Sower tops the capitol tower. *Photo courtesy of the Unicameral Information Office.*

U.S. senator George Norris, left, and Dr. John Senning, below, chairman of the political science department at the University of Nebraska–Lincoln, were two of the primary forces behind Nebraska's move from a bicameral to a unicameral legislature. *Photo courtesy of the Nebraska State Historical Society,* RG3298-PH-30-71.

seems like I'm dealing with 49 independent, sometimes very independent, people on a particular issue."[48]

Johanns got several emphatic lessons in legislative independence in 2002 and 2003 when the legislature overrode five major gubernatorial vetoes. On April 10, 2002, the legislators mustered the required thirty votes to override Johanns's line-item veto of many parts of the legislature's appropriations bill. Of the thirty senators voting to override, sixteen were Republican, eleven Democrat, and three registered independents.

The following day, the legislature overrode the governor's veto of proposed tax increases. Again, the vote to override was thirty, the bare minimum required. This time eighteen Republicans voted in favor of the override along with ten Democrats and two independents.

In 2003 the legislature was even more dominant. With the state facing a large revenue shortfall, Governor Johanns proposed an austere budget that required slashing spending for social services, higher education, and state aid to school districts, among other things, and raising taxes only on cigarettes. The legislators took a different approach, cutting spending by about a third of what the governor requested and increasing taxes to make up the difference. The bills passed with thirty-seven and thirty-six votes in favor, respectively.

On May 26, the governor vetoed both bills in total, remonstrating senators to return to the budget he proposed in January. Johanns told the Associated Press on May 27 that he had met with twenty-five of forty-nine senators in person and that his staff spoke with nearly all the others in an attempt to forestall veto overrides. But the arm-twisting was in vain. On May 27, the legislators voted emphatically to override both vetoes. The overrides passed with thirty-seven votes each, comfortably higher than the required thirty-vote supermajority.

Of the thirty-seven senators voting to override the spending bill and the tax increase bill, twenty-three were Republicans and two were independents. Only one Democrat voted to sustain the veto.

When the legislature took on a third veto, this one of a proposal to allow K–12 schools to increase property taxes five cents per one hundred dollars of property value—without the vote of the people previously required—the senators were even more united. They overrode the veto forty-four to four. The four votes to sustain the veto all came from Republicans, but that means the other twenty-nine Republicans voted against their fellow Republican in the governor's office.

In a partisan legislature, one would expect no more than one or two senators from the majority party to defect on such hot-topic votes. In Nebraska in 2002 and 2003, however, a majority of Republicans, the party whose members held an informal majority in the legislature, voted to override five high-profile vetoes by a Republican governor. In the test of wills, it was the legislature—not any political party—that triumphed.

In 2002 and 2003 the unicameral's nonpartisan coalitions worked to accomplish the body's will. But some believe that was an exception rather than a rule. Vard Johnson, who served in the unicameral from 1979 to 1989, said he believed the body would be better off if whatever informal party influence exists were made formal. Party discipline in a legislature, he said, gets legislative objectives accomplished better than loose coalitions based on some other factor.

In the unicameral, most coalitions must be based on some other factor. Even if senators' votes are sometimes influenced by their party affiliation, the fact remains that party organization and party discipline are, by definition, absent from the legislature: no party leadership positions, no expectation that members will vote as the party tells them to. That opens the field to any individual or group that can gather and sustain a coalition. Without party as the organizing factor, coalitions form in a variety of creative ways.

Scholars who have studied Nebraska's system note that regional representation on the Committee on Committees, for instance, "substitutes geography for partisanship in the nonpartisan Nebraska Legislature," and many observers believe the same situation exists when legislators form coalitions to make policy.[49] In fact, the explanation heard most often in casual conversation seems to assume a rural-urban split in many legislative decisions. Some senators said that's true.

In his experience, Peter Hoagland said, rural versus urban was frequently the dividing line.[50] A number of other current and former senators agreed, including Ardyce Bohlke—at least to a point. Bohlke said she thought coalitions formed on an urban-rural basis less than half the time, "but it does come up fairly often." On the other hand, she said, coalitions often simply shift when the topics shift.

Vard Johnson had much the same opinion. He said some coalitions were based on the urban-rural geography and others were more ideologically based. Either way, despite his wish that the legislature would be organized on a partisan basis, Johnson said the coalitions were always informal.[51]

Dennis Baack disagreed about the rural-urban split. Baack said, emphatically, that urban and rural allegiances were not behind any kind of ongoing or overarching coalition.[52] On major issues, Baack said, a bloc of middle-of-the-road senators has a lot of say in what gets done in the unicameral. But in many cases, he said, coalitions were built around "communities of interest." Each legislator brings some expertise to a subject, he said, and senators turn for leadership to those with expertise. Many other senators said similar things, indicating that no one senator or small group of senators dominated the process of coalition formation.

Coalitions in Nebraska form on the basis of self-interest, David Landis said. "You have to show people where it benefits them and their constituents directly or the state and their constituents indirectly."[53]

DiAnna Schimek said on any given set of issues, she usually sees a core group on either side of the question because of the senators' basic philosophical underpinnings. But people outside those core groups can move around a lot, she said. Those who make up the core have to reach out and convince additional senators to vote with them on a particular issue.[54]

Hoagland agreed: members of the unicameral had to be in touch with each other all the time. "You could count on the votes of those you agreed with philosophically," he said. "So you line up your supporters first and then go talk to the people undecided."[55]

That kind of coalition-building requires personal skills like talent, knowledge, and the ability to get along with other people, skills that are all the more important in the absence of partisanship, Doug Bereuter said.[56] A big majority of senators (91 percent) responding to the survey agreed strongly or somewhat that coalitions often formed on the basis of personal relationships, which meant getting along with one's fellow senators was important (see appendix 1, table 8).

Furthermore, without party structure and party discipline to get votes in line, each legislator is involved in shepherding the bills he introduced through committee and out of special file on the floor. No party leadership will do it for the introducer. Every senator's intimate involvement in the entire process almost guarantees a degree of logrolling and vote trading.

Don Dworak admitted it happens. "There's some dealing," he said. For instance, Senator A, with no strong feelings on a bill, may agree to vote yes or no to please Senator B, who will, in turn, support a measure that is really important to Senator A. But a senator's conscience and his or her constituents are always the primary parts of the equation, Dworak said.[57]

Senators responding to the 2001 survey were nearly evenly divided on the subject of whether or not unicameral members trade votes. And the even division appears to have remained relatively constant over the decades (see appendix 1, table 9).

"Vote trading" sounds like one of those things citizens hate about politicians. But the process of legislating is the process of negotiating, and, in every setting, negotiation means Senator A may give in to Senator B at one point with the hope—or even the understanding—that Senator B will give in at another point.

Don Wesely pointed out that absence of parties and the resulting fluctuation in coalitions meant senators had to pretty much start over on every issue. "It forced you to not burn bridges," he said of his years in the legislature. A senator may oppose a colleague on one issue but need that opponent's vote on the next.

Doug Kristensen used the same bridge-burning metaphor. Senators in the unicameral work with each other on an individual basis, Kristensen said, and need to keep their relationships intact.

Scott Moore agreed. "You need that person on the next coalition," he said. But the coalitions themselves are based not on returning legislative favors but on "what's right," or on what senators believe is right, Moore said. That's different from a partisan structure where tactical strategy may take the upper hand, he said.[58]

Legislative scholars say bargaining and compromise are essential parts of the legislative process because issues and bills are connected, and legislators have to confront trade-offs. DiAnna Schimek said much the same thing but added that that doesn't mean senators give up their core principles. They simply negotiate on bits and pieces of the larger picture, she said. "It keeps us from going off the edge" and takes the legislature, instead, to generally moderate positions.[59]

All the compromising and negotiating and persuading necessary to build coalitions in the unicameral generally slow things down, but that's not all bad, Schimek said. Without a second house to check legislation, the legislature needs to take its time and consider issues thoroughly, she said.

In general, senators seem to think they're accomplishing enough and that the absence of party discipline is not a hindrance. More than two-thirds of those responding to the 2001 survey agreed that senators actually get more done because of the absence of party labels (see appendix 1, table 10).

Citizens also seem convinced the legislators don't need party discipline and structure to get their work done. More than two-thirds of the citizens responding to a 2000 survey took positions that agreed with those of the senators. They think the legislature accomplishes more thanks to the absence of parties (see appendix 1, table 11).

Whether or not the average citizen pays close enough attention to the legislature to be able to determine how nonpartisanship may influence legislative activity is less important here than the fact that Nebraskans believe the unicameral is living up to one of its founders' promises: that nonpartisanship improves their legislature's functionality.

While the sheer amount of legislation passed is surely not the only indicator of a legislature's productivity, it is one measure sometimes applied. Because Nebraska does not limit the number of bills its senators can introduce, productivity may be better measured by considering the number of bills actually passed. The national average is about 20 percent. In 1999 Nebraska legislators introduced 883 bills, and 327—37 percent—were enacted, nearly twice the national average. The implication is that the unicameral is more efficient than most state legislatures in dealing with proposed legislation.

Members of the public often grumble that the unicameral introduces too many bills in the first place. But Nebraska's 883 in 1999 placed it forty-first among the fifty states in total bills introduced. Connecticut and Hawaii both introduced nearly four thousand bills in 1999, New Jersey nearly six thousand.

Fostering a "Guiding Force"

Senators firmly assert that the speaker's position has been steadily strengthened and is now the most powerful in the legislature. Those interviewed for this book were unanimous on that count. And it's a good thing, Jim Pappas said. The unicameral needs someone with leadership authority to be the "guiding force of all legislation and legislators."[60]

Doug Bereuter and Ardyce Bohlke agreed, using almost identical words. The two senators, who served in the 1970s and 1990s, respectively, both said the speaker is powerful because of his power to set the agenda, a power that has been enhanced in recent years.[61] That is real power, said Bob Wickersham, who also served during the 1990s.[62]

Scott Moore expanded on the speaker's influence. Controlling the calendar and the agenda influences what is discussed and what becomes law, he said.[63] Walt Radcliffe, a Lincoln lobbyist, said the legislature needed the organizational structure provided by the stronger speaker.[64]

But, although the speaker's influence has grown, Dennis Baack, who was speaker in the early 1990s, said the speaker's power over the agenda is still not ironclad. "You have to build a consensus around the agendas."[65]

Ron Withem also said the office was still weak. But he said the rules changes of the mid-1990s, which took place when he was speaker himself, did move the position well beyond being purely ceremonial. And those formal changes also gave the position more informal clout. Before the rules changes, "there was not much expectation of moral authority" connected to the office, Withem said.

However, he added, reflecting once again the underlying populist philosophy, power in the unicameral is intentionally dispersed. Because the body doesn't have two houses to keep checks on each other, the legislature must be careful not to give too much power to a few leaders who might take over and run the entire process.

Bereuter saw things from the other side. He said it is precisely a lack of strong leadership that can result in one or two people's having overwhelming influence. If leaders don't have considerable authority, an individual member can "completely define the process" by filibustering and manipulating procedures at the expense of the rest of the legislators.[66]

Withem said he thought the speaker had become more influential because of changes in both rules and norms of the legislature. The speaker today is expected to manage legislative business, Withem said, in the face of a workload that has become steadily heavier and in a body that is less congenial than it used to be. The changing expectations allowed Doug Kristensen, who succeeded Withem as speaker in 1998, to do things "that would have caused open rebellion twenty years ago," Withem said.[67]

Current and former senators who responded to a 2001 survey supported the proposition that the speaker has, indeed, become more influential in recent years. Senators were given the following scenario: "Your office hires a new staff member to answer the phone. On his/her first day, he/she leaves you a list of four calls that must be returned. The list, however, does not include the time or reason for the call. Please list the order in which these calls would be returned."

Respondents were asked to rank the following choices: the chair of your most important committee; the speaker of the legislature; a senior colleague representing your region of the state; a junior member you have been mentoring. When responses are divided according to the decade in which a senator served, a trend becomes obvious. Senators serving in the 1990s indicated they were considerably more likely to return the speaker's call first than were senators who served in the 1950s (see appendix 1, table 12).

The survey responses seem to support the notion that the speaker has become more influential over the years. But that doesn't mean he has always used the powers granted him. Ardyce Bohlke said Doug Kristensen, speaker from 1998 through 2002, was reluctant to use some of the power he had, specifically the authority to declare some bills super-priorities. "If you're on the other side of the issue, it's [super-priority designation] not a very popular thing for the speaker to do," she said. "So if you're a speaker who tries to keep all the troops happy rather than shove through a piece of legislation, I think you would be reluctant to use it.[68]

David Landis, one of the legislature's longest-serving senators in 2004, said the speaker's power in the unicameral was different from what it is in other states where partisanship is part of the equation. In the U.S. House of

Representatives, for instance, the body's time is owned by the speaker, "who doles it out and takes it back," Landis said. In the unicameral, though, "time is owned by everybody."

The rules themselves dole out time, he said, allowing senators to speak only three times to a single issue but to offer an unlimited number of amendments. "The rules give you this; the speaker doesn't," he said.

In the unicameral, the rules may give the speaker authority to say, "We'll debate one hour and then go on but *not* the authority to say we'll debate one hour and then *vote*," Landis said. The rules are designed to facilitate debate, not to block it.

"Our rules are fairly short" compared to legislative rules in other states, Landis said. "They mainly set the traffic patterns at intersections, but you (the senator) get to drive the car."

The most powerful people in the legislature, he said, are those who are regarded as credible sources of information and analysis. Committee chairs have some formal power, but most of whatever authority they have stems from their opportunity to develop expertise on specific issues.

Committee chairs have power if they know what they're doing, Bob Wickersham said. But the positions themselves don't confer power. Every bill must have a hearing. Any committee member can ask to have a bill scheduled for debate. The chair may be able to exert some influence by the way he or she sets the schedule for hearings and debate, but if a member wants to declare a bill his or her priority, that can automatically move the bill higher on the agenda.

However, most of the senators interviewed indicated that at least some committee chairmanships are reasonably influential. "In some ways, it's [being a committee chair] like the speaker is at the floor level," Ardyce Bohlke said. The chair gets to set the agenda for the committee.

And some committee chairmanships are perceived as more influential than others. Scott Moore, among others, cited the Appropriations Committee because it sets the state's budget and controls how state money is spent. Dennis Baack added the other "money" committee, the Revenue Committee, to the list.

DiAnna Schimek said she thought the chairman of the Executive Board could also be powerful, depending on who held the position. That board, officially the Executive Board of the Legislative Council, is responsible for many day-to-day functions of the legislature and also coordinates business when the body is not in session.

But even the chair of the Executive Board does not have a great deal of authority. Some senators note that many of the duties are more procedural than substantive. Wesely said the board "can make life hard for you," in terms of the way the members assign staff and arrange legislative workings, but it "can't make things happen."

Another potential leadership group, the Legislative Council, was the group for which the original unicameral promoters had high hopes. As noted above, the first council, formed at the end of the 1937 session, declined to accept the option to determine a general agenda for the following legislative session. The council declined to become the kind of leadership group its founders had wanted it to be.

Instead, the council decided to concentrate on educating all senators and citizens about current state issues. Today, that takes the form of interim studies, usually led by the standing committees into whose jurisdiction a matter falls. All members of the legislature are considered members of the Legislative Council. The Executive Board functions as a leadership group during the months the legislature is not in session but also has been granted some important duties during the session itself, as discussed above.

In general, though, senators give the unicameral's leadership structure the same kind of marks Goldilocks gave to the porridge: the unicameral does not offer leadership positions with lots of authority, and the lack of strong leaders can prevent the body from working efficiently but, on balance, the system itself is "just right."

Pappas said the unicameral's lack of hierarchy continues to provide lots of opportunities for all senators to participate in decision making. But simply being in a potentially powerful position doesn't guarantee that a senator will use the authority available, Pappas said. Some committee chairs know how to use their power effectively. Others are "good guys" who try to appease everybody, with the result that they aren't very effective for anybody.

Baack agreed that a senator need not be a committee chair to be able to influence legislation. The unicameral is a small group, he noted. Members get to know each other. And since seniority plays no role in committee assignments, a senator could, theoretically, become a chair soon after he or she was elected.

Survey data from 1994 support Baack's assertion that seniority plays no role in senators' voting for committee chairs. Asked to indicate the top three factors that influence their votes for those positions, the thirty-nine then-senators who responded put seniority at the bottom of the list, below knowledge, respect, fairness, confidence, ideology, and friendship. Only four of the respondents indicated seniority played any role at all in their vote choice.

Data from a 2001 survey of current and former senators casts a slightly different light on how much importance senators place on seniority in a body where, officially, it counts for nothing. For instance, 56 percent of the respondents agreed strongly or somewhat that seniority is an important indicator of a senator's political influence. The 10 percent who placed themselves in the neutral category may be significant, though, because that left only about one-third of the respondents strongly disagreeing that seniority is important (see appendix 1, table 13). Regardless of whether seniority confers informal influence, the fact remains that seniority is not an important factor in the selection of legislative leaders.

While senior senators may be seen as more influential than their juniors, survey respondents also indicated overwhelming support for rules that allow junior senators to have a significant impact on the body's proceedings. Only about 3 percent of the respondents agreed that junior members are allowed too much influence; 85 percent disagreed (see appendix 1, table 14).

On the other hand, almost three-fourths of the survey respondents did see some value in seniority: that members become more realistic about legislative processes. The longer a senator serves, these answers imply, the more he or she will understand and be able to use the legislature's processes (see appendix 1, table 15).

Furthermore, most senators (68 percent) agreed that those who had served longer were more knowledgeable than newcomers. And many believed that junior members should accept guidance from their elders. Not surprisingly, the percentages in favor of that kind of informal exercise of seniority were largest among the cohort of senators who had served longest, although the group that had served longest of all is sharply divided on the question with one-third agreeing strongly and two-thirds disagreeing strongly with no responses in between (see appendix 1, table 16).

Still, while seniority may lead to additional knowledge and confer additional respect on legislators, it has no formal influence on their selection for committee memberships or chairmanships. But the importance of committee appointments is open to question, anyway.

The unicameral's rules indicate that Nebraska has a strong committee system, Ron Withem said, but that's not how things play out in reality. People assume bills will move forward through committee, he said, but if a committee encounters strong opposition to a measure, the members will think twice before advancing it. In other words, committees may be wary of having their decisions dissected and second-guessed on the floor, an indication that the old populist ideal of participation by all is still respected in the unicameral.

Current and former senators surveyed in 2001 were nearly evenly divided in their opinions about the importance of committees and whether an individual legislator's most important work is done in committee (see appendix 1, table 17).

Senators were also divided when asked whether more of the legislature's work should be done in committees. Almost 37 percent agreed, but 44 percent disagreed. It may be significant that almost 20 percent were not sure whether they approved or disapproved of the proposal (see appendix 1, table 18).

Interestingly, the distribution of responses was similar when senators were asked whether they thought members of the unicameral should specialize. The opportunity to specialize and increase one's expertise in a particular subject area was one of the original unicameralists' concessions to assigning at least some authority to committees. But it appears many current and former senators (about 39 percent of respondents) are not so sure specialization is an advantage in the unicameral (see appendix 1, table 19).

Despite all that, almost 80 percent of senators responding to the survey seem to believe committees do have some clout in the legislature and that committee recommendations are respected. About three-fourths agreed that a committee's recommendations are usually followed by the legislature as a whole (see appendix 1, table 20).

And, although attitudes toward the committee system may be ambivalent, the vast majority of the survey respondents (88 percent) agreed that committee chairs were important to helping the legislature achieve its goals (see appendix 1, table 21). Of course, the help senators were thinking of may have included not only whatever formal power is granted to committee chairs but also the informal power to persuade and cajole that may often accompany any leadership position.

Even the power of persuasion may vary from person to person, of course. "Chairs don't exercise strong control in committees," Withem said. Some chairs enjoy using the power of their positions; others resist using the authority they have. And nothing in the institution compels them to use it.[69]

Leaders in the unicameral have less power than those in other legislatures, Howard Lamb said. Elsewhere, a committee chair could just stick a bill in his pocket and be sure it is never even considered. In Nebraska, if a chair tried something like that, the committee members would take control. The rank and file members have a lot of authority, he said.[70]

Wickersham, chairman of the Revenue Committee at the time of the interview, said that situation suited him fine. He said the legislature didn't need to invest more power in some positions. "It's not necessary. We're getting along okay without it," he said.[71]

Current and former state senators responding to the 2001 survey generally supported the notion that power in the unicameral is dispersed. Only about one-third agreed with the statement that a handful of members have a lock on legislative power (see appendix 1, table 22).

The people of Nebraska don't seem to have a strong collective view of just how dispersed or concentrated their legislature's leadership is. In a 2000 survey, citizens were almost evenly divided about the truth of this statement: "Just a few members of the Nebraska unicameral have all the power" (see appendix 1, table 23). Because most Nebraskans' contact with the legislature comes via the media, the assessment that a few senators have all the power may reflect that the speaker and chairs of prominent committees are the senators most often cited in the media. Since citizens see the same faces and hear the same voices much of the time, they may assume that a handful of senators dominate the body. But that point of view is held by only 43 percent of those surveyed; 40 percent disagreed with that perspective.

Then-senator Jenny Robak's observation may do well to summarize the relationship between formal leadership positions and actual leadership in the unicameral. "The ability to present yourself on the floor gives you more power than any chairmanship," she said. "In other states that wouldn't be true. They don't have a right to speak like we do here. We have a very nonhierarchical structure."[72] As illustrated, it is a structure with both costs and benefits to the senators themselves and to the state they serve.

In the midst of the 1996 debate about increasing the speaker's power, Senator Dave Maurstad noted, "[W]e are forty-nine independent contractors."[73] The phrase has been used to describe the Nebraska unicameral on many occasions and in many contexts. It echoes the intent the original unicameralists had for the legislature: independent members, weak leadership, rules that give plenty of voice to every senator.

To a large extent, it is still true. But as the demands on the legislature have grown, the body has adjusted its rules and procedures to grant more authority to some members—at the expense of others. For better or worse, coalitions are still formed on the basis of the issues and without benefit of party discipline. The unicameral's small membership contributes to nonpartisanship's success in that regard. But in an attempt to allow those informal coalitions to deal with legislation that has grown both more complex and more abundant, the senators have recognized the need for additional formal leadership.

The unicameral's structure is a bit more of a pyramid now than it was in 1937, but only a bit. George Norris and his compatriots would probably be happy to see that parties still don't play much of a role in coordinating interests and that committees are still kept under tight control by the body as a whole.

But they wouldn't be happy about the trend toward hierarchy, weak as it still may be in comparison to other state legislatures.

In general, the scales that once came down heavily on the side of equality have been counterbalanced a bit on the side of efficiency. But it hasn't been easy. The legislature has searched its collective soul over every step away from the populist egalitarianism promised for the unicameral.

5 / We, the People

The Progressive Philosophy Reflected in the Legislature

It sounds like a truism: A representative body in a democracy should be representative of the people.

To George Norris and the other promoters of the nonpartisan unicameral, that meant a legislature that would respond to "the people," not to powerful business interests or powerful political parties. It meant a legislature independent of the governor and able to serve as the people's voice in government. It meant a citizen legislature but one that would be professional enough to do the people's business efficiently and well.

Among all the other virtues they attributed to a small, one-house legislature, the Nebraska unicameralists included representativeness—both in terms of districts and elections and in terms of participation in legislative processes. Norris admitted that, in theory, a large legislature where each member represented a small area would provide more complete representation of the entire citizenry at the electoral level. In practice, though, he said a large body was a detriment to real representation because members' involvement in actual decision making had to be limited for sheer logistical reasons. And, of course, a two-house body required those nasty conference committees, which narrowed representation even more. That meant some voices never got heard, he said.

The proposed unicameral form, Norris promised, would offer more representative and efficient government. It would have a direct influence on social legislation, on laws affecting business and on legislation that labor and farmers wanted. Elimination of the second house would speed the passage of legislation the people needed and demanded, making it easier for the legislature to take action on the people's behalf.

The unicameral's supporters also promised that the new form would change the relationship between the legislature and the governor. Making the legislature nonpartisan would free it from the governor's influence as head of his party and would make the body more independent, they said. The implication was that such independence would also improve the legislature's ability to represent the people.

Professionalization would also advance that goal, according to the unicameralists. Good progressives all, they were certain that simplified procedures and more reliance on experts would make the legislature more businesslike. And they were sure such a situation would be beneficial to the interests of Nebraskans. Norris also had been preaching the benefits of decent pay and longer terms of office for legislators long before the unicameral amendment actually passed, saying such benefits would draw better people to run for office and also allow them to devote more time to their duties. That, too, would make the body more professional and businesslike.

The new system proposed for Nebraska would do all those things, its supporters promised: be more representative, more independent, and more professional.

Representativeness

The unicameral's promoters wanted to institutionalize representativeness in a manner they believed would be more effective than what Nebraska had experienced to that point. They wanted to assure what scholars have called the fundamentals of representation: that government would be truly responsive to the people's interests and opinions and that the people would, thus, be present in the actions of government.

Norris rejected what scholars call "descriptive" representation, the idea that a legislative body should be big enough that the members would proportionately "mirror" the various peoples they represented. Instead, he thought a small body would offer better representation as well as more openness and egalitarianism.

The idea drew plenty of criticism. Some argued that a legislature should be large enough to represent every section and interest—the descriptive model—and that the legislative districts themselves should be small in order to keep representatives in close touch with their constituents. But others argued that a small body would be more businesslike and easier for the public to keep an eye on.

Norris was particularly insistent that the legislature should be small. In his *New York Times* piece in 1923 and again in his 1934 speech in Lincoln, explaining and promoting "the model legislature," Norris asserted that one of the evils of the Nebraska bicameral was that it was too big. In theory, he said, a larger legislature would provide better representation of the entire citizenry. But in order to get anything done, a large body must give up too many independent rights and prerogatives to a few leaders and must limit members' right of debate and right to offer amendments. The result would be loss of representation for citizens whose elected legislators didn't happen to be part of the leadership structure.

Perhaps Norris believed in a unitary will of the people that could be represented in just a handful of representatives—at least in Nebraska. In his 1934 speech, he conceded that a state with varied, conflicting interests might need a larger legislature but asserted Nebraska did not. But he could have reached the same conclusion in favor of a small body if he had agreed with Senning, who argued that no legislature of any size could truly reflect the "multiplicity and continued variation" of interests existing in the citizenry.[1] Either way, a small legislature would concentrate power and assure that it was exercised in public view.

Norris originally proposed a legislature of only twenty-one members, but as noted above, his fellow unicameralists eventually prevailed on him to think bigger, believing any number between thirty and fifty would furnish a fair representation of a cross-section of the population of the state and would reflect the interests of urban and rural areas as well as diverse religious and ethnic groups. That approach was a compromise of the populist ideal that the people are unitary entity with a single voice and a recognition that even so small a populace as Nebraska's included a variety of interests and voices.

When the last bicameral reapportioned the state and settled on forty-three districts, it had tried not just to create districts of approximately equal size but also a number of districts that would approximately balance the "west" and the "east." But Senning and others stressed that every senator was expected to represent not only the interests of his own constituents but also those of Nebraskans as a whole.

Norris and his compatriots never really settled the question of representative theory on which they based their plan. Their public statements and writings give a mixed picture. Sometimes it looked as if they believed in a unitary people; other times they appeared to recognize a greater diversity. One scholar who analyzed the first session of the unicameral was more specific about the basic theory behind the new system: the people are simply one great, unified whole.[2]

Proponents and supporters of the Nebraska unicameral, Douglas Weeks said, believed the citizenry to be one great democratic family with common aims and purposes "whose general will or at least whose majority will and general good are consistently flouted by the divided responsibility and intricate machinery of the bicameral, which is peculiarly susceptible to the demands and pressures of selfish interests and minorities." The solution was simply to provide one single, upstanding, straightforward, responsible representative body to translate the common will and common good into law.[3] The unicameral was designed to be just such a body.

But, Weeks asked, "What proof is there that there is a common public will independent of group wills?" and that any conceivable public policy could work to the good of all? Weeks put his finger on the philosophical problem: he saw the populist ideal in the unicameral structure but doubted whether it could really work in practice.

For all his enthusiasm for the unicameral, Senning may have agreed with Weeks about representation. Representative government should reflect the community, he wrote, but terms like "the people, the community" suggest an ideal unity when the actual situation is "one of endless multiplicity and continued variation."[4] A legislature, he wrote, must weigh the voices of many groups and come to some compromise. But first, legislators should recognize the general interest as a compound of many lesser interests. It looks as if Senning, too, believed legislators represented not a single voice of the people but the aggregate of a variety of interests.

Many supporters of the unicameral, however, appear to have taken a more populist approach to citizen representation in the new body. Praising the unicameral as "a more perfect democracy," one observer said it put control over government more directly into the hands of all the people. Everyone must be allowed to participate in decreeing what the law shall be so that the majority's will can be accomplished.[5] The majority, in this case, is "the people," attempting to curtail the "exploitation powers of a minority," a sentiment prominent in the doctrines of both populism and progressivism.

A 1913 legislative study group looking for ways to improve lawmaking in Nebraska had recommended a small, unicameral body to make government by the people direct and responsible. Norris preached the same message when he campaigned for the constitutional amendment.

Senning's suggestion that a legislator's constituency was based more on communities of interests than on geography put a different twist on the theory of representation. It meant every legislator could be seen to be a statewide representative—not quite representing the will of "the people," perhaps, but certainly representing the interests of people who may or may not reside in his district.

But when it came down to actually drawing the districts for the new legislature in 1935, people's belief in the reality of multiple, specific interests became obvious. If legislators were truly to represent "the people," they could have been elected at large. Geographic location wouldn't matter if representatives simply discerned and acted on the common will of a unitary people or even on, as Senning suggested, geographically dispersed communities of interests.

As it was, however, farmers and people in rural areas, especially, were concerned that they would lose representation in the smaller unicameral. The legislature had not been reapportioned since 1921, although the population of the state had increased and shifted in the ensuing years, and population in the legislative districts was far from equal. In fact, according to figures from the 1930 census, some house of representatives districts were twice or almost three times as populous as others; the disparity among senate districts was not quite as great, but even there some districts included at least one-and-a-half times as many constituents as others. By 1935 one house district had a population 250 percent larger than another; one senate district included 50 percent more people than another.

The last bicameral body decided to try to fix the lopsided apportionment before settling on a specific number of districts for the new unicameral. Senning drew up more than thirty maps to illustrate the possibilities of districting, combining counties with common backgrounds and mutual interests wherever possible. Many of those maps made their way into newspapers, and delegations from various parts of the state appeared before the committees to argue for a realignment of a county or to have it set off in a single district. The sparsely populated central and western parts of the state, with agriculture as their primary economic interest, wanted to be on an equitable basis with the more densely populated eastern part of the state where, some claimed, economic interests were more diverse.

Many saw a natural rural versus urban conflict, a concept fostered by populism and, in part, by progressivism, both of which enshrined the common people—usually rural residents—as the "real" people. Some said fewer and larger districts would give rural communities less representation.

The editors of *The Nebraska Farmer* issued a brochure opposing the unicameral amendment. Remaking the legislature according to the proposal, they said, would result in far fewer farmers and small-town people in the body. Farmers had made up a much larger proportion of the hundred-member Nebraska house of representatives than of the thirty-three-member senate, the brochure said, allowing for better representation of rural interests. "Nebraska is a purely agricultural and small-town state," the brochure said, implying that the state's interest was nearly unitary, despite the editors' worry that rural citizens would lose representation in the proposed unicameral.[6]

On the other hand, some observers used the very same logic to conclude that a unicameral would be just fine in Nebraska, a state that was "so rural that it is homogeneous," with no rural-urban conflict to worry about. After all, the state had only two cities—Lincoln and Omaha—with populations of more than twenty-five thousand.[7]

Before the amendment was passed and the districts drawn, some proponents tried to calm the fears of those who were afraid that the voice of rural people would be muffled by the new system. The smaller body meant that representation from rural areas would decrease only in the same proportion as representation from urban areas, they pointed out.

And even urban Nebraskans indirectly depended on the agricultural economy for their well-being and were believed to be "primarily interested in the same things to a greater or lesser degree."[8] The chief industry of the state was diversified agriculture, Senning said. "Everyone rises or falls as it does." The resulting interdependence diminished the feeling of conflict between groups, he asserted.

The legislative committees' 1935 public hearings on redistricting, Senning said, served as a popular referendum on the process, helping people to understand the legislature's "scientific" approach to reapportionment. Despite the voices that insisted the state was largely homogeneous, the 1935 legislature was sensitive to demands that it be sure to balance the eastern, more populous one-fourth of the state and the western three-fourths of the state. Eventually, legislators settled on forty-three districts, believing that gave the least margin of population variance among the districts and generally equalized the two regions.

Once the members of the first unicameral had been elected, observers noted that eighteen of the forty-three members were farmers or retired farmers, actually a larger proportion than in most bicamerals since 1900.

Although Norris and other unicameral supporters had preached that the new system would better represent "the people," the arguments over apportionment indicate that neither legislators nor citizens really bought the notion that a unitary people existed. The suspicion over a perceived rural-urban clash and the manifest concern that the western three-fourths of the state be as well represented in the unicameral as the eastern fourth indicate an underlying belief that a legislature listens to and negotiates among varied interests. It does not simply serve as a conduit for "the will" of a unitary people, despite the happy democratic ideal that idea may represent.

If citizens were well represented in the unicameral, it was because districts were carefully drawn to give voice to regions with interests that most people perceived as varied. Of course, both populist and progressives designated the rural and working classes as "the people," distinct from the economic elites more often found in urban areas. Thus, they would be concerned that apportionment not give unfair advantage to the elites at the expense of the true people, and that concern could be what is reflected in the 1935 commotion over redistricting.

The unicameral proponents had said a small body would provide "real" representation of the people through more proper deliberation and discussion. And early assessments of the unicameral concluded that the smaller body had, indeed, engaged in less oratorical posturing and more meaningful argument. "While members may differ as to the method of solving a problem, nevertheless they share an individual responsibility of finding a satisfactory solution," Senning said.[9]

That was the flip side of the promise of better representation. Not only would legislators be elected representatively but the unicameral's size and structure meant the voices of all Nebraskans would be better heard because every member would be able and expected to participate in all the policy making.

In a small body, the unicameral's promoters asserted, every member would have the same rights to be heard. Perhaps the only way to guarantee total participation in every aspect of the process would have been to abolish the committee system or to make the system so open and so accountable to the entire body on the floor as to be nearly powerless, but that was not the course the members of the first unicameral chose. They adopted a standing committee system that was more streamlined and, thus, more open than its predecessors, but they gave their committees at least some decisive authority, as discussed in previous chapters.

In the process, John Norton lost one of his battles.

Norton, acknowledged father of the unicameral's rules, had hoped to abolish the Committee of the Whole, a practice the bicameral body had used regularly. The practice went as follows: the legislature would hear committee reports and then form itself into a Committee of the Whole to discuss those reports "off the record." The legislators would adjourn the Committee of the Whole, return to regular floor procedures, and move to pass or kill legislation, usually without further discussion.

Norton thought getting rid of the Committee of the Whole would go a long way toward making the unicameral more efficient and more open. He said it was an unnecessary procedure and that doing away with it would save time, remove duplication, fix responsibility, and simplify procedure. Norris, too, had no love for the committee, which he said had been used "chiefly to avoid going on record with roll calls."[10]

Senning said a Committee of the Whole was not necessary in a small body like the unicameral but advised that, if the legislators decided to retain the practice, they should be sure—via the rules—that all the constitutional provisions that applied to the legislature also applied in Committee of the

Whole, especially the provision that roll call votes could be demanded by any one member.

Ultimately, that was the Rules Committee's recommendation: an effort to balance plenty of opportunity for debate and discussion with the unicameral's promise of openness. The Committee of the Whole would be retained, but one member could demand a roll call vote, and such votes would be recorded in the daily journal. The members of the legislature were divided on the question. Some members said it would be better not to "encumber the proceedings" with all that went on in the Committee of the Whole. But others said the Committee of the Whole would encourage free and full debate and would slow down the legislative machinery so bills wouldn't be turned out in a haphazard way.

Senator Charles Warner, newly elected speaker of the legislature, argued that the Committee of the Whole, long recognized as a brake on hasty legislative action, would be a double check on legislation. He proposed amending the Rules Committee's report so that no vote on a bill would be taken until three days after it had been discussed in Committee of the Whole. Other proponents said the press would give thorough coverage to discussions in the Committee of the Whole—the constitution, after all, required that the committee's sessions be open to the public—and the lapse of three days would give people time to advise their senators about the pending legislation. That plan was adopted January 15 on a twenty-four to eight vote.

The legislators seemed to feel that whatever they lost in openness by adopting the Committee of the Whole they made up in deliberative, careful action. They were aware that a lot of critics were predicting that a one-house, non-partisan body with simple procedures might rush to judgment without careful consideration of the issues and measures before it—might make uninformed and ill-advised collective choices. Warner's proposed double check was an appealing solution to that potential problem.

Some observers, however, saw the adoption of the Committee of the Whole as a defeat for Norris's unicameral plan. The vote on Committee of the Whole was the "dividing line between the conservative and the progressive trend of thought," and the conservatives had their way on this point, slowing action and, potentially, decreasing accountability.[11]

At least one legislator apparently believed the unicameral eventually came to use the Committee of the Whole as the forum in which to make final decisions, not simply as one more step in the process of debate. In a letter to Fred Wachtler on April 5, 1937, Senator Charles Tvrdik of Omaha said once a bill had passed the Committee of the Whole and advanced, "[i]t is just a matter of procedure before it is enacted into law."[12]

Getting everyone involved in the discussion and decision making probably did help assure that all interests were represented, but it also threatened to slow the process to a crawl. The unicameral was torn between wanting all members to give all ideas careful consideration and wanting to make progress on legislation.

When a group faces that kind of dilemma, one solution is to refer items to subgroups—like committees—for a first cut at the issues, reducing the complexity of the decision-making environment. But at the same time that handing off duties improves the efficiency of the body, it decreases the representativeness of the process.

The 1937 legislative rules tried to strike a balance between those goals in the way they empowered but also constrained standing committees. The rules assured committee honesty by mandating public hearings on all bills, but they also assured that committees would play a role in the legislature's policy decisions. Committees were to gather information via hearings and the use of experts and also to make decisions about the fate of bills. They could, in fact, decide to postpone bills indefinitely—to kill them. Or they could amend them before reporting them to the floor.

Standing committees had "an appreciable effect" in deciding the final disposition of bills in the 1937 session, Senning said. By and large, the committee system worked as intended, relieving the parent body from further consideration of nearly half the bills introduced. Those who demanded representation of every voice in every decision may have resented the influence committees had on narrowing choices—and voices—but those who also wanted to live up to the unicameral's promise of efficiency probably saw the committee system as a positive trade-off.

The Essence of Democracy
Frustrated with state government that seemed unwilling or unable to meet citizens' needs, Norris and his colleagues promoted their unicameral plan as an expedited way to take action on behalf of the people. Eliminating a second house was one factor intended to speed legislative decision making, as discussed previously. But the one-house, nonpartisan body would also be stronger vis-à-vis the governor and better able to be the people's representative in state government. Independence can be thought of as a subcategory of representativeness.

Legislative independence from the governor was not a big selling point among the unicameralists, however. Instead, they often found themselves defending the elimination of the second house's check on action by reminding critics that the governor's veto power would still be in place.

Some critics said the one-house body would invite control of the legislature by the governor, who possessed patronage, the power of publicity, and popular appeal. If the governor also had ulterior or selfish motives, he would be able to exercise them freely in a government with a unicameral. After the first session, some observers said the new system increased the governor's responsibility and, thus, his power because the unicameral looked to him to act as the "other house."

That, however, seems to have been a minority opinion. Senning said the legislature, originally dominant in Nebraska, had lost ground to the executive branch in the 1920s and 1930s. He hoped the creation of the unicameral might effect a better balance between the two branches despite the fact that the new legislative system did not in any way curb the governor's constitutional powers. But the relationship under the new structure was simpler, he said, making it harder for the governor to shift blame to the legislature and giving the direct representatives of the people as much power as that held by the chief executive. The shift, Senning said, was the essence of democracy.[13]

Robert Cochran, governor in 1936 and 1937, told the *Lincoln Star* before the first unicameral session that he wasn't worried about the fact that the new body was nonpartisan, nullifying much of his political clout with legislators. By the end of the 1937 session, however, Cochran was not entirely happy with the result. The 1937 legislature had passed a biennial appropriation of almost fifty-five million dollars, about five million dollars higher than what he had recommended, and Cochran complained that under the unicameral system, the governor had become "only an advisory officer when it comes to budget matters."[14]

The trend continued. In its first meeting, on September 13, 1937, the newly created Legislative Council asked that the governor supply a study of every state agency that spent money and the budget requirements of the different departments before the legislature convened for its next session. No Nebraska legislature had had that information before, Senator Frank Brady pointed out, and couldn't get it during the session. "We aren't directing the governor's budget, but we want to know how each department is spending," Brady said. The legislature would not be overstepping its bounds to demand public information from the auditor, Brady added.[15] Getting its hands on that kind of basic information—and simply asserting its right to have it— dramatically boosted the legislature's equality as a branch of government.

In other ways, too, the legislature asserted its authority vis-à-vis the governor. The unicameral, with sessions only in odd-numbered years, adopted a rule that allowed it to call itself into session in even-numbered years by a two-thirds vote. The governor's authority to call special sessions remained in force, but the rule allowing the legislature to get into the act helped set the legislators "free of the power of the governor on special sessions."[16]

But it was probably the absence of party structure in the unicameral that did most to increase the legislature's power at the governor's expense. In an article analyzing the changes made by the 1934 constitutional amendment, the *Lincoln Star* wondered whether the new arrangement would cause more conflict between the governor and the legislature or whether the legislators would simply become a "rubber stamp for the governor."[17] As things turned out, the rubber stamp scenario never materialized.

Senning hoped the legislature would regain its independence and prestige under the new system. He didn't like that the governor and his party had been dominating the legislature.

From the start, the unicameral began to reverse that situation. Appraising the first unicameral's performance, Senning said the new system had liberated the legislature "from domination by the governor as titular head of his party" and had simplified the relationship between the governor and the legislature.[18] Neither could shift blame for inaction or action contrary to the public will onto the shoulders of the other, he said.

Nonpartisanship created a striking change in the relationship. No longer could the governor look to the legislators from his party to rally support for his program. Partisan appeals and threats of political punishment would have no effect. The nonpartisan unicameral, some said, had "thrown off the dominance of the executive."[19]

The point was all too clear to the frustrated Cochran, who said the governor needed the strength of party organization and party discipline to carry out the pledges he had made to the people. A legislature elected on a nonpartisan ticket and free of party responsibility "is tremendously upsetting to our traditional balance," Cochran said.[20]

Without any party structure and party discipline, the governor had virtually no leverage to use on the legislature other than the veto, a power Cochran exercised sixteen times in 1937. And nearly 100 percent of his vetoes were successful. The legislature overrode only one veto—on LB438, which allowed a father and son from Omaha to file suit against Cuming County for injuries they incurred on a road south of West Point.

Governor Cochran did not enjoy working with the nonpartisan unicameral. The old system provided lines of communication that allowed the executive and legislative branches to compromise, even on highly controversial measures, he told a reporter. With parties out of the picture and the legislature made up of forty-three independent actors, "the chance for intelligent compromise is correspondingly decreased," Cochran said.[21]

The increased authority of the legislature, the people's branch, over against the governor wasn't something the unicameral's promoters had used as one of their selling points, but it was undoubtedly a consequence of the new structure. Under the nonpartisan unicameral, "the people are the driver," some observers said.[22] Nebraskans seemed comfortable with their governor in a "caretaker role."[23]

The situation reflects the unicameralists' belief in the populist/progressive ideal. The legislative branch is considered the hallmark of popular sovereignty. If the people are truly in charge, then it is their representatives in the legislature who should determine the people's preferences and make policy according to those preferences. The governor's role as a check on the legislature should be eliminated or, at least, greatly diminished; he should stay out of the way of the people's will being accomplished through the legislature.

Open for Business

"Professionalization" of a legislature can be a catchall phrase. It can include Norris's insistence that the state be run like a business corporation with the legislature serving as the board of directors and with a cadre of experts hired to inform and advise the elected representatives. But it can also include Norris's desire to increase legislators' pay and term of office in order to attract better personnel and to give legislators better opportunity to concentrate on their public service.

Even before it became a unicameral, the legislature already had some staff, some specialists. But the 1937 body expanded the resources available to legislators, working to arm its members with "scientific information" so they would not be "deluded by specious arguments from lobbyists."[24]

Besides affecting the relationship with lobbyists, the increased reliance on experts was one way, Norris believed, to make the legislature more businesslike. It was advice Senning enthusiastically endorsed. In a 1937 Omaha lecture, he said state government in the 1930s needed to make prompt adjustments to the "new era in industry and science" by using scientific methods in government.[25]

The 1937 unicameral looked at its job as a business, and it wanted to run that business efficiently, said newspaper reporter Curtis Betts in a detailed examination of the body's first session.[26] The legislature expanded the services of the bill drafter into the Legislative Reference Bureau, an office Senning said was invaluable during the session, and hired three attorneys to advise on the constitutionality of all bills before they were passed.

The 1937 legislature also made the clerk of the legislature's position permanent. Instead of serving only during the months every other year while the legislature was in session, the clerk was now on duty year-round so that the public could have access to all public records available in that office. The unicameral created a standing committee, the Committee on Enrollment and Review, to make recommendations "relative to arrangement, phraseology, and correlation" of language in a bill (Rule XIII.6) and to avoid messy rewrites in midstream.

Later in the session, the legislature passed LB306, creating the Office of Constitutional Reviewer, to be hired by the Legislative Council, subject to approval by the legislature. Senning said the reviewer would study the bills for phraseology and constitutionality and to see whether they were likely to require amendment of existing statutes. That would help cut back on the flood of bills the legislature usually faced each session. The reviewer was also expected to prevent introduction of more than one bill on the same subject.

Looking back at the first session, Senning was pleased with what he saw. He believed the legislature had tried, throughout the session, to improve the mechanics of legislating and do its work in a businesslike manner.

The Legislative Council was another attempt to develop more expertise among legislators. Although the fifteen-member council declined to accept all the authority originally intended for it, as noted previously, it did agree to direct the study between sessions of various matters before the legislature. A *Lincoln Star* editorial on March 21, 1937, pointed out that the legislature often complained it hadn't the time to make a necessary investigation regarding a particular bill or issue. The Legislative Council, it said, would help solve that problem, putting the legislature on a more informed and more businesslike footing when it was time to make decisions.

Senator Charles Tvrdik, a member of the first Legislative Council, said at the group's first meeting that legislators "need scientifically gathered data of unquestioned authenticity from which to draw our conclusions. That's what this council is for."[27] The council planned to employ a "corps of researchers" to collect data on specific problems.[28]

The council considered having the clerk of the legislature double as its director of research but finally decided that would be overloading an already overloaded employee. So the council hired University of Nebraska political science professor Roger Shumate as director of research and put him in charge of the reference bureau. Senning said hiring an "expert" to handle research and data collection would make the legislature far more efficient and would give the senators more time for direct contact with the people of the state. That meant they could "keep pace with the changing needs of every community."[29]

In its 1937 session, the unicameral also made use of a state bill-drafting service to put bills into technically correct form and hired an assistant clerk to help the clerk of the legislature. While designating to the Committee on Legislative Administration the authority to hire and supervise staff, the rules made it clear that all employees "shall be selected without reference to party affiliation, and shall be chosen upon the basis of merit" (Rule III.2). In other words, no patronage. The unicameralists were determined that their businesslike body would not turn into a pot of political plums.

Analyzing the 1937 session, Aylsworth noted that the unicameral spent less money for legislative processes and procedures than any bicameral legislature had in more than a decade. The new body spent more than its predecessors on only one thing: expert assistance and counsel.

Although bureaucrats are the butt of plenty of jokes and complaints, a strong bureaucracy can help legislators be more effective in deciding which of their business is most urgent and important. The unicameral adopted the progressive notion that a permanent organization of experts and specialists would help the legislature operate efficiently and effectively to do the people's will. It also decreased the body's reliance on the executive branch for information, increasing its own independence and power. And for unicameralists, who had eliminated political parties and wanted to decrease the influence of lobbyists, the addition of expert information and advice was almost essential.

All in all, the unicameral made major strides early on toward a businesslike approach to legislating. But Norris had less success with his other goal for professionalizing the legislature: increasing salaries.

When the Model Legislature Committee was formed in 1934 to develop a plan for Nebraska's new legislative system, Norris wanted each member of the proposed body to receive $2,400 per year in salary, not a bad figure in the depths of the Great Depression. Members of the bicameral legislature were paid $800 per member for each two-year term, not enough to allow most people to leave their businesses for four months of legislative service each year, committee members thought. The total salary figure for the bicameral body had been $106,400 per biennium.

Perhaps in an effort to "sell" their proposal on the basis of its thrift, the committee members decided to set the total salary level for the unicameral at $37,500, to be divided among however many legislators between thirty and fifty the redistricting process would produce. Had they stayed with Norris's proposed twenty-four members, each legislator would have received about $1,500 per year. Because the membership in the first session turned out to be forty-three, each received $872 per year, nothing like Norris's original proposal but more than twice what their brethren in the bicameral body had earned.

Norris also gave in on the term of office. He had wanted legislators' terms to be increased from two to four years; a two-year term meant legislators served during only one actual session and could, theoretically, mean that every session would be comprised of entirely new personnel. But Norris's fellow committee members convinced him to stick with two-year terms so that the amendment would not have to build in a mechanism for a recall election. Apparently, the unicameralists thought voters wouldn't want to wait four years to get rid of someone who had fallen out of favor with his constituents.

Neither the low salary nor the short term limit was a very progressive notion. And the fact that the aggregate salary figure was actually written into the Nebraska constitution as part of the amendment that created the unicameral (Article III.7) has come back to haunt the state over the years. If the legislature wants to increase salaries for successive bodies, it must put the proposal on the ballot for approval by the voters. That approval has proven to be exceptionally difficult to come by.

Experts—Not Elites

Populists believe political power is rooted in the people, that the sensible voice of the common people—not a few elites—should be the guiding force in government. Progressives share that high ideal but add to it a belief that experts and expertise can make all life's institutions better, including government. They see the bureaucracy of trained professional servants as the means to educate the public and to provide the vision and leadership that will guarantee the future of democracy.

Progressives enthusiastically promote experts and technology to solve and prevent problems, but the experts are on a tight rein. The democratic theory underlying progressivism demands that all members of society together control their public affairs. Managing some of those affairs may require experts or specialists, but those specialists act solely to carry out the will of the people.

As George Norris and his fellow unicameralists set out to propose a new legislative design for Nebraska, they translated that big-picture populist/progressive ideology into a specific legislative structure and into the procedures they believed would help to make the legislature more representative and more professional. Much of what they put in place in the 1930s remains in place in 2002, although some things, of course, have changed.

One Person, One Vote—Mostly

The forty-three legislative districts adopted for the first unicameral were, as noted above, nearly equal in population. According to the 1940 census, District 1 (Pawnee, Richardson, and Johnson counties, in the southeast corner of the state) had the largest population at 36,354; District 43 (Morrill, Cheyenne, Banner, and Kimball counties, in the panhandle) had the smallest population at 24,257. The average population per district was 29,616, and the standard deviation from the mean was 3,356.

It was a good start. But the legislature seemed reluctant to deal with redistricting in the following years, despite the fact that the state's population continued to grow and to shift toward urban areas. Neglecting to draw new districts after the 1940 census could be excused because the districts were only five years old at that point. But it seems the legislature's may have failed "accidentally on purpose" to make changes following the 1950 census. By that time, the districts' populations were far from balanced, but folks in rural areas wanted to avoid redistricting because they were wary of its impact on their influence in the legislature.

So the various interests worked out a compromise. In 1961 the legislature placed on the ballot an amendment to provide that legislative districts be redrawn primarily on the basis of population but with some weight given to area, an attempt to allow rural areas to maintain clout in the legislature even as they lost population. The voters approved the amendment in 1962, but the measure was doomed to fail in the courts in light of the U.S. Supreme Court's one-person, one-vote decisions. The unicameral was forced to return to drawing districts on the basis of population alone and has done so ever since, redistricting after each census report.

As the state's population slowly grew, the unicameral tried in 1957 to increase the maximum size of the legislature to a number greater than fifty, but the proposal was defeated by the voters in 1958, perhaps because it was linked to a salary increase for legislators. A 1961 proposal to increase the legislature's size never got out of committee. But a 1965 proposal to increase the number of members from forty-three to forty-nine was approved by the voters in 1966.

The number of citizens in each of the forty-three districts in the 1960s was not a lot greater than it had been in the mid-1930s. But the population had continued to shift east, and districts in urban areas had much larger populations than those in rural parts of the state. Adding six senators helped to equalize matters, although it probably also narrowed the number of interests represented in some districts. Norris would probably have complained that the increased size actually decreased the legislature's representativeness.

However, the unicameral's nonpartisanship has eliminated one pothole many other legislatures have trouble avoiding when they draw their districts. In a partisan setting, the dominant party often tries to increase its advantage by drawing district lines to capitalize on its voting strength in certain geographic areas. The result is overrepresentation of one party in the legislature.

Nebraska senators admit that partisan considerations may play a role when the unicameral draws lines for federal congressional districts, but it is unlikely that partisanship is much of a factor in legislative districting. Even if one party managed to construct districts that favored its constituency, that gain wouldn't be worth much in a body that does not organize itself or function along party lines.

The unicameral also has made some changes in the way it manages representativeness in its internal procedures. It began almost immediately. The Committee of the Whole, for instance, was history at the end of the 1937 session.

By April 10, after seventy legislative days had passed, the unicameral was dealing with an average of seven bills a day in the Committee of the Whole. Most reports from the Committee of the Whole were automatically approved. Finally, the legislature voted on May 7 to suspend use of the Committee of the Whole to try to determine whether it served a real purpose. On the final day of the session, May 15, the legislators voted unanimously to abolish the Committee of the Whole from the rules, having found it "useless in a one-house legislature."[30] To many, "it had become obvious that the extra delay only slowed procedure without adding anything to the thoroughness of consideration."[31]

The change, Senning said, did not reduce the number of times the legislature examined a bill. It just meant that standing committee reports had to follow the regular rules of house procedure: the vote of each member on every motion had to be a matter of public record in the daily journal, a process that proponents of Committee of the Whole had promised to follow but seldom had. As a result the Committee of the Whole actually circumvented the openness the unicameral's proponents had preached. Once the Committee of the Whole was eliminated, standing committee reports were thoroughly debated and amendments carefully considered on the floor of the legislature in full view of press and public.

Deliberation and participation were not substantially reduced when the legislature dumped the Committee of the Whole. In fact, full participation in the legislature's deliberative process has been a hallmark of the unicameral throughout its history. The standing committee system has changed little over the years; committees are still subservient to the legislature as a whole. While committees do narrow choices by killing some bills and revising others before they reach the legislative floor, they are still expected to function in the open and to report their proceedings to the body as a whole. Furthermore, a committee's decisions to kill a bill may be second-guessed by a three-fifths majority of legislators voting to pull it from committee.

Changes in floor procedures that somehow limit debate and deliberation have been hard-fought, as reported in chapter 4. In addition, no party discipline intervenes in senators' decision making, and no second house can negate it. The result has been a legislature that is still open to freewheeling discussion by any and all senators.

The deliberative process makes the unicameral very different from direct or participatory democracy, where citizens take policy making into their own hands. Although the unicameral's supporters had promised a body open to full view and to providing full representation for the people, they purposely did not set up a system that would make elected legislators simply a conduit by which the people called the shots. The unicameral's rules have always stressed full debate and plenty of opportunities for lots of viewpoints to be expressed—and to be negotiated.

The bargaining and compromise built into the system are essential ingredients of the legislative process. The various issues the legislators discuss are connected, and legislators have to confront trade-offs and long-term effects. Debate and deliberation help build consensus for policy outcomes that everyone will have to live with.

Representativeness has not suffered in the nonpartisan unicameral, scholars say. Debate is abundant and free-flowing. And, without the demands of party loyalty, legislators can more easily widen their focus to encompass the entire state.

The 1971 report from the Citizens' Conference on State Legislatures ranked Nebraska eighteenth among the fifty states in representativeness. "Representativeness" was measured by citizens' awareness of their legislators (the small size and unicameral nature helped with that); reasonable qualifications for office; adequate salaries (which had to take Nebraska's rating down a notch); and streamlined operating procedures that allowed each legislator to represent his or her constituents fully.

At the turn of the twenty-first century, legislators and citizens from the western part of the state continued to worry that they were losing representation as the state's population moved east and became more urban. However, as long as districts must be drawn solely on the basis of population—and as long as Nebraskans refuse to increase the number of districts—the trend will continue: rural districts will grow larger geographically, but legislators from rural districts will be outnumbered by legislators from urban districts.

Some observers have suggested that representativeness in Nebraska—in the broader sense—might be enhanced if the legislature were made partisan and bicameral once again. Reinstating political parties would offer a vehicle for political affiliation that would cut across the rural-urban division. And a second house with longer terms might produce legislators more willing to place the interests of the entire state ahead of those of their own district.

As of 2002, however, that seemed unlikely to happen. Support among citizens and legislators alike for their nonpartisan unicameral remained high. (See survey results in chapter 3.)

Senator DiAnna Schimek did propose returning to a bicameral in 2003, introducing a resolution early in the session to place an amendment to the constitution to that effect on the next statewide ballot. The resolution would have provided for no more than sixty-two representatives and thirty-one senators, elected from identical districts: two house members from each senator's district.

But the resolution was pure political maneuvering, designed to make a point. The point was Schimek's opposition to the term limits—two consecutive four-year terms—imposed on the legislators by the voters in 2000. The senator said the public had not thoroughly considered the drastic impact term limits would have on their small, one-house legislature.

"In other states, if you are precluded from running again in the house, you would be eligible to run for a seat in the senate. So you would be taking your experience to the second house. In Nebraska, there is no second house," so term limits assure that no legislator will have more than a maximum of eight years of experience.[32]

Furthermore, Schimek said she hoped her proposed amendment would help Nebraskans understand that returning to a bicameral structure would not provide more representation for rural parts of the state. "The second house would be based on population just like the first," a situation demanded by no less an authority than the U.S. Supreme Court.

As for her true feelings about unicameralism, Schimek agrees with the majority of her fellow citizens that it is a good thing for Nebraska. She had no intention of shepherding her proposal for bicameralism through to legislative passage.

Keeping the Executive in Line
Outside of her or his fellow members, the single most important political force a legislator must deal with is the governor. And it is easier for the governor to exercise influence in the legislature when that body is a unicameral, some scholars say. But that assumes that the unicameral is partisan and that the

governor can use party ties and party discipline to work his or her will on the legislature. Other scholars say unicameralism strengthens the legislature's hand vis-à-vis the governor.

The latter goal is what the Nebraska unicameralists hoped for. The American system of government is based on a fear of concentrated power, and most states initially tried to assure that their governors would be relatively weak. However, by the beginning of the twentieth century, governors had carved out a distinct advantage over legislatures in most places. To those of the populist/progressive persuasion, that advantage, with its tinge of elitism, cried out for correction.

Governors do have distinct authority: to propose the state's budget and other laws, to veto bills, to make appointments. And, in all states but Nebraska, the governor is head of his or her political party in the legislature. Furthermore, because he or she is the ceremonial head of the state, the governor is visible and can develop a personal relationship with the state's people more easily than a collective like a legislature. All those things add to a governor's influence.

Nebraska governors have as many constitutional powers as their counterparts in other states. Nebraska's governor can veto a legislative bill in whole or in part, and an override requires a three-fifths vote of the legislature. But governors are at a disadvantage if their party is the minority in the legislature, scholars say. The fact that the governor's party—whichever it may be—does not even exist officially in the unicameral is an even bigger disadvantage. No partisan ties bind legislative leaders or members to the governor and his or her programs.

That makes the unicameral a pretty independent group, and that independence can be a source of friction with the governor. Some say the lack of partisan coordination between the branches makes state government less efficient than it might be, but supporters of the legislature's nonpartisan nature seem to believe government should not take hasty action anyway and seem to be pleased with the body's independence. In Nebraska the idea that the executive and legislature make up independent coordinate branches has been true both in theory and in fact.

The legislature did lose some independence in 1970 when the voters approved a constitutional amendment, which took effect in 1971, that provided for annual sessions but set a time limit on those sessions: ninety days in even-numbered years and sixty days in odd-numbered years. Legislatures that must work under a time limit have somewhat less independence than those who may meet as long as necessary to get their work done. However, Nebraska is not alone in this regard; only twelve of the fifty states have no limits on the length of sessions.

The late senator Jerome Warner said the move to annual sessions was part of a nationwide movement to improve and professionalize state legislatures in the late 1960s and early 1970s. Proponents said it would be easier to retain staff if the legislature met every year and that quality people would be more likely to run for and stay in the body if they could count on fitting annual sessions into their lives and work.

But the demand for time limits on sessions came from members of the public who thought "the less the Legislature meets, the less harm they do," Warner said. The result of the limitations, he said, was that both senators and the public have less time to learn about the issues behind the legislation.[33] The result is also less independence for the unicameral.

Going "Pro"

Life is more complicated and time more limited for legislators today than was true in the 1960s. Legislatures have responded by adding staff and improving scheduling to boost their capacity to do business, and the result has been bodies that are a bit less seat-of-the-pants and a bit more professional than they formerly were.

That is exactly what happened in Nebraska, according to Patrick O'Donnell, clerk of the legislature. The legislature beefed up its staff over a period of years but staff expansion began in earnest about 1977 and 1978 and continued into the early 1980s, O'Donnell said. Before that time, senators shared the services of clerical staff. Once the growth in government duties really began, the legislature provided staff for its standing committees first and then made provision for senators to have their own year-round legislative staff.

Capacity and professionalism grew again when senators were assigned their own offices, either shared with another senator or occupied individually. Through the 1960s senators had had no space of their own other than their desks in the legislative chamber. As the state built new office buildings for executive branch agencies, the legislature acquired the vacated space for senators' offices and for expanded research and fiscal offices.

Legislative salaries are another measure of professionalization—and have been a matter of frustration for legislators over the years. Norris and the other promoters of the unicameral said their new system would save money. The importance of that selling point was probably the reason Norris backed down from his wish to set a salary that would attract good people to legislative service and enable them to concentrate on their legislative work without being distracted by having to make a living outside the body.

Not surprisingly, the smaller legislature was cheaper. The 1952 total for salaries was just $75,000 per year—about $1,745 for each of the senators—not all that much more than the $53,200 total per year for the last bicameral that met almost twenty years earlier in the midst of the Great Depression.

Nebraskans have always seemed to think of their senators as citizen legislators who should work part-time and for little pay. The senators themselves, however, have tried almost since the first session of the unicameral to increase salaries for their successors. Proposals to do so were introduced in all but fifteen sessions between 1937 and 2000. Some years, senators tried several different proposals.

Increasing salaries for any public official is always hard to do under the harsh light of taxpayer scrutiny. Increasing salaries for legislators who are, officially at least, part-time employees may arguably be even harder. But when a salary increase requires a change to the state's constitution and, thus, a vote of the people, it can be well nigh impossible to accomplish.

The whole process would undoubtedly be easier if salaries weren't written into the constitution, and the unicameral has suggested a number of alternative ways to set legislators' pay: by legislative law; by creating a commission on legislative compensation; by creating a citizens salary control committee; by giving salary authority to the State Board of Equalization and Assessment; by adopting a formula based on the governor's salary; by adopting the minimum wage rate; by creating a compensation review commission; by using the increase in the cost-of-living index. Several of these alternatives have been proposed more than once since 1939.

Despite their best efforts, though, the senators have not been able to get out from under the constitution when it comes to determining their pay. Every salary increase they have received over the years has had to be approved by the voters. In 1959 the salary went to two hundred dollars per month. In 1962, when the voters approved the switch to four-year terms, they reaffirmed the two-hundred-dollar-per-month salary but added reimbursement for one round-trip per session between the senator's home and the capitol. In 1968 voters doubled the senators' pay to four hundred dollars per month, or forty-eight hundred dollars annually. A proposal advanced to the ballot in 1972 and 1978 would have paid per diem expenses to senators on legislative business between sessions, but the voters turned it down both times.

In 1973 and 1976 citizens defeated a proposal to increase pay to $675 per month, or $8,100 per year. Finally, in 1988, after granting their legislators no raises for twenty years, the voters apparently felt generous and increased senators' pay to $1,000 per month, or $12,000 per year. The legislature has not placed a salary increase on the ballot since then. Neither have the citizens.

Still Progressive after All These Years

In his progressive zeal for the new system he proposed, George Norris had promised that a nonpartisan unicameral legislature would give the state a "business administration" in which every member could participate in every decision and in which each member would help to shape the body's shared interests.

In 2002 the unicameral was still trying to live up to those promises.

Representativeness Maxed Out

Unless legislators can convince the people to amend the constitution to increase the number of legislative districts, the legislature has done about all it can to increase representativeness through reapportionment. It has no choice but to use population as the basis for drawing districts, and the current forty-nine districts are only one district short of the maximum allowed in the constitution.

It seems unlikely that the legislature or anyone else in the state will try anytime soon to add a second house or reinstall partisanship. Though some have argued those may be ways to improve representativeness in response to a population that continues to concentrate in a relatively small geographic area, they haven't gained a large following. On the contrary, a number of senators responding to the 2001 survey commented that nonpartisanship was good for representativeness, allowing legislators to represent the people rather than being beholden to a political party.

But in its internal procedures, the legislature has made changes that may have had an impact on representativeness. For instance, as the speaker is given more authority to structure debate, individual senators' right to participate is limited. On the other hand, if the speaker can't structure debate, any individual senator can simply highjack the proceedings and block other senators from participating.

Some observers say that is exactly what has happened in recent years. One former senator said in an interview that the unicameral is set up so that it is possible for one member to have overwhelming influence. Strong leadership from someone like the speaker is necessary in order "to be sure one person or a small number doesn't completely define the legislative process," he said.

Another senator interviewed said a legislator or two with strong, dominant personalities can make it nearly impossible for newly elected senators to be involved in debate and deliberation. People like that can "run the show," he said, forcing newcomers to the margins.

In response to exactly those concerns, the legislature has not only strengthened the speaker's power but also changed its rules, making it easier for senators to end debate. In fact, a 2002 change eliminated any minimum time allowed for debate and made it possible for the body to vote for cloture at any time; however, the motion requires thirty-three votes to succeed. Senators admitted the rule was specifically aimed at quieting one particular senator who was known to use the rules to tie up bills in filibuster and long debate.

Throughout the unicameral's history, specific individual senators have known how to use the rules to their own advantage. And senators who have done so usually have received plenty of attention in the press. It may be those senators, rather than senators in formal leadership positions, that citizens were thinking of when they responded to the 2000 survey. Forty-three percent agreed just a few members of the unicameral have all the power. (See appendix 1, table 23).

George Norris would probably be horrified at the thought that senators' opportunity for full participation was being cut off—either by the rules themselves or by someone's manipulation of the rules.

Yet, senators said, legislators who want to speak out and want to participate can usually do so in the small, nonpartisan unicameral with its nonrestrictive structure and rules. Each member has a chance to participate in easy interaction both in committee and in each of three rounds of debate on the floor, former senator Dennis Baack said.[34]

Other senators agreed that rank-and-file members have plenty of opportunity to be involved in debate and decision making. "The average member is limited only by his willingness to work hard and learn the issues," said former senator Sandy Scofield.[35]

Senator DiAnna Schimek said the unicameral's democratic structure boosts individual senators' opportunities. Senators feel they can be heard and can influence policy making. "It's empowering. It's invigorating," she said.[36]

It also appears to be representative. All in all, both citizens and legislators themselves seem to think the unicameral remains reasonably representative of the state. About three-fourths of those responding to a 2000 citizen survey about the unicameral said they thought it represented various interests quite well (see appendix 1, table 24).

Senators surveyed in 2001 seemed to share that point of view. When asked to agree or disagree with the same statement, about three-fourths of the senators agreed. However, the percentage of the current and former office-holders who agreed "strongly" that the unicameral represents the people's interests well was higher than the comparable category of citizens (see appendix 1, table 25).

Several senators noted on their surveys that legislators try to respond to the needs of all the people and represent the entire state, not only their own districts. Another saw the other side of representativeness: the legislators come from the same walks of life as the general public, he said. But several others disagreed with the notion that the unicameral was representative in the descriptive sense. They said the legislature was dominated by wealthy people and does a poor job of representing low- and middle-income people. Another said the unicameral needed to attract a broader age, gender, and minority membership. A current senator agreed that the legislature did not reflect the makeup of Nebraska but still said "there are some very talented individuals serving."

Finding a balance between descriptive representativeness and representativeness in a broader sense will always be difficult in a state and legislature with a populist orientation like Nebraska's. Populism's distrust of elites and fondness for "the people"—as wonderfully democratic as it may sound—can lead to a desire to cut everyone down to the same size at the expense of benefiting from senators' varied talents and abilities.

"The Governor Proposes; the Legislature Disposes."

As the unicameral has become more professional over the years, it has also shored up its independence from the governor. Having its own research staff and its own personal staff has helped the legislature institutionalize its role as an independent and powerful branch of the government.

And while the legislature's nonpartisan status may be its biggest asset regarding independence from the governor, the fact that it is one-house may also have an effect. In most legislatures, the two houses contend not only with the governor but also with each other. In Nebraska, those kinds of intralegislative battles are nonexistent. The legislature is "one" and can put all its energies toward protecting legislative prerogatives from encroachment by the executive.

On the other hand, one former senator responding to the 2001 survey commented that it is too easy for a governor to "tie up" a twenty-five-vote majority for his programs in the small, one-house legislature—nonpartisan or not. "I just don't think one person should have that much power in a democracy," the senator wrote.

The Nebraska governor who worked with the first unicameral certainly didn't think he had all that much power. Governor Cochran complained that he had become pretty much irrelevant in the budget-making process.[37]

One might expect all of Nebraska's governors to echo Cochran's distaste for Nebraska's unique system. But a 1996 survey of the current and former governors (updated in 2001) found mixed reaction to the legislature's nonpartisanship. Asked whether the legislature should be elected, organized, and operated on a partisan basis, two governors strongly agreed and one agreed; one was neutral, three disagreed and one strongly disagreed. However, the respondents did seem to believe the governor's job would be easier if the legislature were partisan (see appendix 1, table 26).

But the governors didn't question unicameralism. None of the current or former chief executives expressed distaste for the one-house arrangement. None of the eight who responded to the survey said Nebraska should revert to bicameralism.

The governors also said the legislature should not be increased in size, return to biennial sessions, or meet in longer sessions. And seven of the eight respondents said they had found the legislature easy to work with. Perhaps one reason for that assessment was the governors' belief that they had been successful in getting their programs through the legislature. Asked approximately how much of their program was enacted, three respondents said nearly all, four said most and one said some.

While the numbers involved here are too small to allow firm conclusions, the governors' responses seem to indicate that it is the legislature's nonpartisan status that makes the Nebraska governor's job at least different from that of other governors—if not more difficult.

A 1994 study places the Nebraska governor at the midpoint of a five-point scale measuring governors' institutional powers.[38] The governor has a line-item veto, a leading role in budgeting, the ability to call and circumscribe special sessions, and a reasonable amount of appointment power, which makes the governor a force to be reckoned with in Nebraska. But the absence of party in Nebraska's legislature counters some of the power the governor has and keeps the legislature relatively independent, a situation populists and progressives would applaud.

The governor can propose—the state's budget, various other programs, or changes to programs. And the governor can veto. In between, the legislature has the upper hand, particularly in Nebraska, where the governor can bring no partisan pressure to bear on the legislators. As one senator said, "The governor proposes; the legislature disposes." Nebraska's fiscal problems in 2002 provide a good illustration.

In autumn 2001 the state realized its tax revenues had declined dramatically, and the forecast was that the decline would continue. The governor called a special session to deal with the first and most immediate problems, but the regular 2002 legislative session was also consumed by the budget shortfall. So, as he was expected to do, the governor developed a plan to increase revenues slightly and cut spending more than slightly in order to create a balanced budget, which is required by Nebraska law.

Then the plan went to the legislature, which had, of course, been generating its own ideas about how to balance the budget. The unicameral voted down several key parts of the governor's plan, on both the income and the spending side, and began to suggest other solutions to the problem, much to the governor's consternation.

Interestingly, at one point the governor, a Republican, and the chair of the Revenue Committee, a Democrat, found themselves on the same side of a losing battle to impose a surcharge on tax breaks that Nebraska corporations received for creating jobs. It was a situation unlikely to occur in many other states but a good demonstration of the lack of party clout and discipline in the unicameral and of how nonpartisanship keeps the governor at arm's length.

Overriding a governor's veto is not exactly a snap in the unicameral: the constitution requires a three-fifths vote to do so. But that supermajority is not historically hard to come by, at least not in recent years. In 1998, when the governor vetoed fourteen bills, the legislature voted to override eight of those vetoes. In 1999, when he vetoed nine bills, the legislature overrode all nine.

In 2002 the governor and legislature debated fiercely for months about the best way to deal with the state's revenue shortfall. The governor insisted the budget be balanced almost solely on the basis of cuts in spending; he threatened to veto any appropriations or revenue bill that did not follow his mandate.

Legislators, on the other hand, came up with an appropriations bill that did cut spending but not far enough to result in a balanced budget. Instead, they passed a revenue bill to increase sales and income taxes enough to cover the shortfall. True to his word, the governor vetoed both. But neither of the vetoes stood up to the legislature's determination. The body overrode almost 60 percent of the governor's line-item cuts to the appropriations bill and completely turned back his veto of the revenue bill.

In 2003 the override votes were even more powerful; thirty-seven senators joined forces to override vetoes of the budget and appropriations bills. And the senators did it by a clearly nonpartisan vote, as reported in chapter 4. That kind of record gives credence to the claim that Nebraska's legislature is a powerful counterbalance to the executive branch.

Struggling with Professionalization

When Paul O'Hara started lobbying the legislature in 1969, "nine secretaries served 49 senators," he said. Nebraska has increased its staff support for legislators dramatically since then. It is now one of twenty-three states that provide year-round personal aides for legislators—in Nebraska, an administrative assistant and a legislative assistant for each senator—and one of thirty-six that provide both professional and clerical staff for all standing committees—in the unicameral, a committee clerk, a research analyst, and legal counsel for each committee.

But legislative leaders have little more staff help than their brethren who do not hold leadership positions. Doug Kristensen, speaker from 1998 through 2002, said the speaker of the Iowa house of representatives had eleven staff members; Kristensen had three, just one more than all the other senators. Furthermore, Kristensen said, staff salaries are appallingly low, and turnover is high. That creates problems, he said, because senators depend on staff to help them gather and confirm information.

Walt Radcliffe, who lobbies the legislature, said increased staff has made a big change in the way the body works. It has given lobbyists "someone else to talk to" if a senator is busy and can't hear the lobbyist for himself or herself. Other lobbyists said much the same thing.

Bill Mueller, who had been lobbying for seventeen years, said staff may help a senator handle a steadily increasing workload, but he doesn't think information provided by staff has taken the place of information provided by lobbyists.[39]

But Paul O'Hara disagreed. He said he thought senators get more information now from staff than from lobbyists. That's a good thing, he added, because information from research staff is likely to be more independent than that provided by lobbyists.[40]

Current and former senators surveyed in 2001 indicated they do get information and opinions from staff. Interestingly, those who have served in the legislature most recently are less likely than those who served in earlier decades to believe they rely too heavily on staff for that information. Perhaps the disparity reflects the fact that members of the legislature in the 1950s and 1960s had virtually no staff and, thus, see less benefit from staffing available today (see appendix 1, table 27).

On the other hand, senators indicate that they do, indeed, make use of the resources legislative staff have to offer. Asked whether they use the legislature's research office when deciding whether to introduce a bill, more than 70 percent of the senators indicate they do at least sometimes fashion bills on ideas they get from that office (see appendix 1, table 28).

The growth of legislative staff is one measure of professionalization, and the Nebraska legislature has moved up the scale in that regard. "We could run it on the cheap, but we haven't," Senator Dave Landis said of the legislature's increased staffing.[41] Although staff salaries are low and turnover high, good people have generally been willing to work for the legislature, Landis said.

But legislative pay is another measure of legislative professionalization, and on that one the unicameral is lacking. Kristensen said legislators' salaries are as appallingly low as those of staff.

Senator Bob Wickersham said the legislature had failed to live up to Norris's goals when it came to salary. Norris believed legislators should be well compensated, Wickersham said, so that the best-qualified individuals would be more inclined to run for office. The state has paid less attention to its legislators' salary level than it has to other parts of Norris's vision, he said.[42]

Several former senators responding to the 2001 survey said better pay for senators would improve the legislature by making it possible for more diverse candidates to run for the office. As long as salaries remain low, they said, many qualified people will be deterred from running, and the body will be dominated by retirees or independently wealthy people.

Nebraska is not the only state that keeps its legislative salaries low. According to the Council of State Governments, seven states paid their legislators less in 1999 than Nebraska did, while four others offered more than Nebraska's $12,000 per year but still less than $15,000 annually. New Mexico pays legislators no salary at all but does provide $124 per day to cover living expenses during the session. New Hampshire was even farther down at the bottom of the barrel, paying $200 for a two-year period and nothing to cover living expenses.

Nebraska legislators are also lacking another possible benefit: the opportunity to participate in state retirement funds. Only six other states do not offer legislative retirement benefits. Nebraska is also one of only eight states that do not provide at last some additional compensation for the speaker.

That the speaker receives no extra pay is not surprising, given Nebraska's historically populist, egalitarian approach to its legislature. But the low legislative salary is not so easy to explain, considering Norris's promotion of good pay for good people.

Current and former senators responding to the 2001 survey nearly all agreed that salaries should be increased, although those serving in the more recent decades seemed even more convinced than those who served earlier (see appendix 1, table 29).

The group that designed the Nebraska unicameral believed wholeheartedly that the new structure and the kind of rules anticipated for the legislature would enable senators to cast off the influence of powerful elites and, instead, represent the real people of Nebraska. But Norris and his supporters also saw the benefit of a professional legislature that would rely on information and expertise as it made its decisions and that would offer salaries sufficient to attract excellent public servants. Those tenets of progressivism seem sometimes in conflict with the populist desire for representativeness. And, it must be said, they have been only partially met in Nebraska.

Yet the expertise, information, and quality personnel the progressives touted were all designed to assure that the will of the people would be done in and by government. To a reasonable extent, that goal has been met via the unicameral's representativeness and professionalization.

Setting Limits

At the 2000 general election, Nebraska voters approved a measure to limit state senators to two consecutive two-year terms. The voters had approved term limits at two previous elections—in 1992 and 1996—but both of those amendments had been found unconstitutional, primarily because they included limits on Nebraska's congressional delegation; the courts said the state could not designate limits for representatives in national offices. The 2000 proposal was written to encompass only members of the state legislature and has not been successfully challenged in court.

Candidates running for election in 2002 were the first to fall under the limit, so the effects of the restriction will not be felt for a while. But when they are felt, they may well be most obvious in matters related not only to efficiency—caused by absence of institutional memory—but also to representativeness, independence, and professionalization.

Such esteemed politicians as Edmund Burke and James Madison both argued that legislators should not sacrifice the interests of the state for the particular views of their constituencies. But the interests of the state are not necessarily just the sum of the local constituents' desires. Working with colleagues in an institution like a legislature helps members learn to think in terms of the whole, not just the part that elects them, scholars say.

Members new to a legislature tend to put more stock in what they think their own constituents want than do legislators who have been around for a while. After some years of service, legislators often develop a more statewide perspective because of their experience and additional responsibilities and obligations and because they develop commitment to the institution itself. Term limits will limit legislators' opportunity to acquire the broader, longer-range view of public policy and, in that sense, decrease their representativeness.

Term limits are also likely to make the legislature less independent of the governor. A less experienced body will be more dependent on the executive for leadership and information. Inexperienced legislators will have trouble making the machinery of government function, and the executive will likely become, once again, the more dominant of the branches.

Staff will become increasingly important, too, since they will be the only legislative employees with in-depth institutional memory. And, of course, lobbyists will rise to fill the void left by experience.

Legislative leaders could, by default, become more powerful in a situation where no member has more than four years' more experience than any other and no one has time to develop the kind of respect and expertise that have conferred leadership in the past. Or leadership could, for the same reasons, be crippled and even less effectual than it has been in the nonhierarchical unicameral.

Furthermore, term limits will probably have an effect on accountability. Legislators who know they cannot serve more than two terms may feel completely free from the pressures of constituents or state interests during the second term. One can hope those lame-duck senators will use their freedom from electoral pressures to do what is right for the state as a whole. But, regardless, constituents will have no way to hold the legislators accountable for their actions. The public is often tempted to sneer at candidates' eagerness to be elected or reelected, but it is through the electoral process that citizens hold public servants' feet to the policy fire. Remove that process, and accountability is decreased.

Legislative term limits were undoubtedly not something the framers of the unicameral imagined. It is impossible to say exactly what they would have thought about the idea, but considering their concern that legislators think broadly and act on behalf of the entire state, that they develop expertise and be professional and that the legislature be strongly independent from the governor it seems likely they would not have approved.

Although senators and citizens alike in recent years have increasingly worried that the rural areas of Nebraska are losing representation in the legislature, the state's redistricting hands are firmly tied by federal requirements that districts be drawn proportionately according to population. Some have suggested that a return to two houses might ease the problem caused by the state's population slipping steadily eastward, but Nebraskans' fondness for their one-house body makes that kind of change seem unlikely at present.

Increasing the number of legislative districts might help assuage concerns about lack of representation for rural areas, and that very idea was proposed in 2002. It is a less drastic move than a return to bicameralism, but it, too, would require a constitutional amendment and a good effort to sell the idea to the voters. In an era of falling state income and tight budgets, increasing the number of representatives runs counter to the trend toward cutting everything in sight.

In the meantime, Nebraskans may have to give up their concern that the unicameral doesn't live up to the descriptive model of representation and be satisfied that the small numbers mean all legislators can quite successfully be involved in all aspects of the policy-making process. In that sense, the body remains representative, as Norris had hoped it would.

The unicameral also remains strong vis-à-vis the governor. Norris would undoubtedly be pleased to see the people's branch of government holding its own in the balance of power. How that balance will be affected when term limits take effect remains to be seen.

In regard to professionalism, too, the unicameral has done reasonably well in living up to the goals its promoters set for it. Certainly, the first body adopted the progressive model, which insisted on the importance of experts to aid lawmakers in their deliberations. Of course, the legislature didn't keep up that pace, and increases in legislative staff languished for nearly fifty years after that first flourish of improvement. But the unicameral of the last several decades appears to have institutionalized the importance of good staff support for individual legislators and for the body as a whole. On the other hand, maintaining that support by providing adequate salaries for staff continues to be a struggle.

Salaries for legislators themselves have been a struggle from the beginning. They were not as high as Norris would have liked in the first unicameral session, and they have not even kept pace with inflation since then, much less been increased to a level that would allow senators to make legislating a full-time job. Norris and his compatriots would probably be disappointed about that.

On the whole, then, Nebraska's unicameral has met at least some of the goals the unicameralists set for it in regard to representativeness, independence, and professionalization. It may not have been a smashing success, particularly when it comes to professionalization, but it has done pretty well.

6 / "You Lie, You're Gone"

Lobbyists' Role in the Unique Unicameral

Lobbyists had a bad name in Nebraska in the early 1930s. Many citizens regarded them as representatives of elite special interests, sneaking around behind the scenes to promote benefits for their wealthy employers and block measures that would benefit the people. Reducing the influence of the lobby was one of the unicameralists' most vaunted goals. Governor Charles Bryan said special interest lobbyists had learned how to take advantage of the bicameral's complex system and knew how to cover their tracks as they did their dirty work. George Norris said the unicameral would mean an end to lobbying by special interests and the end of secret lawmaking.

A small, one-house, nonpartisan legislature, Norris said, would give corrupt special interests and the corrupt representatives they influenced nowhere to hide. Those infernal lobbyists, mistrusted in the 1930s as much as they are today, would be exposed to the light of day and unable to do their nefarious deeds.

Norris claimed lobbyists' influence would be diluted in a number of ways. Because the legislature would be small, it would be hard for lobbyists to hide their dealings with individual members. Because it would be nonpartisan, lobbyists would be unable simply to go to a few party leaders and persuade them to take the lobbyists' preferred position. And because it would be one-house, conference committees would be eliminated. It was in those small, secretive groups that Norris suspected the worst of special interest pressure was brought to bear.

Proponents of bicameralism had defended conference committees as vital to the check that each house of the legislature had over the other. Norris's reply to the assertion that a two-house body provided necessary checks and balances was widely quoted, including by himself in his autobiography: "As a matter of practice, it has developed frequently that, through the conference committee, the politicians have the checks and the special interests the balances."

Norris and the other framers of the unicameral appear to have believed that the new structure of the unicameral would, in and of itself, pretty much take care of the lobbying problem. They made few if any suggestions for rules and procedures to control lobbyists. But Norris made counteracting special interests one of the themes of his campaign in favor of the unicameral, a theme founded on his populist belief that special interests had been able to influence the legislature at the expense of ordinary people. Undoubtedly, that theme found an eager audience among suspicious, populist-minded Nebraskans.

Lobbying and its role in the legislature is, of course, closely related to openness, accountability, and accessibility, to equality and efficiency, to professionalization and representativeness. It could, perhaps, have been dealt with in each of those chapters. But because controlling the lobby was such an important part of the unicameralists' case and because it remains high on the public's agenda today—a 1998 poll found nearly 80 percent of Americans believe special interest groups exert too much control over government—it is the basis for a separate chapter in this work.[1]

Keep It Small

When Norris, John Senning, John Norton, and the others kicked off their campaign for the restructured legislature in 1934, Norris addressed a huge rally in Lincoln on February 22, 1934. His speech laid out all the basic arguments in favor of the small, one-house, nonpartisan body, including proclamations that special interests would be far less powerful in the unicameral than they had been in the old bicameral legislatures.

While Norris had given in to his compatriots' insistence that a twenty-four-member legislature would be too small, he had not lost his faith in the benefits of decreasing the membership considerably from the 133 that served in the 1933 bicameral body. A small legislature, he told the crowd that February day, would be more free from corrupt influences than a larger, two-house body.

"I have been told by lobbyists that the easiest legislature to control is the one which is large in number," Norris said in his Model Legislature speech. In a large body, much authority must, of necessity, be delegated to only a few members. Thus, lobbyists need work only with those few in order to get their way.

The idea was not new for Norris in 1934. He had been convinced for many years that a small legislature would better resist the influences of special interests. In a 1927 letter, he said he had talked with a lobbyist who told him he preferred to work in a large legislature because there an individual legislator could more easily hide from his constituents.

In the spring of 1934, as he promoted the proposed new legislative structure, Norris told the *Washington Post* the Nebraska plan would drastically decrease the influence of lobbyists who, he said, "have a picnic in large legislatures where members get small salaries."[2] The implication was that lobbyists' favors helped pad the legislators' income, the kind of bribery or near bribery Norris hoped to fend off by paying members of the unicameral a living wage.

In a statement after the end of the unicameral's first session, Norris continued to support its small size, despite the inadequacy of the salaries. Professional lobbyists will admit, in confidence, that it is easier to handle a legislature of two hundred than to control a small body of seventy-five to a hundred, Norris said. Of course, the unicameral, then at forty-three members, was considerably smaller than even the "small body" Norris mentioned in his statement.

No Way to Cover Tracks

Norris had been talking about the benefits of a small, one-house legislature long before the formal campaign for the unicameral got under way. In a 1933 *Sunday Journal and Star* interview, he had laid out all the arguments in favor of a small body, including its salutary effect on the influence of special interests. A two-house body, he said, gives a legislator who represents some special interest a chance to cover his tracks by shifting responsibility through parliamentary maneuvers and conference committees. He admitted critics said a small legislature could be "purchased" more easily than a large one but said eliminating the structural means for legislators to hide their intentions would prevent that from happening.

After the constitutional amendment was approved in November 1934, Norris continued to tout the benefits of Nebraska's new plan in a December 16, 1934, radio address. The text of that address was reprinted the following February in the *Congressional Record*. Norris reiterated how much the openness afforded by a one-house structure would neutralize the influence of special interests.

"The professional lobbyist would find his occupation gone, because his success depends upon his ability to assist the unworthy legislator to make such a record that his constituents cannot easily determine just what it is," Norris told his listeners. That would be well nigh impossible in the new unicameral with its public hearings, open records, and open votes, he said.

Furthermore, lobbyists' influence via conference committees and political maneuvering was about to be eliminated. People thought their legislature had had two houses, he said, "but as a matter of fact, we have three." The third house was the conference committee, where lobbyists were able to be especially effective. As noted earlier, conference committees were small—often only six members—met behind closed doors and kept no records of their proceedings. A lobbyist could kill legislation there or change it dramatically from what the house and senate had done in open session, and "the people are unable to fix responsibility."[3]

A unicameral would put a stop to that. No more opportunities for lobbyists to succeed by getting cozy with just a few legislators. "In a one-house legislature, special interests desiring to control legislation would have to control a majority of the legislature itself," a far more difficult feat, Norris contended.[4]

But critics said without the check of a second house, a unicameral could be stampeded into action by pressure groups. In fact, some said the lobby would become the second house. After the first session, Senator O. Edwin Schultz said elimination of conference committees hadn't eliminated pressure by lobbyists, and he said some special interest bills that had failed in previous sessions were passed by the unicameral.[5]

But Senning said that wasn't because of the absence of the second house. On the contrary, Senning argued, thanks to the lobbyists, the two houses in a bicameral had never efficiently checked each other. Lobbyists, he said, brought the action of the two houses to a common point of interest, eliminating the beneficial effects of checks and balances. Besides that, the complexities of the bicameral procedure helped the unscrupulous lobbyist work his will on the legislature. The unicameralists were convinced that having just one house in the legislature would make both lobbyists and legislators more honest in their dealings with each other.

Parties vs. Lobbyists

The unicameral promoters said getting rid of party apparatus and party loyalty in the legislature would make life harder for lobbyists. No longer would they be able to persuade only a few party leaders to their point of view and be able to count on the support of all the legislators of that party. Under the new system, senators were to be independent thinkers, and lobbyists would have to persuade at least twenty-three of the forty-three members to support a particular issue. Theoretically, that should have made the lobbyists' job harder.

Not everyone was convinced. Some critics said that without parties to organize voting majorities, legislators would be overwhelmed by "trained and captained and well-oiled minorities grasping for some advantage."[6]

Others also have suggested that the nonpartisan unicameral may be a productive arena for special interests. Without parties to collect and represent citizens' views, lobbyists may provide the most important connection between constituents and legislators. That is not necessarily bad, but it does elevate lobbyists' importance by eliminating parties as a means of making that connection. Lobbyists also gain by the simple fact that, because legislators need to spend no time listening to what party leaders have to say, they can spend more time listening to lobbyists. And they need not divide their loyalties between party demands and persuasive lobbyists.

The arguments for nonpartisanship as a tool against special interests are not as strong as the arguments for a small, one-house body and the resulting simplified procedures. In fact, scholars suggest that the weaker the political parties, the stronger the special interests. Special interest groups are perfectly legitimate; they represent many of the multiple interests that make up America's pluralistic society. But political parties are far more representative, umbrella-like organizations that embrace a host of groups and interests and are formed around a broad philosophy rather than the specific, narrow interest or objective a lobbyist is likely to represent.

Removing political parties from the field is compatible with the populist belief that "the people" are one and should not be artificially separated by party labels. And it was definitely compatible with George Norris's progressive goal of making state government more simple and directly accountable to the citizens. Nonpartisanship did, indeed, eliminate the possibility that lobbyists could narrow their targets to only the party elite. But the absence of parties left an organizational and informational vacuum that lobbyists may have rushed to fill. Whether the openness and accountability offered by the simplified procedures was adequate to counterbalance that force was open to question in 1937—as it is today.

Cut "Special" Interests Down to Size

John Senning recognized the lobby's presence and potential power. Writing in 1939, he noted that in both the unicameral's sessions the registered lobbyists had outnumbered the legislators four to one, although he believed the legislature's new structure was keeping the lobbyists at bay. "Powerful interests have attempted to force members to support their bills, but the legislative procedure is so direct and open that no member can conceal his vote, and none wishes to admit that he is the tool of a lobby."[7]

But unlike George Norris, who derided lobbyists with populist fervor, Senning admitted lobbyists could and did provide worthwhile information and even leadership in legislative matters. Listening to lobbyists on different sides of an issue helped legislators sift data and draft conclusions, he said.

Senning, a political scientist as well as a political activist, understood what political scientists today say about lobbies and special interests: that they represent the legitimate interests of ordinary people—often in conflict with other legitimate interests of other ordinary people. In fact, scholars commonly assert that lobbying is the primary way Americans exercise their First Amendment right to petition their government.

Many citizens and much of the media—in both eras—tend to believe, however, that special interests are the embodiment of evil. The term "special interest" in American politics conjures up the notion of a group that gets more attention than it deserves. The notion is not without historical foundation.

In Nebraska, for instance, the rise of populism was fueled at least in part by the very real and disproportionate power of special interests, particularly the railroads, and the power people perceived those interests to wield in government. In the late 1800s Nebraskans and other "common people" began to question the American ideal of the rugged individual unfettered by government interference. They believed a privileged few rugged capitalists were exploiting the struggling common folk, the farmers, and laborers.

It wasn't just that the government was too "hands off" in its attitude toward big business; big business interests actually had control of government, the populists believed. These fat cat capitalists used their wealth and power to get special privileges for their industries, to keep government regulation at bay, and to maintain their monopolies. The populists saw a real divide between private interests and the public's interests.

In the early decades of the 1900s, the progressives picked up where the populists had left off. Men of wealth—special interests—were still influencing politicians, still getting favored treatment. The progressives said the situation should be the other way round: government should protect the common interest against special interests.

With that history no more than a decade or two behind them, with incentives to influence government policies growing during the New Deal era of government expansion, and with the progressive spirit of reform coursing through their veins, Norris and his fellow unicameralists can be forgiven for conceiving of special interests as taking advantage of "ordinary" people. One can understand that "lobbyist" and "special interest" were pejorative terms in 1937.

Undoubtedly, some lobbyists and some special interests in the twenty-first century still pursue nefarious goals on behalf of elites. But American politics is replete with example of ordinary people banding into groups to advance their interests. As government has grown and become more complex, citizens increasingly rely on groups and associations and the lobbyists who work for those groups and associations to represent their interests in government. Nearly eight of every ten Americans are members of some organized group with a policy agenda. Special interests are no longer the enemy; "they are us."[8]

It is still true, though, that what most people know about lobbying is what they read in and hear from the mass media, who tend to focus on lobbying gone awry, which it sometimes does. Thus, the public generalizes from the worst possible scenarios and cooks all lobbyists in that same corrupt pot, assuming that lobbyists, in general, try to buy legislators' votes and that legislators, in general, will do anything for lobbyists' money.

But lobbyists say they support candidates simply to get access to present their clients' views, not to obtain promises of votes. Legislators say most of what lobbyists do is provide information, not try to buy legislative promises. Some scholars say all of that is undoubtedly true but add that lobbyists often do want a bit more than just access and that legislators do get a bit more than just information. The purpose of the information, after all, is to persuade a legislator to take a certain action.

Lobbying in state capitols today is far different from what it was in the unicameral's early decades. Ethics laws, requirements of financial disclosure from both lobbyists and legislators, a vigilant press, and public perceptions combine to keep relationships between lobbyists and legislators more at arm's length than they once were.

Regulations and disclosure requirements have been put in place, at least partly to counteract the very real fact that some interest groups have more resources than others—not just lots of money but also lots of members, such as in teachers' associations—and that the public has a right to know who has the resources and how they are being used. All that has helped keep special interests in their place as only one of many influences on legislators who also pay attention to information gleaned from their constituents, their staff, and their own research as well as their own core beliefs.

Like its sister bodies in other states, Nebraska's legislature has changed its approach to and dealings with special interest groups as times and circumstances have changed. In fact, the first unicameral session was barely over when Senning recommended that the unicameral pass some laws to regulate the lobby. He said the one-house legislature was well equipped to be able to take quick action to "circumscribe activities of the lobby."[9]

Perhaps one of the obvious activities Senning wanted to circumscribe was the lobbyists' having made themselves at home at the back of the legislative chamber. Nebraskans were making the switch from a two-house to a one-house body at about the same time their new state capitol was being built—with two legislative chambers. The forty-three-member unicameral moved into the space designed for the hundred-member house of representatives. That left more than fifty empty chairs at the back of the room, and some of the 187 lobbyists registered that session just filled in the gaps. It may have been logical from the lobbyists' point of view, but it didn't look good to outsiders.

The situation didn't last long. The *Lincoln Star* reported on January 25, 1937, that the members had taken care of "a little problem of dignity that's been bothering them." The unicameral adopted a motion to rip out a row of ten chairs and stretch a rope across the aisles at that point in order to separate the forty-three members from whoever might be sitting in the seats at the back. Apparently, the legislators had not anticipated that lobbyists would close in on them from the rear the way they did, and they didn't much like it. In a review of Alvin Johnson's 1938 book about the unicameral, Senning states clearly that the unicameral did not give even tacit approval to the lobbyists' being seated immediately behind the legislators.

Despite the rope and the missing row of seats, the fact remained that the lobby was an influential presence in the unicameral—as it had been in previous bicamerals. Some said the lobby had more influence in the new institution. Opponents had warned that a lobbyist's ability to sway lawmakers to his particular point of view would be all the easier in a small, one-house, nonpartisan body. Writing in the *Official Debate Handbook*, Door and Kitchin supported that contention. They found some evidence in the 1937 unicameral, they said, that lobbyists' task is easier in a unicameral body, where only one house must be persuaded to take action.

One newspaper story indicated the lobbyists watched over the session like "hawks over prey" and that many senators and lobbyists consulted each other at the back of the chamber. But the same story added that the contacts between lobbyists and members were so open to public scrutiny that many lobbyists said their work was harder in 1937 than it had been in previous sessions.[10]

The late Jerome Warner served his first term in the legislature in 1963, when lobbyists still filled the seats at the back of the chamber. He admitted the arrangement didn't look good to the public, but on the other hand, "[e]veryone knew who was talking to whom," and if another senator or member of the press wanted to listen in on a conversation between a lobbyist and a legislator, it was easy to do. "It was very public," Warner said.

Senning noted that lobbyists' old formulas were ineffective in the new unicameral. The absence of a second house meant lobbyists had no foil with which to play one group against the other. And, he said, the field of forty-three was too small to allow opportunity for "that finesse which is the lobbyist's stock in trade."[11]

Some said the legislature's simple structure and open procedures meant lobbying was not the threat of corruption in Nebraska that it was in some other states. No member was able to conceal his vote, and no member wanted to admit he was a tool of the lobby.

Senator Emil Von Seggern said after the 1937 session that the lobbyist "could not avoid placing his friends on the spot. His allies on the floor were plainly known in the unicameral and not concealed as in the two-house sessions."[12] Senator John Norton said the unicameral's open procedures meant the lobbying problem would "take care of itself" and that legitimate lobbying by ordinary citizens would increase under the new system.[13]

The unicameral's provision for public hearings on every bill meant lobbyists had fewer advantages of access or information over private citizens than had been true in the past. And veteran legislators reported they received five to eight times more letters during the 1937 session, which they identified as a form of "citizen lobbying,"[14] a welcome consequence of a more open, accessible system.

Senator W. H. Diers told the *York Republican* on June 10, 1937, that "the organized minority groups endeavoring to put over a program of selfish self-interest did not get far; but other lobbyists who had something for the public good to recommend got a respectful hearing."

Other early observers agreed that lobbyists were forced to behave under the bright light of the public scrutiny in the simplified legislative structure. The actions of lobbyists and members alike, one said, were now out in the open where the press could report on them and the people of the state could see just who was doing what at who's behest.

By pushing lobbyists and their work into the open, the unicameral was able to use the information lobbyists provided but also to curb any improper influence lobbyists may have wielded in previous legislatures. The new system forced legislators and lobbyists to do business in the public eye; the results, proponents hoped, would be better behavior from both groups.

But just in case publicity wasn't enough to keep everyone in line, Nebraska put regulations in place, regulations that have been updated and strengthened periodically.

Some of the changes came in the form of legislative rules. Some were directed specifically at lobbyists; others were intended more to improve decorum in general and simply included lobbyists in the provisions. For instance, a 1959 amendment to Rule 16 said no printed material could be placed on members' desks unless its source was clearly printed on the front of the items and distribution had been approved by at least one member of the legislature. That measure assured that lobbyists could not just hand out their own propaganda without attribution and without permission.

Also in 1959 the legislature adopted a Rules Committee recommendation that no one be allowed to sit next to a member while the legislature was considering a bill on final reading. No longer could legislators leave their seats to talk with lobbyists, nor could lobbyists sit down with senators at that point in the proceedings. Significantly, though, the rule did not ban lobbyists from the floor during other parts of the legislative proceedings.

A pair of 1965 amendments tightened things further. One amendment, offered on January 5, proposed that an area on the main floor, behind the senators, be reserved for temporary visitors and families of senators. A substitution was proposed that clearly stated no lobbyists were to be on the floor except in designated areas and by invitation of a legislator. The amendment also proposed that identification cards be issued to senators and that reporters requesting an interview with a senator send their requests via the sergeant at arms or his assistant. The substitute amendment was adopted forty-one to one on January 18. That was the permanent end of lobbyists' sitting in the seats at the back of the chamber.

The other amendment was proposed and adopted on January 5. It said no one but senators' immediate family were to sit next to them on the floor—and not even they were to be present during final reading. That still didn't keep lobbyists from wandering in to talk with senators on the floor, but it did keep them from plopping down and making themselves comfortable.

Then in 1969 Senator Terry Carpenter moved to further define just what the legislative "floor" was to mean. Carpenter suggested it be all space forward from the metal railing behind the senators' desks, including the space under the balcony. And he suggested no one be admitted to the floor except members, their families, employees of the legislature, and reporters. Significantly, that left lobbyists on the perimeter. Carpenter's motion was adopted on the first day of the legislative session.

Then the legislators got serious about protecting their physical space. The body adopted a rule change in 1988 that forbade even immediate family members from being on the floor except by permission of the chair and never during final reading. In 1989 they adopted another amendment, this time clearly stating that no lobbyist should be admitted to the chamber and that other guests should also be allowed only in the roped area at the back of the room, not under the balcony along the sides of the legislative floor. As a result lobbying was actually relegated to the lobby or rotunda of the capitol, the area that gave the activity its name in the first place.

During debate on the 1989 amendment, Senator Ron Withem told his fellow senators they might be surprised to know that what they assumed was "an ironclad rule and law that no registered lobbyists are allowed in the chamber really doesn't appear in the rules anyplace." While registered lobbyists generally recognized they were not to be inside the chamber, Withem noted that other people with interest in legislation—like teachers' groups or mayors of Nebraska cities who were visiting the capitol—were sometimes invited to sit under the balcony and observe the legislature at work. At times, the discussion the group might be observing was "of direct concern to them." A situation like that compromised the "integrity of the chamber," Withem said. His fellow senators agreed, and they changed the rule on a thirty-four to zero vote.

The legislature had come a long way. In 1937 lobbyists had just walked in and made themselves comfortable in the chairs behind the senators. Slightly more than fifty years later, they were standing on the other side of the doors.

That took care of one very obvious part of legislative life where lobbyists may have been an embarrassment. But it was not until 1976 that the unicameral got around to assuring that details of the lobbyists' dealings with legislators were out in the open and accounted for. Lobbyists had been required to register with the clerk of the legislature ever since the unicameral began meeting in 1937, but the requirement was loosely enforced at best, according to Frank Daley, executive director of the Nebraska Accountability and Disclosure Commission. That changed in 1976 with the passage of the Accountability and Disclosure Act that created the commission.

The 1976 act was intended primarily to require campaign finance disclosures from legislators and candidates, Daley said, but it also made the commission responsible for enforcing regulations regarding lobbyists. Lobbyists have continued to register with the clerk's office, and their names are listed in the *Legislative Journal* at the beginning of each session. But the Accountability and Disclosure Commission sees to it that the lobbyists report appropriately and on time. And because both senators' campaign expenditures and lobbyists lobbying expenses are open to misuse by those involved and to misunderstanding by the public, the two subjects seem to fit logically under the commission's umbrella.

The regulations are almost exactly what they were when they were enacted in 1976, Daley said, with just a few exceptions. For instance, until the mid-1990s lobbyists were required to file monthly reports of income and expenditures during the legislative session, a process they found burdensome during the time they were most busy. However, if lobbyists got behind on their filings, they faced no penalties. A change in 1996 dropped the monthly reports and made them quarterly but added fees for late reporting. "It was a trade-off," Daley said. [15]

Another change came in 2000 when the reporting form was changed. Until that time, Daley said, the forms had simply required that lobbyists fill in their expenditures in various broad categories, one of which was entertainment. "Entertainment" often included a so-called legislative day, when all members of a particular association came to Lincoln to visit the legislature and have lunch or dinner with senators. Sometimes, Daley said, of the total number attending the event, only a dozen or so were legislators while another 100 or 150 were members of the association.

But the expenses would be lumped together in a lobbyists' report, and the cumulative effect of a number of such events sponsored by a number of lobbyists on behalf of a number of organizations would give the impression that senators were being wined and dined at a rate far more intense than they really were. Those were the numbers the media reported, Daley said, and senators didn't like the false impression they said was created. So now lobbyists' reports break out what part of the "entertainment" category was spent specifically on members of the legislative or executive branch and which part on "others."

The preamble to the 1976 act notes both a general interest and a "compelling state interest" in ensuring that elections are free of corruption and of the appearance of corruption. That goal can be achieved only if both income and expenditures are fully disclosed, it says.

Furthermore, public officials must be independent and impartial and must not use their offices for "private gain." Recognizing that even the appearance of conflict of interest can damage the governmental process, the preamble concludes, "although the vast majority of public officials and employees are dedicated and serve with high integrity, the public interest requires that the law provide greater accountability, disclosure, and guidance with respect to the conduct of public officials and employees."

The act goes on to delineate what must be included in a senator's "disclosure" report and then launches into lobbying regulations. Before they may lobby the legislative or executive branch, lobbyists must register with the clerk of the legislature. The registration must list who is paying the lobbyist (and details about the business or group) and on what subjects he or she plans to lobby. Annual registration costs are a hundred dollars per client—or principal—for a paid lobbyist and fifteen dollars for an unpaid lobbyist. But if that unpaid lobbyist suddenly begins receiving payment for his or her work, he or she must go back and reregister and cough up the additional eighty-five dollars.

To be sure lobbyists' names are out in the open, a list of all registered lobbyists is printed in the *Legislative Journal* during the first week of the session each year. Lobbyists and their principals—the groups employing them—must file separate quarterly statements showing the total amount received or spent on lobbying expenses. If lobbyists receive or spend more than five thousand dollars for lobbying purposes during a single month, they must file an additional report within fifteen days after the end of the month. Fines for missing the deadline are a hundred dollars per day. At the end of the legislative session, lobbyists have forty-five days to file a report that lists all the legislation on which the lobbyist acted.

All those provisions are designed to keep lobbyists' work and money out in the open. But the act also set limits on gifts to public officials, and here, too, the act has been adjusted slightly over the years, Daley said. Originally, lobbyists were limited to gifts equivalent in value of no more than ten dollars per month for any legislative or executive branch official or staff member or family member. That was increased to twenty-five dollars in the 1980s and to fifty dollars in the 1990s, Daley said. Meals at which the lobbyist is present are excluded from the regulation. So taking a senator to breakfast is okay, but a hundred-dollar gift certificate for a senator and his family to a nice restaurant is not. A coffee mug is okay. But a coffeemaker plus a few bags of Starbucks coffee to go along with the mug will probably exceed the fifty-dollar limit, at least if all arrive in the same month. Knowingly going over the limit is a Class III misdemeanor. It won't land a lobbyist in prison, but it's more than a slap on the wrist.

What the public most dislikes and suspects about lobbyists is, black-on-white, prohibited by law: the act says lobbyists must not lie. It says they must not try to influence legislation in order to create jobs for themselves. And significantly, it says they must not promise to give or threaten to withhold campaign support in the future in order to influence an official's stand on a matter of public policy. In other words, no vote-buying allowed.

But the official prohibitions laid out in the act probably aren't enough to keep citizens from continuing to suspect that money-for-votes is the underlying relationship between lobbyists and public officials.

Compared to other states, Nebraska requires a great deal of disclosure from its lobbyists but places relatively few restrictions on their activities. For instance, Nebraska law does not prevent lobbyists from making contributions to legislators' campaigns. Nine states ban such contributions entirely; twenty-four ban them during the legislative session. Twenty-five states say officials may not solicit contributions from lobbyists; Nebraska is one of the twenty-five that does not prohibit such solicitations.

On the other hand, Nebraska is one of only seven states that require registered lobbyists to file disclosure reports at least quarterly. Eleven states ask for monthly filings; the other thirty-two require less frequent reports. And Nebraska requires a lot of information on lobbyists' reports: what legislation the lobbyists are seeking to influence; their expenditures benefiting public officials or employees; total compensation lobbyists receive from their clients;

their expenses broken down by category; their total expenditures; a list of names and addresses of individuals giving more than a hundred dollars in contributions or gifts to legislators via the lobbyist; disclosure of honoraria or other money loaned, promised, or paid to officials or staff in the legislative or executive branches. Only ten states ask for more information than Nebraska does.

Lobbyists are not going to go away, nor should they. As long as multiple interests demand attention from government, groups will form and will hire lobbyists to promote those interests. In general, government response has been not to try to eliminate lobbying but to set certain standards that narrow the scope of acceptable behavior and require disclosure that lets citizens watch and judge how lobbyists and legislators interact.

Heaven or Hell?

If observers of the first unicameral session in 1937 were dismayed that the 187 lobbyists outnumbered 43 legislators more than four to one, they would probably be apoplectic in 2002. The 2002 *Nebraska Legislative Journal* recorded in its Day Four proceedings that 265 lobbyists had registered, more than five lobbyists for every one of the 49 legislators.

Of the 265 registered, at least 14 were previously members of the legislature themselves. Another half-dozen or so had served in the executive branch or as legislative aides. That pattern of moving from service in government into the private sector to lobby the government is common in the United States where former legislators can drawn on their skills and experience to continue to be involved in public affairs—and make a better living than they could in the legislature. Nebraska has no "revolving door" law that prohibits a state official or employee from leaving government to work as a lobbyist. But, as scholars note, nothing is inherently wrong with lobbying or the people who do it.

The number of lobbyists in Nebraska is not unusual, either. Lobbyists far outnumber legislators in virtually every state because for every one legislator, numerous interest groups want to be heard. Scholars note that citizens should not look at lobbyists' numbers and automatically equate presence with power.

But observers disagree as to just how influential lobbyists are in Nebraska's unique legislature. Some say the unicameral is a lobbyist's paradise. Other say a lobbyist's job is harder in Nebraska than it is elsewhere.

"Forty-nine Free Thinkers"

A 1978 study found that Nebraska legislators had generally positive attitudes toward lobbyists, on whom they rely for information, and concluded that interest groups may be more important in a nonpartisan body. Furthermore, the study found that lobbyists' attitudes toward the nonpartisan unicameral were also positive.

Whether those attitudes solidly reflected lobbyists' conviction that they were more influential in the nonpartisan legislature than they would be in a partisan body is not completely clear. In interviews in the summer and fall of 2001, lobbyists without exception expressed or implied admiration for and satisfaction with the unicameral's structure—and also, almost without exception, declared it was harder to lobby there, for one reason or another, than it might be in a state with a traditional legislature.

Nebraska lobbyists indicate they have many of the same goals that scholars have identified for lobbyists nationwide. They aggregate interests; they contribute to the substance of public policy as sources of technical and political information; and they educate legislators and citizens about public issues. And because they would like to see people elected who generally share their point of view and are sympathetic to their clients' cause, Nebraska lobbyists, like those in other states, contribute to political campaigns.

Ron Withem has seen the process from both sides. He served in the legislature from 1983 to 1997, the last four years as speaker. Now he lobbies the unicameral on behalf of the University of Nebraska. He said the most important thing lobbyists must do is have all the facts together before they go to talk with legislators. That includes background about why the issue is important in the first place and the policy rationale for making a change.

The second most important thing, Withem said, is to "just be there." Questions may arise on the spur of the moment, and it's imperative that lobbyists who want their position understood be available to answer questions promptly and thoroughly.

Herb Schimek, who has lobbied on behalf of the Nebraska State Education Association (NSEA) since 1974, said communication was the key to effective lobbying: Present the problem, the reason policy needs to change, and how that change will help solve the problem. In past years, he said, the vast majority of his lobbying was in favor of changing something. "Now we have accomplished a lot of our goals," he said, and he finds he spends the bulk of his efforts lobbying against change the NSEA fears could be detrimental to its interests.[16]

Scholars say that lobbyists who work for business and professional groups, especially, spend the majority of their time trying to keep the state from imposing more regulations or getting more involved in the group's functions. Furthermore, it is easier for special interests to block policy change than to promote it, so groups that lobby in favor of the status quo are more likely to be successful.

Walt Radcliffe, who has lobbied since 1977 and represents a long list of clients, agreed. Most people are comfortable with the status quo and afraid of change, he said. But most legislation is intended to solve problems. It may be easy for legislators to come up with prospective solutions, but they often involve unintended consequences, consequences that would adversely affect Radcliffe's clients. "So if I'm affected, I play defense," he said. [17]

Stopping legislation is his primary task, too, Paul O'Hara said. O'Hara has lobbied since 1969 for a variety of interests. Usually, he said, his relationship with a client begins because the client wants the legislature to do something. But things gradually evolve to the point that most legislative issues that would affect a client would have a detrimental impact. Then the lobbyist's job is to try to block the change, which is a lot easier to do, O'Hara said. For instance, a lobbyist can simply try to slow a bill's progress so that it ends up getting lost in the rush of business at the end of the session. [18]

Lobbyist Mary Campbell said she, too, often plays defense, although some of the groups she represents are looking for "affirmative things" like state funding for educational programs. Either way, she said, she sees her job as a form of teaching and sees herself, the teacher, as successful only if she is knowledgeable and builds credibility with the legislators she hopes to "teach." [19]

Radcliffe agreed that knowledge of the system and the people in it were invaluable "so you can ask the right questions." And Bill Mueller, a lobbyist at the unicameral since 1984, said the biggest part of the job was communication.

But being successful also has to do with building a relationship with the legislators, Mueller said. Lobbyists don't buy access, he said; they earn it over time as legislators learn a particular lobbyist can be trusted to provide honest information.

That is the common denominator for lobbyists across the nation, scholars say. Lobbyists work to build a reputation for honesty, establishing credibility with public officials so that the information the lobbyists provide will be more effective. Successful lobbyists everywhere understand exactly what Bill Mueller said. Without trust and credibility, the process simply wouldn't work. As laws have changed to tighten regulations on lobbying activities and demand disclosure of lobbyists' expenses, trust and credibility have become increasingly important. A lobbyist may be able to deceive a legislator, but it will only happen once. A legislator burned by a lobbyist will have no reason ever to listen to her in the future.

"You lie, you're gone," Herb Schimek said.

Ron Withem, now a lobbyist for the University of Nebraska, said he relied on lobbyists for good information when he served in the legislature. Generally, he said, he got forthright answers to his questions. If he didn't, that was the end of his relationship with the lobbyist.

"Trust is critical," Withem said. "On a hundred issues, you could get ninety-nine straight responses, but if there's one where you think there's deliberate shading of the truth, it's over."[20]

Kim Robak agreed. "You must be honest," said the former lieutenant governor who is now a lobbyist for the University of Nebraska. Lobbyists play a valuable role by providing information to senators, she said. Because Nebraska's nonpartisan, one-house system gives each legislator so much autonomy, the senators "have to know everything." But, of course, that's impossible. So senators rely on honest information from interest groups to help them form their opinions.[21]

Frequently, senators hear from lobbyists representing several points of view. "If there's money involved, you'll hear from both sides," former senator Don Dworak said. He added he often appreciated hearing from lobbyists, getting information on issues he knew little about.[22]

Still, Nebraska's legislature is not necessarily an easy place to lobby. Tim Hall, a senator from 1984 to 1995, said lobbyists in the unicameral have to help individual senators understand an issue in order to convince them to vote for or against it. Lobbyists can't rely on working with party leadership or conference committee members to push their ideas.[23]

Mary Campbell agreed that the unicameral system complicates matters. She said lobbyists from other states had told her they did their best work in conference committees, an option not available to Nebraska lobbyists.

Schimek heard otherwise. He said colleagues in other states told him conference committees, made up of senior legislators with little to risk, are not easily susceptible to lobbyist influence. So lobbying is probably easier in a one-house body, he said.

But Larry Ruth saw it differently. "If you're playing defense, a bicameral is better. If you lose in the house, you can go to the senate," he said. Ruth has lobbied since 1974 and has also worked in the U.S. Congress. The two-house structure gives a lobbyist more ways to stop legislation, he said.[24]

But Ruth said the nonpartisan feature in the unicameral had even more effect on lobbying than did the one-house structure. "You have forty-nine free thinkers," he said, any one of whom can become a leader. That means lobbyists must deal with all forty-nine senators instead of just a few party leaders, which makes the job a bit harder. Other lobbyists said much the same thing. So did several senators.

The late senator Jerome Warner offered an example to support that point of view. He told a reporter in 1993 that he had spoken with a lobbyist who came from Texas to work on an issue in Nebraska. "He said in other states he'd just get in a motel room to talk to the majority leader and minority leader and would be done," Warner said. "Here he had to convince twenty-five people [a majority of the forty-nine members], one at a time."[25]

On the other hand, some say the small number of senators in the unicameral makes it easier for an experienced observer to figure out who is making the decisions, Ruth said. And without party discipline keeping legislators in line and with so many stages of debate on every issue, it's easier for a lobbyist to help foster compromises, he said.

But Mueller said he thought lobbying would be easier in a strongly partisan body where a lobbyist would have to deal only with leaders of the majority party. "Here the majority is twenty-five—and it's different on every issue," he said.[26]

Dennis Baack, a former legislator and now a lobbyist, said, "This is a tough body to lobby." His job would be easier, he said, if the unicameral were a partisan body, in which case he would have to convince only a few leaders to support his position. "Now, I need twenty-five people," Baack said. "On one issue, I went to all forty-nine."[27]

Kim Robak thinks the unicameral's structure generally makes life harder for lobbyists. Norris was right about the dangers of conference committees, she said. The lobby in a bicameral, partisan system needs to influence only a handful of people—possibly only the chair of the conference committee. In the unicameral every member is autonomous, and the system is exceptionally open to public view. Lobbyists from other states are amazed at the lack of hierarchy and the openness of Nebraska's system, she said.

O'Hara agreed it would probably be easier to stop legislation if the legislature had a second house that could block action by the first. In Nebraska, he said, legislation can move very quickly, and an interested party has to pay close attention. But nonpartisanship in Nebraska may have a different effect, giving lobbyists more opportunities to influence the legislature, O'Hara said. In a partisan system, if the majority party leader says no, "you're done. Here, if the most powerful person says no, I can go to forty-eight others," he said.[28]

That may give a lobbyist more options, but it also exponentially increases the workload, and some lobbyists see that as making the job more difficult. Walt Radcliffe said lobbyists in a partisan legislature work with six to twelve people in leadership positions. Here, the number of leaders may be about the same, but they're different leaders on different issues, so lobbyists end up working with all the senators.

Ron Withem said he wasn't sure whether the unicameral's system made lobbying harder or easier. He knew it made it different. In the unicameral, "the expectations are that you'll work with all forty-nine," he said. And nonpartisanship disperses power and influence so that a lobbyist cannot concentrate on just a few leaders.

He added that stopping legislation in the unicameral is probably harder than it is in other systems. Once a bill is reported out of committee and hits the floor, "there's a sense it will pass. . . . [T]he assumption is it must be a good idea if it's on the floor."[29]

Despite the consensus that lobbing may be harder in the unicameral than elsewhere, the lobbyists interviewed expressed affection and admiration for Nebraska's system. "We have a very open, democratic system," Mueller said. "I like it. It's a good system."[30]

Campbell said she respected the openness and cleanness of Nebraska's structure and procedures and thought the nonpartisan nature meant senators decided issues on the merits rather than on the basis of party dogma. "I respect what Norris envisioned," she said.[31]

Kim Robak said her experience in state government had made her a strong supporter of the unicameral. Before becoming personally involved, she thought the legislature should be partisan, but she had changed her mind. "It works, and it should stay that way."[32]

Money vs. Citizen Voices

If citizens in America believe they have some good ideas and want to be directly involved in making public policy, the first thing they must do is get elected. Getting elected—and, possibly, elected again—requires name and message recognition, contact with potential constituents, campaign organization. And all of those things cost money.

Some of that money comes from individuals, but much of it comes from groups that believe a candidate shares or can be persuaded to share their interests. It often is funneled through lobbyists who represent those groups. Getting involved in election campaigns is different from providing information for and building relationships with legislators, and it is a big part of what has given lobbyists a bad name.

Studies indicate that special interests contribute to campaigns most often in order to show support for and elect or reelect candidates and to gain or improve access to legislators. Evidence indicates that those contributions almost never "buy" votes. Contributions seldom are responsible for changing a candidate's or official's mind. Instead, most candidates or legislators receiving the contributions are already sympathetic to the contributing groups' point of view. Campaign contributions, most lobbyists say, have an effect on issues mostly at the margins. But they do seem to improve access, the chance to make a group's case to a legislator.

Nebraska lobbyists agree. "Money is a megaphone," Radcliffe said. His voice may not be inherently any more influential than that of any other citizen, but his lobbying activities make him better known, he said.[33]

But it's not just money that is influential. Sometimes a lobbyist's ability to organize a group in support of or opposition to an issue can be equally effective. "Grassroots organizing has taken on a new life in the last fifteen years," Larry Ruth said.[34]

Mary Campbell said that organizing had become an important part of her job. She helps people she represents prepare the testimony they will give during committee hearings. They have the knowledge, she said; she simply organizes the presentations for them.

When a lobbyist works for a big organization like the Nebraska State Education Association, with members all over the state, the endorsement he can offer may be more important than a campaign contribution, Herb Schimek said. Every candidate for a unicameral seat has NSEA members in his or her district.

But Schimek gave a moderate twist to his association's impact: "[w]e don't 'deliver' an election." Nebraska voters are too independent for that, he said, although he admitted research has indicated that an endorsement from the NSEA can have a positive influence on a campaign.

Even if citizens are willing to believe that lobbyists don't use campaign contributions or endorsements to buy legislators' votes, many still resent lobbyists' access to lawmakers. They're afraid ordinary citizens will be shut out of the process. In fact, Nebraskans surveyed in 2000 overwhelmingly agreed that lobbyists have too much influence in the legislature. Eighty-one percent of those surveyed agreed with the statement; only 19 percent disagreed (see appendix 1, table 30).

Senators surveyed in 2001 responded differently to the same statement. What is interesting about their responses is the nearly even division between those who agree, at least somewhat, that interest groups have too much influence and those who disagree, at least somewhat. Perhaps the upswing among those who served in the 1970s and 1980s and agreed that the special interests were too powerful (almost 60 percent) indicates a dissatisfaction with special interests that led to passage of the Accountability and Disclosure Act in 1976 (see appendix 1, table 31).

In comments added to their 2001 surveys, some senators had harsh words for lobbyists and special interests. "Their influence is tremendous," one said. Several others said interest groups had too much clout or too much influence on legislators and legislation. A senator who served in the 1980s said he thought special interests dominated too much legislation, at the expense of "Joe Citizen."

The lobbyists and senators interviewed for this book, however, said it was not true that lobbyists' voices overwhelm the voices of individual citizens. Countless times when he was in the legislature, Withem said, he was influenced by what his constituents told him or took action on matters in which they had expressed interest. Lobbyists' voices did not drown out constituents' voices.

The fact that the unicameral holds a public hearing on every bill works against special interests, Bill Mueller said. If a hearing were not required, a lobbyist could try to convince the committee chair just to file away some issues the lobbyist would prefer never saw the light of day. Mandated hearings prevent that from happening and give the citizens an opportunity to be heard, he said.

Scholars find that public hearings can, indeed, make a difference in a legislator's thinking. The common wisdom may be that testimony at hearings seldom changes votes, but hearings let both groups' and individuals' positions become part of the record. They get media attention. They officially transmit information to legislators.

Lobbyists do have an initial advantage over citizens "off the street," Mueller said, because the lobbyist has already established a relationship with the legislators. "Once past that, though, it becomes evaluation and analysis of an issue" he said, and the citizens' voice will be part of that analysis.[35]

The individual is not squeezed out of the process, Kim Robak said. The Nebraska legislature is very accessible. Citizens can simply walk into any senator's office and make their wishes known. In addition, senators are responsive to citizens who contact them by phone or mail or testify at hearings, she said.

Current and former senators responding to the 2001 survey were in nearly unanimous agreement that, while they got ideas for bills from lobbyists, they more frequently listened to their constituents when deciding to draft a bill (see appendix 1, table 32). They also said they listened to constituents' opinions when they made policy decisions (see appendix 1, table 33).

Former senator Tim Hall said no lobbyist can defeat individual citizens who need or want something from the legislature. But, he added, "lobbyists are there to represent the people who can't be there."[36]

On some issues, Larry Ruth said, senators are particularly interested in how a proposed law applies to individual people. That's when an individual citizen can be very influential, he said. But a lobbyist generally has an advantage because senators "know me and can trust me."[37]

Paul O'Hara agreed. "I have better access," he said. "This has been my calling for a long time. It's my business to maintain relationships that give me access to plead a case." On the other hand, O'Hara said he had also seen nonprofessional citizen groups that were very patient, persistent, and effective.[38]

Dennis Baack, who said nonpartisanship made lobbying harder, also said he's glad the legislature is nonpartisan. The openness that results from the absence of parties "really works well for the citizens of the state," he said.[39]

Despite the access that lobbyists may have, they are less likely than they may have been in the past to be able to exert unethical influence, O'Hara said. The disclosure laws mean lobbyists' business is out in the open for everyone to see, and that's a good thing, he said.[40]

Other lobbyists also said they approved of the increased openness that results from the disclosure requirements. The detailed forms are a nuisance, Campbell said, "but I have no quarrel with the motivation."[41]

Legislators—even in George Norris's custom-designed legislature—do respond to lobbyists. For one thing, lobbyists provide information, support and money. But for another, lobbyists are a vehicle through which citizens' needs and desires are communicated to the legislators.

Legislators tend to be very responsive to citizens, even when those citizens may be acting through interest groups. Critics say the system is still unfair because the groups with the most money to spread their message get the biggest response, but others answer that the ground is leveled by the fact that nearly every American is represented by at least one interest group. Although populists of every era may instinctively suspect that all special interests are elite interests, those who face the facts of lobbying in the early years of the twenty-first century must realize the suspicion is at least partly unfounded.

For one thing, the definition of special interests has changed, at least somewhat. "If we [citizens] care about it, it's special," lobbyist Mary Campbell said. No longer are special interests equivalent simply to big business and big money. Today nearly every citizen is, formally or informally, represented by some special interest group.

Doug Kristensen, speaker of the unicameral from 1998 to 2002, admitted George Norris hated special interests and lobbyists. But Kristensen said it was unfair to measure lobbyists' influence by the amount of money they spent.

Kristensen said lobbying should not be done behind the public's back, and he praised the accountability and disclosure laws. "We must be open to scrutiny," he said. But with transactions between lobbyists and legislators out in public view, he said, it is simply impossible for a lobbyist to contribute to a legislator's campaign and then expect the legislator to repay him or her with votes.[42]

Echoing scholars of politics, his fellow senators and many Nebraska lobbyists, Kristensen said the lobby helps in two ways to solve a problem most everyone experiences in an increasingly busy world. First, the lobbyists provide valuable information to legislators too swamped with issues to be able to research everything on their own. Second, they promote citizens' interests when citizens don't have time to do that themselves.

Those sentiments may hold true in every state, but Nebraska lobbyists work with a unique system. The house that George Norris built grants special interests both advantages and disadvantages, depending on one's point of view. The unicameral is neither a heaven for lobbyists nor a hell. It's just different.

7 / Promises Fulfilled?

Has the Unicameral Done
What the Founders Said It Would?

The basics have not changed. Just as it was in 1937, Nebraska's legislature is a small, nonpartisan, one-house body. A majority of Nebraskans have never seriously considered changing that structure. In fact, many are proud and fond of their legislature. As the *Lincoln Journal Star* editorialized in 1995, "Nebraskans like what they've got in the state Capitol, a unique state government system that works well."

But sometimes familiarity breeds contentment. And in most cases, it's easier simply to live with the institution one has than to go through the nearly Herculean efforts required to change it. To apply the philosophy of the pop song, if you can't be with the one you love, love the one you're with.

That wasn't good enough for George Norris, John Senning, John Norton, and the others who joined them to reform and refashion Nebraska's state government in the 1930s. They were convinced the system in place was failing the people of the state, and they were willing to go to enormous lengths to improve it. What they accomplished was not just incremental change, not just change at the margins, but revolutionary change to the legislature and, by association, to the state government.

Norris and his fellow travelers knew that institutions matter, that how a governmental body is structured and the way it functions makes a difference in what it can and will produce. Political democracy, according to this point of view, depends not only on economic and social conditions, not only on the actors on the political stage, not only on the voters serving as principals to the actors' agent, but also on the design of the political institutions themselves. Instead of assuming political action is simply choice based on individual values or expectations, this approach assumes political action is the fulfillment of institutionalized duties and obligations.[1]

The unicameralists understood, long before the idea became a recognized political theory, that the forms and institutions of a legislature have a direct bearing on the performance of that legislature. They believed that if they could improve the institution, they could also improve its work.

This book does not attempt to examine Nebraska's laws and policies to determine whether they are "better" having been produced by the unicameral than they would be if they had been produced by a traditional legislature. But it does attempt to discover whether the institutional structure put in place by the people's 1934 vote has lived up to the broad promises its promoters made on its behalf: openness, accountability, accessibility, efficiency, egalitarianism, representativeness, professionalization, and most fundamentally, responsiveness to the needs of the "real" people.

Nowhere to Hide

You can lead a constituent to his legislature, but you can't make him pay attention. A 1978 survey indicated about two-thirds of Nebraskans knew their state had a one-house legislature, but only about 20 percent realized it was nonpartisan. Only one-third could name their own legislator.[2] Twenty-five years later, the figures probably have not improved.

Even had they known in 1937 that Nebraskans would be woefully ignorant about their state government a few decades later, it probably would not have deterred the unicameralists from designing an open, accountable, and accessible system. If citizens failed to take advantage of that openness, the framers would have considered it regrettable. But it was government's obligation, not the people's obligation, that Norris and his friends were concerned about.

The 1971 Citizens' Conference survey found the unicameral exceptionally open. Indications are that the situation still holds. Senators, both current and former, are convinced the legislature is wide open to public scrutiny. They attribute the openness to the institution's structure and rules.

Senators cited the legislature's small size, which makes the body's collective actions and each individual legislator's activities much easier to track than they might be in a larger group. And just as Norris had hoped, the small size means all legislators are involved in most every decision. Each senator's vote counts for something, and constituents can see their representative's impact on legislative decisions.

Unicameralism also improves openness, senators said. In a one-house body, "there's no place to hide," former senator Scott Moore said. The unicameral cannot pass a difficult decision along to the other house or blame the other house for its actions when no other house exists. And citizens can watch all the action in one place; so can senators. "You can be *in* the room where we're making law," Senator Dave Landis said. With no second house and no conference committees, law is made in only one place: the unicameral chamber.

The absence of conference committees is another big plus, senators said, just as Norris promised it would be. Neither citizens nor senators need be surprised by legislation that emerges from the secret recesses of the conference committee.

Nor can parties dictate legislative processes or outcomes. Senators in the nonpartisan unicameral are responsible not to party bosses but to the people, many said. Those who believe party labels would improve citizens' vote choice and make legislators more accountable were in the minority among those surveyed and interviewed.

Furthermore, most citizens responding to the Bureau of Sociological Research (NASIS) survey said the absence of party labels on legislative ballots did not make their vote choices harder. The fact that only about 15 percent of those who vote for president fail to vote for a nonpartisan legislative candidate seems to reinforce the survey respondents' assertion.

Theory aside, Nebraskans seem content with their nonpartisan legislature. Only 22 percent of the citizens and 17 percent of the senators surveyed indicated they would like to see the state return to a partisan body.

Within the structure designed to be open to public view, the legislature has fashioned rules that also promote openness and accountability. The requirement that every bill receive a public hearing in committee may be at the very top of the list. Senators may or may not hear a lot of new information at the hearings, but the sessions do meet another need: allowing citizens access and input and promoting coverage of the issues by the media. And that coverage is likely to focus on the issues and impacts involved rather than on party rivalry and jockeying for advantage as is often the case in coverage of partisan bodies.

The mandatory hearings are truly open to all. In fact, people don't even have to sign up ahead of time; they can simply wander in from the hall and get in line. That's about as accessible as it gets.

Other factors that promote openness include absence of a limit on the number of bills a senator may introduce. Critics say that means too much legislation is placed before senators each year, but defenders say it means issues are more likely to be considered via normal procedures—with public hearings—than to pop up as amendments to other bills and without a hearing.

In addition, records of the legislature's proceedings have been available to the public since the unicameral's 1937 session. Since 1971, citizens have been able to watch floor proceedings on cable television. Now they can keep track of bills on the unicameral's Web site.

On balance, the unicameral seems to have preserved and even expanded the provisions that Norris said would make it open, accountable, and accessible. As U.S. representative Doug Bereuter said, "George Norris would not be disappointed."

Getting the Job Done—Together

Equality. It is at the base of the democratic credo. Everyone was created equal, democrats believe, and everyone should have an equal shot at everything—including equal participation in making public policy. For most citizens, that equal participation comes at the polls. For legislators, it comes in structures and rules that assure no elected representatives will be left out of the decision-making process.

That was another of the unicameralists' goals when they designed the new institution. Removing a second house and the accompanying conference committees, and eliminating party structure and discipline, they believed, would put all legislators on an equal footing. That way all the people's voices would be heard through elected representatives.

Of course, unicameralism and nonpartisanship upset what had become familiar and accepted decision-making procedures: party leadership, seniority influence, conference committee decisions. In their place, the unicameral promoters installed nothing but a hope and belief that right-minded people would get together to make right-minded policy choices.

Observers and senators provide a number of explanations for just how senators do get together and form coalitions. Geography is one suggestion. Urban versus rural is a variation on that theme. But even senators who recognize a rural-urban split said that, unlike party discipline, it is not present on a formalized and ongoing basis.

Many senators said coalitions were formed around communities of shared interest. Many said coalitions changed with the issues. Senators said the fact that coalitions fluctuated meant senators spent a lot of time building coalitions. That requires knowledge of the subject and personal skills that enable senators to work with each other. It also results in some vote trading, senators admitted.

But former senator Scott Moore said it was a different kind of vote trading than would occur in a partisan setting where tactical strategy may take precedence over the issues themselves. In Nebraska, he said, coalitions are based not on trading favors but on where senators fall out on the issue at hand.

Both citizens and senators surveyed resoundingly agreed that state senators get more done without party labels. Coalitions do form, legislation does get advanced, and bills do become law—all without the hierarchy that partisan organization imposes.

However, the unicameral recently has made its system at least somewhat more hierarchical by strengthening the speaker's position. Hard-fought changes in the rules have given the speaker increased influence over the legislative calendar and over its debates: what topics are discussed and for how long. That is real power, Moore said.

But former speakers Dennis Baack and Ron Withem said the position still wasn't all that powerful. Baack said the speaker still had to build consensus around the agenda. Withem said taking care not to put too much power in a few people's hands was all the more important in a unicameral body without the check of a second house.

Without some authority granted to the speaker, though, floor debate can be dominated by one or two strong personalities who know how to use the rules to their advantage. The attempt to find a solution to that problem is behind at least some of the legislature's moves to increase the speaker's power, although senators noted that speakers have sometimes been reluctant to use the power granted them.

Despite his growing influence in the unicameral, the speaker in Nebraska is still less powerful than he would be in a partisan setting, where his or her party would dominate legislative action. For instance, in Nebraska the speaker may now have the authority to put a stop to debate and take the legislature to its next subject, but he still cannot stop debate and call for a vote on the matter at hand as his counterparts in most other states could do.

After the speaker's position, committee chairmanships are considered to be the most powerful slots in the unicameral, conferring agenda-setting authority and leadership within the committee. But again, the positions do not automatically bring power. Senators said whatever authority committee chairs may have stems from their opportunity to develop expertise on specific issues and their ability to work with their committee members. An enthusiastic 88 percent of those current and former senators responding to the 2001 survey said committee chairs helped the legislature achieve its goals, an acknowledgement that the positions do carry some weight.

In general, senators said, the unicameral today does not offer many more leadership opportunities than it did in the past. It remains generally nonhierarchical, a place where even junior members are expected to participate.

And much of the most important participation is still expected to happen on the legislative floor. Despite the division-of-labor benefits offered by a strong committee system, some senators said the unicameral's committees are relatively weak. And the senators surveyed were almost evenly divided about the importance of committees' work.

They were also divided as to the importance of a senator's specializing in some particular subject area. Although senators' comments and survey responses indicated that legislators with expertise are respected and looked to as informal leaders, only about 48 percent of the survey respondents agreed that members of the unicameral should specialize—the logical way to gain expertise. Perhaps the results indicate an innate recognition that the floor is still the place where the action is and that senators need to be generalists who can be particularly effective there.

The power in the speaker's position today may be a far cry from what the original unicameralists intended, but it is also a far cry from the power the speaker wields in most partisan, two-house bodies. The unicameral has recognized the benefits of granting leadership to its presiding officer and its committee chairs, benefits that allow the body to move forward toward its policy goals. But in general, the legislators continue to share and practice the unicameral framers' belief in equality, even if it sometimes comes at the expense of efficiency.

Representativeness in Question, Independence Established, Professionalization in Progress

Norris wanted the unicameral to be small for several reasons. First, he believed larger geographic districts would actually be more representative because they would encompass a variety of interests, giving legislators a broader focus than they might otherwise have. Second, Norris wanted every member to be able to participate in all the decision making. It was a cornerstone of the populist need to assure that all voices would be heard in the legislature.

In accord with federal mandates, the unicameral's districts today are drawn on the basis of population. On one level, that would seem to make them representative since it assures that the groups of constituents represented by each legislator are fairly equal in size. Surely that is more fair than giving one small group the same voice in the legislature that a large group has.

But on another level, Nebraska's geography and demography raise questions about the legislature's representativeness. Yes, it is true that the vast majority of the population is concentrated in a vast minority of the state's area. But many of those who are spread out across the western majority of the state believe their interests and voices are being lost in the din created by all the folks clustered in the eastern part of the state.

It could be that increasing the size of the body is the only way to respond to the concerns of those who believe they are being left out. More and smaller districts would increase the number of representatives from the urban areas too, of course, but they might give the rural areas enough additional representatives to bring them closer to some kind of critical legislative mass that would make them feel more included.

Thus far, the legislature has taken no action on the matter. A proposal to increase the number of members beyond the fifty allowed in the constitution has been introduced twice but died in committee both years.

Internally, the legislature continues to offer a great deal of opportunity for all representatives to participate fully in the legislative process. The speaker's power to control debate has been strengthened, and the result has been some restriction of completely freewheeling debate and discussion. But it has also made it more difficult for a single senator or two to dominate the process to the detriment of others who may want to be involved. Senators said the legislature remains a democratic body where anyone who wants to work hard can be part of the process.

Citizens seem reasonably content with their legislature's representativeness. About three-fourths agreed the unicameral does a good job of representing citizens' diverse interests. About the same proportion of senators agreed.

The unicameral has also remained representative of the people in terms of its relationship with the governor. The Nebraska legislature maintains a healthy independence from gubernatorial domination, probably in large part because of its nonpartisan nature. The governor cannot work through his political party to influence the legislature in favor of his programs. As a result of its independence, the legislative branch is an effective foil to the executive branch and a stronger representative of the varied interests of Nebraskans.

One reason the legislature has been able to continue as a powerful separate branch of government is that it has gained staff and resources over the decades. Without access to the information generated by its own research office and without staff assistance to committees and individual senators, the unicameral would be more dependent on the governor and on lobbyists for information and guidance.

Some critics don't like the idea of an elected official depending on hired aides for information and opinion, but in the complicated context of today's legislature, no elected officials have time to research everything for themselves—if they ever did. Senators responding to the 2001 survey said they do get ideas for bills from legislative staff, but the majority said they do not rely too heavily on staff for information or opinions.

Staff are not paid well, though—and neither are the senators themselves. George Norris's goal in that regard simply has not been met. It's true that state legislators across the nation generally are not paid well, but Norris had hoped the unicameral would offer senators a living wage so they would not have to depend on other employment to survive. It hasn't happened.

Legislative salaries are still set in the state's constitution, which means any increases must be approved by a vote of the people, a vote that has been very difficult to come by. Salaries for senators have stayed at twelve thousand dollars per year since 1988. Only two other states pay their legislators less than that.

Norris and his compatriots respected expertise and its role in good government and tried to provide the legislature with staff resources to help build that expertise. Efforts to build on what the framers started languished until the 1960s and 1970s but have come a long way since then. As long as the legislators continue to examine and respond to changing needs for services from professional staff, they will have lived up to at least some of the goals of professionalization.

It's up to the voters of the state to live up to the other part: adequate pay for legislators. How to accomplish that is beyond the scope of this book.

Lobbying: It's Different

The men who designed the unicameral believed that its simplified and open structure would go a long way toward neutralizing the influence of all lobbyists but, especially, corrupt lobbyists. Cutting the number of legislators, eliminating a second house, and above all, the despicable conference committees and getting rid of partisanship would make lobbyists' job much harder, the unicameralists believed. Special interest representatives who wanted to influence legislation in the new unicameral would have to work in the full light of day, unable to use the confusing apparatus of the partisan bicameral to hide their dealings with legislators.

Lobbyists disagree about whether their job is harder or easier in the unicameral, and those who do think it's harder disagree on the reason. Some said it was the single house and absence of conference committees. Others said it was the absence of party discipline. Harder or easier, though, lobbying in the Nebraska legislature is different from lobbying in other state capitols, lobbyists said.

The lobbyists interviewed for this book, considered some of the most successful in the state, all said they were most effective when they could provide solid information to legislators, information the senators find credible because it comes from someone they know and can trust. Trust is something lobbyists earn by building relationships with senators over time, they said, and it pays off in better access than an ordinary citizen may have.

George Norris wouldn't like to hear that. Both lobbyists and senators stressed that citizens also have a lot of access to their legislature, but the lobbyists are a known quantity, and legislators will probably give ear to someone they know before they listen to what a relative stranger has to say. Norris still wouldn't like it.

Nebraska citizens don't like it, either. More than two-thirds of those who responded to the 2000 survey agreed the unicameral is too heavily influenced by special interests when making decisions.

Even many of the legislators themselves think the body is too much influenced by lobbyists. About 48 percent agreed with that statement as it appeared on the 2001 survey.

When it comes to providing information to persuade senators to a certain point of view, most citizens are at a disadvantage because they don't usually have the depth of knowledge a lobbyist makes a point to have. On the other hand, senators surveyed in 2001 said they are prompted to draft a bill far more often by information they receive from citizens than from lobbyists. Seventy-one percent of the respondents said citizens are a frequent source of information in that case; only 27 percent said the same of lobbyists.

Even if the unicameral's structure has not militated against lobbyists as successfully as Norris had hoped, the legislature has taken other steps to control what they know is a source of suspicion and irritation for many citizens. For one thing, the senators removed the lobbyists from the legislative chamber in 1965. Granted, it took almost thirty years to accomplish that, but legislators eventually grew to understand how shady the previous arrangement looked to a disapproving citizenry.

The legislature took things several steps farther with the Accountability and Disclosure Act in 1976. The act put more teeth into what the law already required of lobbyists, and several changes since then have continued the trend. The media and the general public have full access to all the records that disclose who is giving how much to whom.

That kind of openness is something Norris would applaud. It is unlikely he thought lobbying could or should be banished in the unicameral. But he was adamant that special interests plead their case in the open. By and large, that is how things work in Nebraska.

Promises Fulfilled?

If George Norris, John Senning, John Norton, and their fellow unicameralists had had godlike powers, they would have designed the perfect political institution, one that would serve all the highest and best interests of the citizens. They would have used all their special knowledge and special abilities and would have created a perfect structure.

And then they would have had to watch as it was peopled with human beings. So much for perfection.

But, of course, George Norris, John Senning, John Norton, and the others did not have godlike powers. They may have created a very good institution, but it was not perfect. Furthermore, it still had to be occupied and implemented by human beings, who are always imperfect.

Looking at the unicameral after sixty-five years, it would easy to be cynical about whether it has lived up to its promises. Even the most politically naive observer understands that senators talk business in the hall, over lunch, in informal meetings. Not all decisions are made in public hearings or public sessions on the floor.

Even a naive observer realizes that not all legislators are equal, that some snatch power and use it to their own ends—not necessarily to enrich themselves personally but at least to achieve their political goals.

The observer knows, too, that representativeness by the letter of the law may not be representativeness in the spirit of the law. The observer knows professionalization can sometimes be just another word for elitism. And she knows that lobbyists' special relationships with senators can be repugnant even when they're not illegal.

It would be easy to say, then, that the unicameral has not lived up to its promises, that it is nowhere near as open and accountable, as egalitarian and efficient, as representative or professional as its founders said it would be. But that would be to ignore the evidence.

The evidence suggests that, by and large, the institution that is the Nebraska legislature continues to do what it was intended to do. The system is open to citizens, to media, and to the most junior legislator. Because the system is accessible, the legislators can be held to account by anyone who cares to pay even casual attention.

The system remains largely nonhierarchical, despite the additional authority granted the speaker in the last fifteen years. The speaker in Nebraska looks almost powerless compared with speakers in partisan bodies.

The system works with reasonable efficiency. The legislators have tinkered with their rules and procedures over the years, trying to increase their efficiency while remaining true to their other values: openness and equality. Thus far, they seem to have maintained a reasonable balance.

The unicameral remains representative on the most basic level, although the legislators and the citizens will have to think hard about ways to be sure rural citizens do not become a casualty of shifting demographics.

And both the system itself and the laws devised by legislators within the system do a reasonably good job of assuring that lobbyists will not become a shadow legislature. The legislature's level of professionalization helps with that, too.

When the first session of the new unicameral met on January 5, 1937, George Norris addressed the legislators gathered to undertake the legislative experiment he had designed. "You have an opportunity to render a service to your fellow citizens that no other Legislature has ever had," he said.

Were the ardent progressive to be asked today how well he thinks the experiment has worked, Norris would probably say, "Just as I thought it would."

Appendix 1

Survey Results

Table 1. 2001 legislators survey
Nebraska should return to a two-house legislature.

	1950s	1960s	1970s	1980s	1990s	All years
Agree strongly			4.0%	8.0%	3.40%	4%
Agree somewhat			4.0%	2.5%	6.90%	5%
Neutral		11%	11.5%	2.5%	13.80%	8%
Disagree somewhat		22%	11.5%	5.0%	20.70%	13%
Disagree strongly	100%	67%	69.0%	82.0%	55.20%	70%

Table 2. 2000 citizens survey
Nebraska should return to a two-house legislature.

Agree strongly	7%
Agree somewhat	20%
Neutral	3%
Disagree somewhat	28%
Disagree strongly	30%
Don't know	12%

Table 3. 2000 citizens survey
*I have difficulty making voting decisions
without knowing the candidate's party label.*

Agree strongly	10%
Agree somewhat	20%
Neutral	2%
Disagree somewhat	35%
Disagree strongly	30%
Don't know	3%

Table 4. 2001 legislators survey
Nebraska should return to a partisan legislature.

	1950s	1960s	1970s	1980s	1990s	All years
Agree strongly			12%	8%	7%	7.0%
Agree somewhat	14%	11%	12%	8%	3%	10.0%
Neutral				5%	14%	6.5%
Disagree somewhat		22%	24%	8%	10%	11.5%
Disagree strongly	86%	67%	52%	71%	66%	65.0%

Table 5. 2000 citizens survey
We should alter the current system
and adopt party labels for state senators.

Agree strongly	5%
Agree somewhat	17%
Neutral	3%
Disagree somewhat	35%
Disagree strongly	33%
Don't know	7%

Table 6. 2001 legislators survey
The unicameral's procedures make every member's record clearly available to the citizens.

	1950s	1960s	1970s	1980s	1990s	All years
Agree strongly	62.5%	56%	65%	51%	45%	53%
Agree somewhat	12.5%	33%	31%	24%	45%	33%
Neutral	12.5%	11%		3%		3%
Disagree somewhat	12.5%			19%	7%	8%
Disagree strongly				3%	3%	3%

Table 7. 2001 legislators survey
Even though the unicameral is officially nonpartisan, senators' party affiliation often makes a difference in the way they vote.

	Republicans	Democrats	Independent	Other	Total
Agree strongly	8.8%	13.0%	20.0%	0.0%	10.6%
Agree somewhat	67.6%	43.5%	20.0%	66.7%	56.1%
Neutral	5.9%	8.7%	0.0%	0.0%	6.5%
Disagree somewhat	14.7%	21.7%	20.0%	0.0%	17.9%
Disagree strongly	2.9%	13.0%	40.0%	33.7%	8.9%
Number responding	68	46	5	3	122

Table 8. 2001 legislators survey
Friendly relationships among members of the legislature are important.

Agree strongly	55.2%
Agree somewhat	36.8%
Neutral	4.0%
Disagree somewhat	3.2%
Disagree strongly	0.8%

Table 9. 2001 legislators survey
Members of the legislature trade votes.

	1950s	1960s	1970s	1980s	1990s	All years
Agree strongly	28.6%	11.1%	3.8%	7.9%	3.4%	7.3%
Agree somewhat	0.0%	33.3%	46.2%	34.2%	31.0%	35.5%
Neutral	28.6%	11.1%	15.4%	5.3%	13.8%	12.1%
Disagree somewhat	42.9%	22.2%	30.8%	42.1%	37.9%	35.5%
Disagree strongly	0.0%	22.2%	3.8%	10.5%	13.8%	9.7%

Table 10. 2001 legislators survey
State senators get more done without party labels.

Agree strongly	41.8%
Agree somewhat	28.7%
Neutral	11.5%
Disagree somewhat	11.5%
Disagree strongly	6.6%

Table 11. 2000 citizens survey
State senators get more done without party labels.

Agree strongly	23.0%
Agree somewhat	46.0%
Neutral	4.0%
Disagree somewhat	14.0%
Disagree strongly	5.0%
Don't know	8.0%

Table 12. 2001 legislators survey
First person to whom call would be returned.

	1950s	1960s	1970s	1980s	1990s	All years
First call speaker	33.3%	37.5%	63.6%	57.9%	73.1%	60.0%
First call chair	16.7%	50.0%	23.8%	23.7%	19.2%	23.7%
First call sr. colleague	50.0%	12.5%	9.5%	15.8%	7.7%	14.0%
First call jr. colleague	0.0%	0.0%	9.5%	2.7%	0.0%	3.5%

Table 13. 2001 legislators survey
*The seniority (years of service in the unicameral) of a member
is an important indicator of that senator's political influence.*

Agree strongly	9.6%
Agree somewhat	46.4%
Neutral	10.4%
Disagree somewhat	21.6%
Disagree strongly	12.0%

Table 14. 2001 legislators survey

The rules of the legislature allow members
without seniority too much influence.

Agree strongly	0.8%
Agree somewhat	2.4%
Neutral	12.0%
Disagree somewhat	52.8%
Disagree strongly	32.0%

Table 15. 2001 legislators survey

More senior members are more realistic about
the legislative process than less senior members.

Agree strongly	28.0%
Agree somewhat	43.2%
Neutral	14.4%
Disagree somewhat	12.0%
Disagree strongly	2.4%

Table 16. 2001 legislators survey

Less senior members should accept guidance from more senior members.

	0-4 yrs	5-8 yrs	9-12 yrs	13-16 yrs	17 yrs +	Total
Agree strongly	0.0%	8.8%	0.0%	8.3%	33.3%	4.0%
Agree somewhat	56.9%	47.1%	50.0%	58.3%	0.0%	51.6%
Neutral	17.6%	14.7%	35.0%	25.0%	0.0%	20.2%
Disagree somewhat	19.6%	29.4%	5.0%	0.0%	66.7%	19.4%
Disagree strongly	5.9%	0.0%	10.0%	8.3%	0.0%	4.8%

Table 17. 2001 legislators survey

The important work of the state senator
is done in committees.

Agree strongly	7.2%
Agree somewhat	39.2%
Neutral	12.0%
Disagree somewhat	33.6%
Disagree strongly	8.0%

Table 18. 2001 legislators survey

More of the legislature's work should be
done in committees instead of on the floor.

Agree strongly	5.6%
Agree somewhat	31.2%
Neutral	19.2%
Disagree somewhat	34.4%
Disagree strongly	9.6%

Table 19. 2001 legislators survey
Members of the Nebraska legislature
should specialize.

Agree strongly	1.6%
Agree somewhat	36.8%
Neutral	20.0%
Disagree somewhat	30.4%
Disagree strongly	11.2%

Table 20. 2001 legislators survey
Committee recommendations are usually
followed by the body as a whole.

Agree strongly	8.1%
Agree somewhat	69.4%
Neutral	9.7%
Disagree somewhat	12.9%
Disagree strongly	0.0%

Table 21. 2001 legislators survey
Committee chairs help the body to
achieve legislative goals.

Agree strongly	36.0%
Agree somewhat	52.0%
Neutral	6.4%
Disagree somewhat	5.6%
Disagree strongly	0.0%

Table 22. 2001 legislators survey
Just a few members of the unicameral
have all the power.

Agree strongly	4.0%
Agree somewhat	28.2%
Neutral	5.6%
Disagree somewhat	45.2%
Disagree strongly	16.9%

Table 23. 2000 citizens survey
Just a few members of the Nebraska
unicameral have all the power.

Agree strongly	8.0%
Agree somewhat	35.0%
Neutral	3.0%
Disagree somewhat	32.0%
Disagree strongly	8.0%
Don't know	14.0%

Table 24. 2000 citizens survey
The unicameral does a good job of
representing the diverse interests of Nebraska.

Agree strongly	12%
Agree somewhat	64%
Neutral	2%
Disagree somewhat	11%
Disagree strongly	3%
Don't know	8%

Table 25. 2001 legislators survey
The unicameral does a good job of
representing the diverse interests of Nebraska.

Agree strongly	35.5%
Agree somewhat	41.1%
Neutral	9.7%
Disagree somewhat	11.3%
Disagree strongly	2.4%

Table 26. Governors survey
Partisan structure in the legislature would
make it easier for governors to accomplish their goals.

Agree strongly	1
Agree somewhat	3
Neutral	2
Disagree somewhat	1
Disagree strongly	1

Table 27. 2001 legislators survey
Senators rely too much on their staff or the legislature's staff for information and opinion.

	1950s	1960s	1970s	1980s	1990s	All years
Agree strongly	14.3%	11.1%	0.0%	0.0%	0.0%	1.7%
Agree somewhat	42.9%	11.1%	32.0%	27.0%	17.2%	24.0%
Neutral	42.0%	11.1%	16.0%	18.9%	13.8%	19.0%
Disagree somewhat	0.0%	44.4%	36.0%	35.1%	48.3%	37.2%
Disagree strongly	0.0%	22.2%	16.0%	18.9%	20.7%	18.2%

Table 28. 2001 legislators survey
How often do you use the Legislative Council's
research division when deciding to draft a bill?

Frequent source of info	21.4%
Sometime source of info	50.9%
Infrequent source of info	19.6%
Rarely used source of info	8.0%

Table 29. 2001 legislators survey
Nebraska should increase state senators' salaries.

	1950s	1960s	1970s	1980s	1990s	All years
Agree strongly	25.0%	22.2%	46.2%	44.7%	53.6%	47.6%
Agree somewhat	37.5%	22.2%	26.9%	42.1%	28.6%	30.6%
Neutral	25.0%	22.2%	7.7%	10.5%	10.7%	11.3%
Disagree somewhat	12.5%	22.2%	15.4%	0.0%	7.1%	8.1%
Disagree strongly	0.0%	11.1%	3.8%	2.6%	0.0%	2.4%

Table 30. 2000 citizens survey
The unicameral is too heavily influenced
by special interests when making decisions.

Agree strongly	23.0%
Agree somewhat	45.0%
Neutral	3.0%
Disagree somewhat	17.0%
Disagree strongly	2.0%
Don't know	10.0%

Table 31. 2001 legislators survey
The unicameral is too heavily influenced by interest groups when making decisions.

	1950s	1960s	1970s	1980s	1990s	All years
Agree strongly	12.5%	0.0%	23.1%	10.8%	6.9%	12.1%
Agree somewhat	37.5%	22.2%	34.6%	48.6%	31.0%	36.3%
Neutral	0.0%	11.1%	3.8%	13.5%	6.9%	7.3%
Disagree somewhat	25.0%	44.4%	30.8%	18.9%	44.8%	33.1%
Disagree strongly	25.0%	22.2%	7.7%	8.1%	10.3%	11.3%

Table 32. 2001 legislators survey
Please indicate how frequently you use the following sources of information when deciding to draft a bill.

CONSTITUENTS		LOBBYIST	
Frequent source of info	71.7%	Frequent source of info	27.4%
Sometimes source of info	24.2%	Sometimes source of info	53.1%
Infrequent source of info	3.3%	Infrequent source of info	15.0%
Rarely used source of info	0.8%	Rarely used source of info	4.4%

Table 33. 2001 legislative survey
As a state senator, I listen(ed) to my constituents' opinions
and ideas when making my decisions about laws and policy.

Agree strongly	52.8%
Agree somewhat	41.5%
Neutral	4.1%
Disagree somewhat	1.6%
Disagree strongly	0.0%

Appendix 2

George Norris's 1923 Article in the New York Times

This article appeared in the *New York Times* January 28, 1923

ONE BRANCH LEGISLATURE FOR
STATE WOULD IMPROVE RESULTS
Nebraska Senator Presents Advantages to Be Gained
by Doing Away With Bi-Cameral Body—Contends That
Long Delays and Corrupt Influences Would Be Removed
   GEORGE W. NORRIS, U.S. Senator from Nebraska

When our forefathers adopted the Constitution of the United States they provided that the legislative function of government should be composed of a House of Representatives and of a Senate. It would be interesting, but it is not material in the present discussion, to give the reasons why this was done. It is sufficient to know that the Federal Government in this respect was accepted as a model and was followed by all of the States of the Union. The experience of more than one hundred years has demonstrated that the two-branch Legislature at least, so far as the various States are concerned, has been very unsatisfactory in its results. One of the fundamental requisites that should always exist in any Legislature where universal suffrage prevails is to enable the citizen to properly place responsibility, either for the success or the failure of legislation.

In every Legislature composed of two branches, the finishing touches and the only thing that emerges from the conference is the final agreement. The individual legislator must then vote upon a conference report without any opportunity of expressing, by his vote, his opposition to anything that the bill in this form contains. The citizen is deprived entirely of an opportunity to pass a just and fair judgment upon the result. In conference, provisions taken out, where an entirely different result would be obtained if the action took place in the open, where a record could be had upon all provisions of the bill.

A one-branch Legislature would obviate all those difficulties. There would be no way for any member of the Legislature to conceal his opposition upon any legislative propositions that come before the body. The citizen would be able to absolutely and without difficulty place responsibility where it properly belonged for every act of the Legislature.

It is quite a common thing in a double-branch Legislature for one house to shift responsibility for failure upon the other house. Bills on practically all legislation are made by conference committees. A bill that has passed one branch and then been amended in another one must go to conference for adjustment of the differences between the two houses. These conference committees in all two-branch Legislatures are absolutely essential in order that anything may be accomplished. Experience has shown that it is within the privacy of the conference committee room that jokers get into legislation, and that provisions of laws demanded even by a majority of both branches of the Legislature are sometimes not included in the finished product.

When a bill is in conference it is necessary that compromises be made in order to secure any legislation. It very often happens that the most important features of legislation are put into the bills while they are being thus considered. Members of Conference Committees are often compelled to surrender on important items where no surrender would be even demanded if consideration of the legislation were in the open where a public record could be had of the proceedings. When the bill emerges from conference it is not then subject to amendment. It must be accepted or rejected as a whole. The conference is held in secret. There is no record vote on any proposition decided at the conference.

Chance to Cover Up Tracks
The public is excluded from the deliberations often passed when it is known by those who pass them that the bill is to be killed in the other House, and in like manner, bills coming from the other House are pigeonholed in the first one. Responsibility for failure is thus divided, enabling participants in the fraudulent procedure to conceal their own records and to cover up their own tracks. In a one-branch Legislature it would be impossible to thus obscure the record by parliamentary tactics and proceedings that make it impossible for the ordinary citizen to properly judge the record of his Representative.

One of the evils of our Legislatures is that they are entirely too large. In theory a large Legislature is supposed to give a larger and more complete representation of the entire citizenship. In practice, however, it has been demonstrated that a large membership is detrimental to real representation. We should avoid either extreme. A large body of men, in order to accomplish any legislative results, must of necessity surrender many of the individual rights and prerogatives of its members. Members must deny themselves the right in large bodies, on important matters of legislation, to even offer amendments. They must surrender to committees the right to determine procedure. The very size of the bodies sometimes makes it impossible for the necessary and proper deliberation and discussion that should always take place before legislation is enacted.

The House of Representatives in Washington illustrates this point. The members of the House are, as a class, both able and conscientious. They are moved by the highest of motives and are a picked body of fine men. And yet, any conservative critic will say that their work is not only incomplete but is very unsatisfactory and often ill—considered. This result comes about entirely and solely from the huge size of the body. In order to accomplish anything whatever they are often compelled in the most vital kind of legislation, by special rule and otherwise, to deprive themselves of the right to offer amendments and of the right to debate and thus point out errors or suggest corrections, and the result is not only disappointing, but it brings about all kinds of errors in the final enactment. Members are thus often compelled to vote for bills containing provisions that in their own judgment are absolutely wrong, in order to get what in their judgment is right and proper; or they are compelled to vote against bills because in their judgment the evil contained is greater than the good.

It is true, of course, that in the final passage of a bill through any Legislature, members in deciding how they shall vote must weigh the good and the bad and vote as their judgment dictates; but in a smaller body of men there would always have been an opportunity to offer amendments, striking out bad provisions, and to offer amendments suggesting good ones, so that the record of the member upon all the provisions of the bill would clearly appear. If this right were not denied it would mean better legislation and enable members to keep a correct record of their won positions. It would often occur that if the right to debate and the right to offer amendments had not been denied, bad provisions would be excluded on a roll call and good provisions put in.

The exact number that should be contained in the membership of a State legislative body would undoubtedly vary somewhat with the different States. Having in mind a State about like Nebraska I should say that the membership should not exceed twenty or thirty. This would make it absolutely impossible for any member to cover up his record in any respect or to shift any responsibility. It would enable a citizen to be fully informed upon the record of his representative without the necessity of doing anything more than to read the news while the Legislature was in session. Punishment could be meted out to those who deserved it, and the faithful could be properly rewarded. It would give to the State a business administration. It would result in full discussion;

complete deliberation, and the highest possible wisdom in the enactment of laws.

Salaries of Legislators Should Be Increased

A State having the kind of Legislature I have outlined would be able to increase the salaries of its members: Under existing conditions it is a well-known fact that it is extremely difficult in many instances to secure good men in State Legislatures, because the ordinary individual cannot afford to leave his business and expend the time necessary to attend the sessions of the Legislature. The result is that we not only get a less desirable membership, but the good legislator, who is induced to sacrifice himself, must give the greater portion of his time to his private business and never becomes really posted on the propositions that come before the Legislature.

Existing conditions afford inducements to the dishonest and corrupt, who avail themselves of the opportunity to become candidates for the Legislature with a view of recouping themselves after election by their official conduct. There are, of course, many honest and able men who are members of the State Legislatures. Undoubtedly, a large majority of them could be thus designated; but it is oft times much easier to deceive the honest man that it is to buy the corrupt man. The ordinary farmer or business man who goes to the Legislature with the very best of intentions is often deceived by lobbyists and evil influences. He is in attendance upon the Legislature but a short time and devotes the balance of his time to his business or occupation, and it is a physical impossibility, whatever may be his desire, to properly qualify himself for the duties of his office. A member of the Legislature ought to be paid a sufficient salary so that he could devote his time to the duties of his office. This would not only attract better men for the position but it would enable good men to perform better service. He out to be paid a salary that would command all of his time, and he should, in my judgment, be elected for a term of four years. This term, with the right of the people to recall their Representative, would not, in my opinion, be too long.

The plan I have outlined would not only result in better legislation, but it would save money for the taxpayer. If members of such a Legislature were paid a Salary equal to the salary of other State officials whose entire time is required in the performance of the duties of their offices, there would still be in most cases, a large saving of money on the salary item alone. We would not only get better legislators, and not only have the benefit of their entire time, but we would do it all with a less cost than under present conditions. Better results for less money would be the outcome.

Partisanship Would Be Eliminated

The members of the Legislature should be elected by districts upon a non-partisan ballot. The business of the Legislature of a State is in no sense partisan. The evils that creep into State management and State legislation on account of such positions being coupled up with national questions of politics, are exceedingly great. Men are often elected to the State Legislature because they happen to be candidates on some particular party ticket, while the duties they are to perform when elected have nothing to do with the National Administration or with the welfare or success of any political party. If politics were eliminated, members would be elected according to their qualifications for the State Legislature. The State would be similar to a gigantic corporation, and the members of the Legislature would be members of the Board of Directors.

Without being handicapped, on account of any partisanship matters, they would be able to give the best that was in them for the welfare of the state. Their duties would be mainly of a business nature. How illogical it is to elect a man to the Legislature because he believes in a tariff for protection, or because he is a free-trader, or because he believes in a Federal subsidy to the national merchant marine, or is opposed to such subsidy, or because of his ideas on the League of Nations, or what is more probable, because he belongs to some political party and will follow that party regardless of what course it takes, when, as a matter of fact, the duties of the office for which he is a candidate having nothing whatever to do either directly or indirectly with any of these partisan questions.

Elimination of Corruption in Legislative Proceedings

A Legislature like I have outlined would be much more free from corrupt influences than would a two-branch Legislature or a Legislature composed of a very large number. I know that many people at first blush do not realize the truth of this statement, but I am sure that the candid student, especially one who has had experience with two-branch Legislatures, will agree that this is true. The corrupt legislator, or the one who in reality represents some special interest, is always looking for a place and an opportunity to cover up his tracks. The two-branch Legislature gives him many opportunities to ply his trade without being found out.

The lobbyist not only deals with corrupt men—he often deceives honest men. In fact, the actual cases of honest men being misled are far, more numerous than the purchase of dishonest men. With the increased salary we would get men to begin with that on the average would be high class and more difficult to deceive than we do now. The opportunities for deception or corruption would be greatly lessened. The men, therefore, to be deceived would be much less, and the man who would try to practice the deception would be almost powerless, and we would have a Legislature that would be untrammeled and to a great extent untempted. A Legislature that is known to be uncorruptible would be practically free from attempts at corruption.

It is said, I know, that a small Legislature could be purchased easier than a large one, and that one branch could be more easily deceived than two branches. If the opportunities for deception and the caliber of the membership were the same in both instances, then this statement would be true; but when the possibility of covering up the tracks of those who want to deceive is practically wiped out, and when the morale of the membership is raised to the highest possible point of the citizenship of the State, then this argument falls to the ground. Who would say, for instance, that the Judges of our various States are corrupt, and argue that therefore, we should have five or six Judges instead of one presiding at a trial? And yet, if we had the kind of Legislature I have outlined, the members would stand as high as the members of our Judiciary. They would become as expert in their line as Judges are expert in the construction of laws. Perfection, it is true, would not be attained, but the morale and the standing of our State Legislatures would be on the same high place as our Judiciary.

Appendix 3

George Norris's 1934 Model Legislature Speech

This speech was delivered by U.S. senator George Norris on February 22, 1934. It was recorded in the Congressional Record February 27, 1934.

THE MODEL LEGISLATURE

The object of all government is the happiness of the people comprising the government. Democratic governments are established among peoples for the purpose of attaining this object. Originally, when civilization was in its infancy, governments were established by chiefs, by monarchs, by rulers, who assumed authority over their fellow men and were able to sustain that authority by physical power and by the ignorance of the people comprising the government. Kings and monarchs were supreme. They claimed a relationship to Deity. By reason of the ignorance of their subjects, they were able to retain their authority and to impose their rule upon their superstitious followers. But as the people became more civilized and as superstition began to give way to education, the mystery surrounding such governments gradually disappeared and the people began to claim more and more of human liberty and human freedom. There arose contests between the power of the ruler and the claims of the people. The king claimed the right to take the property, and even the life, of his subjects if he found it necessary to do so to retain his power. In these contests the monarch was attempting to retain the powers he had assumed while the people were striving to take some of the power away and place it more directly in the hands of the people themselves. Many of these contests were fought on the field of battle. Later on many of them were fought in the courts of reason, but the principle involved was always the same. On the one hand, it was to retain power; on the other, it was to take it away. The history of our civilization is, in the main, the story of these contests. The contest is still going on. The people are striving to gain more power in government.

Democracy

Out of these controversies have grown the present democratic forms of government. A pure democracy is one in which all the people assemble in one body and make the laws for their own government. Manifestly, such a govern-ment, while perfect in theory, is impossible in application. Our own Federal Government is an apt illustration of the outcome of one of these great histor-ical contests. A successful revolution from the mother country brought forth 13 independent Colonies. This revolution marked in the world's history one of the greatest steps that has ever been taken in removing power from the king and placing it in the hands of the people themselves. It was not known, even after the victory at Yorktown, just what form of government was going to spring up in the New World. The leaders in the cause of human freedom did not know what was going to be the result of their heroic sacrifices. Another great step toward realization for those who believed in human liberty was taken when the confederation was formed, but a still greater step was taken when these 13 colonies united and formed the Constitution of the United States. The form of government was to a great extent experimental. The only precedents they had to guide their future steps were the historic instances of the then past wherein legislatures had been set up to make the laws that should govern the people. Our forefathers, knowing that they were taking a new step in advance, were yet fearful that they should make mistakes that might injure, if not destroy, the beneficial effects of the Revolution.

The Legislature

In setting up new State institutions under the Federal Government, our fore-fathers followed the precedents established by the Federal Government in dividing the legislative authority between two houses. In a general way, out of it grew the common and universal rule of a two-branch legislature, usually termed a "senate" and a "house of representatives." The theory back of this kind of a legislature was a beautiful one. The object to be attained was to have one branch of the legislature as a check upon the other. It was a system of checks and balances. But the dominant reason was one which had descended from a time in the history of the world when the common people comprising the government were not sufficiently civilized and sufficiently educated to govern themselves. The Senate of the United States was originally a body elected by the legislatures. This precaution was taken on the theory that this body would be more aristocratic and would, if thus elected, be more likely to protect the rights of property, than if elected directly by the people. The House of Representatives was elected directly by the people. And thus in the new Government, the only place where the people had a direct voice and vote was in the election of the House of Representatives. This House was intended to represent the people, as against property, and thus the checks and balances were completed with the idea that the rights of property should always be safeguarded and protected, and the people themselves should not have a direct voice, either in the selection of Members of the Senate, or in the selection of the President.

But civilization continued to advance. Universal education improved the ability of the people to act more directly in their Government. And again the age-old contest between retaining the power of aristocracy as against the people exhibited itself in our own Government. As civilization advanced and as education increased the people again demanded a change. We provided by amendment to the Federal Constitution for the direct election by the people of the Members of the United States Senate. The electoral college still lingers, but it has been modified to such an extent that, although retained, it is only a body of men pledged to vote for a particular man without regard to deliberation or discussion. The government of the people is gradually being placed in the hands of the people themselves.

Our people are sufficiently civilized and educated to know what kind of government they want and the laws they want enacted to enforce government among themselves. If we can now improve upon our lawmaking bodies, and if we can give to the people a more direct voice in their State governments, why should we not eliminate some of the things which have been found unnecessary and cumbersome, as well as expensive, in these State legislatures? Why should the Legislature of Nebraska have two branches instead of one? We have in this great State one dominating and all-controlling industry—agriculture. Every person in the State, every business in the State, is dependent for his or its success upon agriculture. If agriculture fails, then the happiness of our people is necessarily taken away. The qualifications of members of both branches of our State legislature are exactly the same. They represent exactly the same idea. The official duties they are to perform are of exactly the same nature. Why should we then have two bodies instead of one, and burden our taxpayers with the necessarily increased expense, to attain the object that can be fully attained by one house instead of two?

Conference Committee

But if we analyze our present Government we find we have three Houses instead of two. We have the conference committee—a necessary adjunct wherever two houses are provided for by the constitution. The conference committee, in reality, constitutes a third house. The members of this "house" are not elected by the people to serve as members of the conference committee. The people have no voice as to who these members shall be. They have nothing to say in regard to their selection. This conference committee is many times in very important matters of legislation the most important branch of our legislature. There is no record kept of the workings of the conference committee. Its work is performed, in the main, in secret. No constituent has any definite knowledge as to how members of this conference committee vote, and there is no record to prove the attitude of any member of the conference committee.

When a bill passes one branch of the legislature and passes the other branch in a different form, the matter is referred to the conference committee. This conference committee, arbitrarily selected by the presiding officers of the different branches, takes the dispute and molds it into a law. It then submits the report to the house and to the senate. The conference committee report cannot be amended by either branch. It must be voted up or voted down as a whole. Members must take what they believe to be bad, in order to get what they believe to be good. If it is rejected entirely, it may mean, and often does mean, the entire defeat of the legislation. If the conference committee does not agree upon a bill then it must necessarily fall in its entirety. As a practical proposition, we have legislation then, not by the house of representatives, but we have legislation by the voice of five or six men. And for practical purposes, in most cases, it is impossible to defeat the legislation proposed by this conference committee. Every experienced legislator knows that it is the hardest thing in the world to defeat a conference report.

Those who are clamoring for a large legislature, those who are asking for a check and balance between the two houses of the legislature, because they claim this represents the voice of the people, do not realize that such a condition results in legislation by a much smaller number of men than is proposed in the contemplated amendment to our constitution. Those who clamor for 133 legislators in our State, because they say that is the only way in which the voice of the people can be heard, forget that in hotly contested matters of legislation, where the most vital issues are at stake, they are, in effect, retaining a legislature of five or six men which enacts the laws that shall govern the entire State.

I am not complaining because of the existence of the conference committee. If we are to have a legislature composed of two branches, the conference committee is an absolute necessity. No man has ever suggested a plan, so far as I know, which would do away with this third branch of the legislature, where the constitution provides for two branches of the legislature. In all the history of the various States of the Union I do not know of an instance where any provision is made, either by the constitution or by the laws, which takes away from this third branch, known as the "conference committee," the power to hold its sessions in secret, the power to hold them without anyone being able to know how the votes are cast, or the power to avoid keeping a record of any of its deliberations or votes.

It would be possible, it is true, to provide by a constitutional amendment that the people themselves should elect a third branch of the legislature to perform the duties of the conference committee, but no one has ever suggested this third branch. If we are to retain the two-branch legislature, it would be a vast improvement to provide by constitutional amendment that the people should elect directly a third branch to take over the jurisdiction and the powers of the conference committee. But no one in this State, so far as I have ever heard, has ever suggested such an amendment. It would be an improvement over present conditions, but would add greatly to the expense and the delay now existing.

It is in conference-committee rooms that jokers frequently creep into our laws, and it is in the conference committee that good things are often taken out of our laws. It seems to me to be sufficient to say that this third branch, under our present two-branch system, is an absolute necessity, and that the people—in the most vital part of this legislative government—are now helpless. If our people are sufficiently educated and sufficiently intelligent to honestly and efficiently govern themselves, then all this machinery can be remodeled and put into the one-branch legislature, and the people, through it, can then secure the kind of laws and the kind of government which they desire. To deny this principle is to deny that the people are qualified to govern themselves. To deny this principle is to put upon the shoulders of the taxpayers of Nebraska unnecessary expenses and, in addition, to deny them the right to have the kind of government they wish.

One of the necessities is a provision in the constitution which will make it impossible for any member of the legislature to shift responsibility. I can point to an instance of recent history in Nebraska where a majority of both branches were pledged in writing to vote for a bill embodying a particular principle of legislation. Notwithstanding this pledge, the legislature adjourned without enacting any such law. It does not follow from this that any member of this legislature was necessarily dishonest in making this pledge. But where he was honest about it or not, he could go back to his people and tell them truthfully that he voted for a bill embodying this particular item of legislation. The difficulty there was, and the difficulty is, in such cases that when the Senate passes a bill on a subject, and the House passes a different bill on the same subject, if the conference committee fails to agree upon a report, the legislation is dead. The bill has died the death that many bills must die in this third branch of the legislature, known as the "conference committee."

A one-house legislature would have made this impossible. It often occurs in the two-house legislature that the senate bill and the house bill are intentionally made different. They die the death in the conference committee that special interests desire them to die. The lobby, composed of experts hired by machine politicians and special interests, is successful in killing legislation before these four or five men who hold their deliberations in secret, and who make no record of their proceedings. The present system affords an opportunity to a dishonest legislator which he could not possess in a one-house legislature. It is, therefore, an open invitation to the disreputable man to seek office in the legislature. He is often enabled to introduce bills with the very object of getting something either of a financial or political nature which he otherwise could not get. Such a legislator sometimes introduces bills which he expects to be killed; he wants to be paid for helping to kill them; and he kills them by getting them into a parliamentary tangle where his own record may appear on the surface as perfect. His constituents will therefore perhaps reelect him without knowing his real record.

The State Like a Great Corporation

The State of Nebraska and its officials may be likened to a great corporation. The Governor is the president of the corporation, the legislature is the board of directors, and the people are the stockholders. The stockholders have a right to know what their board of directors does and how it is done. They have a right to be able by the record of the votes, to know whether the members of the board of directors have properly represented the stockholders. With the complexity which comes from a two-house legislature, it is impossible for them to know this.

In order to fully understand the action of the board of directors, the stockholders would have to become parliamentary experts. They would have to spend a large amount of their time in following the intricacies of parliamentary procedure that winds up finally in the conference committee. A one-house legislature would obviate all this difficulty. The stockholders would then be able to tell just how every member of the board of directors voted on every question coming up for consideration. It would then be impossible to shift any responsibility. The members of the board of directors would be compelled then to make a record that any person could understand, and the stockholders could readily ascertain whether the members of the board of directors should be continued in office or whether they should be replaced. It would then be possible to punish the unfaithful, and it would also be possible to reward the man who had done his duty.

The Fundamental Idea Is the One-Branch Legislature

The fundamental principle involved in the proposed change of our constitution is to embody the legislative authority in a legislature consisting of one house. Upon this principle there can be no compromise. As to the qualifications of the members of the one-house legislature, as to the number of members, as to their term of office, and as to their salaries, there can well be a difference of opinion. On these subjects, those who believe in a one-house legislature ought to be willing to compromise in order to attain the fundamental object to be achieved. While some of these subjects are of vast importance, yet honest men and women can disagree, and some compromise is going to be necessary in order to attain the fundamental principle which we seek.

Membership of the Legislature Should Be Small in Number

One of the evils of our present legislatures is that they are entirely too large. In theory, a large legislature is supposed to give to a legislature more complete representation of the entire citizenry. In practice, however, it has been demonstrated that a membership too large is detrimental to real representation of the people. A large body of men is not deliberative, and in order to accomplish any legislative results they must necessarily surrender many of their independent rights and prerogatives. In large bodies, members must deny themselves, in some degree at least, the right of debate, and even the right to offer amendments. They must surrender to a smaller number of men, or committees, the right to determine procedure. The very size of the body sometimes makes it impossible for the necessary and proper deliberation and discussion which should always take place before legislation is enacted into law.

We must remember, also, that the larger the body, the greater the expense to the taxpayer. One of the important questions in the proposed amendment is the saving of money to those who have to bear the burdens of taxation. The members of a legislative body may be both able and conscientious, they may be moved by the highest possible motives, but the very size itself is sometimes an impediment to the transaction of business. Unlimited debate cannot take place where the membership is too large. Full consideration can never be given to a pending measure if the membership is so large that deliberation is absent. In a large body, the members are, therefore, often compelled, even against their own wish, to vote for bills containing provisions which in their own judgment are wrong, in order to get what, in their judgment, the evil contained is greater than the good. Full discussion and the right to offer amendments and to debate them fully is necessary for the best results in any legislative body. In a smaller body of men they would always have an opportunity to offer amendments, to debate them, and to move to strike out bad provisions which in their judgment ought to be eliminated.

The number of members that ought to comprise a legislature would undoubtedly vary somewhat with the different States. When there are varied and conflicting interests involved, the membership ought to be larger. From my experience of 20 years and from my study of State legislatures during the many years of my public service, I have reached the conclusion that a fair membership in a State like Nebraska should not exceed 20 or 25 members. As I first proposed this amendment, I fixed the membership at 21. When this number was given publicity I received hundreds of letters from representative men and women all over the State of Nebraska. Some wanted a smaller number, but the most of them wanted a larger number. Personally, I would not have objected if the membership had been decreased to less than 21. I have no objection, either, to an increase. It is a subject, it seems to me, upon which honest students may reach different conclusions.

As a compromise I have suggested in the amendment which is now pending a membership which shall not be less than 30 or more than 50. The exact number could be fixed by the legislature itself, in redistricting the State from time to time, and I think the wise plan would be to start at 30. If experience found that number to be too small, it could easily be increased anywhere up to the maximum number by the legislature redistricting the State in accordance with their wisdom and experience. In a State like Nebraska, where the great predominant interest is agriculture, it seems to me that 30 members would be amply sufficient, although I do not want to set my judgment up against the judgment of my fellow citizens. I think on this question all of us should meet the proposition with a mind open to compromise and conviction. The chief thing, after all, is to fix responsibility and to make it impossible for any member of the legislature to avoid this responsibility.

It is extremely important on this proposition that the members of the legislature should be paid a sufficient salary to enable them to study and consider the various propositions of legislation, and it must be remembered that whenever we increase the membership we increase the burden of the taxpayer. In these days of depression this is a consideration that should not be lightly avoided.

Salary of Members

Closely allied to the number of members is their salary. The model legislature, it seems to me, would be one in which the members were paid a sufficient salary so they could devote all their time to the business of their offices. They would become experts in legislation. They would familiarize themselves with all the State institutions and they would be able to improve our laws and our institutions by their study of the various subjects submitted to their keeping. They would, of necessity, in such cases strive to give to the State the benefit of their time and their knowledge. As their experience as legislators increased, they would become more valuable to the State. They would not have their mind and attention taken from matters of state to private business matters. They would be able to give to the State better laws and more intelligent consideration to the institutions of the State. I realize that economy is one of the objects of this proposed amendment. I realize, too, that their active duties in the legislature itself would take but a comparatively small portion of their time. I have tried to reach in my own mind a compromise on this subject—the necessity on behalf of the taxpayers of the State, on the one hand, for a decrease in expenses, and the desirability, on the other hand, of getting the most efficient government possible.

In the amendment which I first proposed I fixed the salary at $2,400. From letters from all over the State, and from conferences with a good many people, I reached the conclusion that my idea of the number ought to be increased, and as I increased the number I felt of necessity that the salary ought to be decreased, and in the proposal now before you I have suggested the sum of $50,000 to pay the annual salary of the members, and that this amount should be divided equally between the members, whatever may be its membership. If we should have a membership of 30, the salary of each member would be approximately $1,650. On the other hand, if experience should show that the membership should be increased to 50, the salary would be $1,000 each. The salary of the members is a very important consideration. I want to be indulged while I am talking on this subject to refer to my own personal experience. When I was a practicing lawyer at Beaver City I had an opportunity on several occasions when I could, I think, without any great effort have been elected to the Legislature of the State of Nebraska. I always declined. I did not decline because I would not have liked the position. On the contrary, I had an ambition to become a member of the legislature, but I necessarily declined for the simple reason that I could not afford to do so. I would have been delighted to have been a member of the legislature and to have remained in the legislature, and to have spent my life in the upbuilding of our great State. I knew, however, I could not afford to do this without great financial loss to myself, so great that to me at that time it would have meant absolute poverty. I had a desire to be of service to my State, but it seemed to me had I followed my ambition and my inclination my business would have disappeared, and I would have found myself in the end an old man without having laid by a sufficient amount of money to keep me and those dependent upon me from abject poverty. I believe my experience can be multiplied by the thousands. If the salary is so low as to keep more men out of the legislature, the tendency will be to have men of wealth control our legislation, and this is a condition that cannot be tolerated in a democracy.

While it is desirable to economize and make our governmental expenses as small as possible, we mustn't forget that we cannot expect always to get good men to work for the public without pay. Moreover, a salary that is extremely small affords inducements to dishonest and corrupt men to avail themselves of the opportunity to become candidates for the legislature with a view of recouping after election, by their official activities. Men sometimes go to the legislature for this purpose. They sacrifice financially and fall into temptation to recoup their financial losses by their official votes. This does not mean there would not be honest men in a legislature, even without salaries. There are men who are so situated financially they could afford to give their time to their state, and there are many honest men who would be willing and glad to do this.

But the point is, if we pay a salary which is too small, we exclude from the legislature many men who would become useful and valuable servants of the people.

Proposed Plan Would Be Economical
The plan outlined in the proposed amendment to the constitution would save money for the taxpayers. It would not only do away with many of the evils which now exist but the business of the State would be transacted at less cost. Many thousands of dollars would be saved annually to our taxpayers. The expense of the legislature is not only the salary that is paid to its members. There are hundreds of other items which enter into the expenses of a legislature, all of which increase as the membership increases.

One of the objects to be attained in the proposed plan is to decrease taxation. We have reached a time in this depression when the importance of this subject cannot be overestimated. Most of us are compelled to sacrifice all of the luxuries and many of the comforts of ordinary life in order to save our Government and our State and bring happiness and comfort to our people.

A democracy is more expensive than a monarchy. We want to retain our democracy, and in these times when there may be a possibility of some danger of the destruction of democratic principles, we must reduce the cost of democratic government as low as we possibly can. Those who are opposed to democratic ideas and who believe in monarchical government would be glad to see democracy become so expensive that the fact could be used as one of the reasons why democracy should be abolished and some form of monarchy established in its stead.

Partisanship Would Be Abolished

The proposed amendment to the constitution provides that members of our legislature should be elected on a nonpartisan ballot. Our State ought to be a business institution. Its government should be conducted on business principles. The issues which divide the great political parties in our country should in no way interfere with the business operations of our State. And yet, under present methods, such conditions exist. The Legislature of Nebraska has nothing to do with the tariff; the Legislature of Nebraska, in its official capacity, has nothing to do with shipping on the great oceans. It has no jurisdiction over interstate commerce. It has no official connection with the appointment of postmasters and other official appointments which under our system of government are dealt out to faithful partisan workers. There is no issue involved in the election of a member of the Nebraska Legislature that is the same as the issue involved in the election of a United States Senator or a Member of the House of Representatives. Yet men are often elected as members of State legislature simply and solely because they are members of a political party pledged to some issue on the tariff, or some other issue of national concern. The citizen who goes into his booth ought not decide the question of election of his member of the legislature simply because he agrees with the voter on some national questions. Neither should he be defeated for the office of member of the State legislature merely because the voter does not agree with him on some questions of international importance. We have our State questions and our State institutions, and these should be the guiding star when we come to elect a member of the legislature.

If politics were eliminated, members would be elected to enact our laws according to their qualifications for the State legislature, without being handicapped by any partisan matters. Members of the legislature should be able to give the best that is in them to the welfare of the State. They should be elected on business principles rather than as a result of partisan considerations. Men may disagree as to whether the Federal Government should pay a subsidy to the international mercantile marine, but the Legislature of the State of Nebraska has nothing to do with that questions, and its members should neither be elected nor defeated on that issue. Men may disagree as to whether our country should join the League of Nations, but the Legislature of the State of Nebraska has nothing to do with that subject.

Why should we not divorce the business of our state completely from partisan matters affecting only national legislation? We ought to have a legislature entirely divorced form partisan politics—a legislature elected on a business basis, transacting its duties along business lines. We cannot do this unless we eliminate partisan politics.

Moreover, men in the legislature, elected on a partisan political platform, are inclined to follow the bidding and the dictates of party machines and party bosses. We have taken our school officials out of partisan politics. We have done the same thing with our judges. Ask yourself the question, Why? If the divorcing of our judges and our school officials form partisan politics is a good thing, if their official duties have no connection with partisan politics, why not extend the same theory to members of the legislature, whose official duties nowhere, nor in any degree, connect them with partisan politics? Partisanship is one of the great evils of our Government, when carried into avenues and into places where, officially, there is no politics.

For instance, our legislature makes the laws which govern the property and the legal rights of our people. The judges enforce those laws. How inconsistent it is to elect the one on the basis of his belief in the tariff, and yet remove the other from the same category?

Term of Office

The proposed amendment we are now considering provides for a term of office of 2 years. When I submitted the tentative draft of this amendment to the public for its commendation or criticism, I had provided for a 4-year term. I still believe a 4-year term is preferable to a 2-year term, but from the Nebraska people with whom I have conferred and from the thousands of letters I have received I believe the people are afraid of a 4-year term for their legislators or, at least, they prefer that the term be for 2 years instead of 4.

I do not regard this as fundamental, but I should like to keep members of our legislature out of political contests as much as I can. I should like them to hold office for a sufficient length of time so that they will have ample opportunity to make a record for the people to either approve or disapprove. I believe a 4-year term is none too long to do that. It would also relieve the expense necessarily connected with the campaign of the various candidates for the legislature.

But, in order to compromise and in order to meet the wishes of the people in this respect, I have changed the proposition so that the term of office shall be for 2 years instead of 4. Personally I think all our State officials ought to be elected for a term of 4 years. I think Members of the National House of Representatives should be elected for a term of 4 years instead of 2. I have gained this idea from my experience as a legislator and from my observation of members of State legislatures. But the question is not fundamental. If the people are not ready to agree to a 4-year term of office, I am perfectly willing, so far as I individually am concerned, to accept the 2-year term. Later on, it would be simple indeed to adopt an amendment to our State constitution providing for the election of all State officials for a term of 4 years instead of 2 years.

Elimination of Corruption

A one-house legislature, composed of a comparatively small number, would be much more free from corrupt influences than would a two-house legislature or a legislature composed of a large number of members. I know many people, at first blush, will not agree with this statement. There was a time in my life when I did not believe it, but I have reached the conviction from my observation that special interests, by unfair and unjustifiable means, are able to influence and corrupt a two-house legislature much more easily than they could a one-house legislature. I have been told by lobbyists that the easiest legislature to control is the one which is large in number. Where the number is large they necessarily have to handle only a few men, who, in turn, do their work with the legislature itself. In the two-house legislature the control of the conference committee is, in fact, for all practical purposes a control of both branches.

There are thousands of ways in which this is done. A conference committee can often be controlled by one man—the man who appoints the conference committee. The control of a large body of men can be handled by the control of two or three men who constitute the committee on rules, or who otherwise have a dominating parliamentary influence on the body.

The smallest legislature, which is now under consideration, may be likened to our judiciary, where the power is vested in one man. We know that our judiciary is comparatively free from such influences. A small legislature such as is suggested would be very similar to our judges. The lobbyist who desires to control the membership does not, as a rule, seek out the individual member, and go through the legislature in that way. He undertakes to deceive men by various methods, mostly of a parliamentary nature. The cases of direct sale of votes are very few. Men in congress or in the legislature are, as a rule, not bribed individually. They are led astray by placing them in hopeless parliamentary predicaments, in which they are deceived. In fact, the actual cases of honest men being misled are far more numerous than the purchase of dishonest men. If the opportunities for hiding beneath the parliamentary cloak brought about by a two-house legislature were taken away, the dishonest man would not be so likely to become a candidate for the legislature. He would know to being with that he could not shift responsibility, he could not conceal his vote, or his official conduct, which would have to take place in the open before all the people of the State, and he would, therefore, seek other avenues of enriching himself. In other words, it would have a tendency to eliminate the dishonest man from the legislature, and if you eliminate the dishonest man and make it impossible to deceive the honest man, you have attained as near perfection as is possible in a legislature.

The plan proposed would therefore tend to decrease deception and the man who tried to practice deception would be almost powerless, and we would then have a legislature which would be untrammeled and, to a great extent, untainted. The possibility of covering up the tracks of those who wanted to deceive would be practically eliminated, and it would be impossible to place the honest legislator in a false light.

The Ideal Impossible

I reach the conclusion, therefore, that the proposed amendment would save money to the taxpayers. It would go far toward the reestablishment of a democratic form of government. It would make it more difficult for dishonest men to get into office and make it more difficult for dishonest men to retain office. It would give the honest legislator an opportunity to have his record known to the people, and it would make it possible for the people of the state to readily ascertain and comprehend the record of the members of the legislature. It would enable the people to reward honest servants and to defeat the dishonest ones.

There would, of course, always be a possibility of dishonest men getting into office. There would be a possibility of dishonest men who were in office deceiving the people. But these possibilities would be very much minimized. Nothing has ever been said that is truer than the saying that "Eternal vigilance is the price of liberty."

To get a good government, and to retain it, it is necessary that a liberty-loving, educated, intelligent people should be ever watchful, to carefully guard and protect their rights and liberties. The proposed amendment is not offered with the idea that it is perfect. It is not offered with the idea that it will eliminate wrong entirely or that it will make it unnecessary for the people of the State to always keep a watchful eye upon their servants, but it will help them to know and to find out what is wrong. It will enable them to get better laws enacted and better men into office, and to this extent it will be a guidepost along the road to human advancement and a higher civilization.

Notes

1. One of a Kind

1. *Washington Daily News*, February 23, 1934.
2. Robert F. Wesser, "George W. Norris, the Unicameral Legislature and the Progressive Ideal," *Nebraska History* (December 1964).
3. Russell B. Nye, *Midwestern Progressive Politics: A Historical Study of Its Origins and Development, 1870–1958* (Lansing: Michigan State University Press, 1959), 136.
4. James Morone, *The Democratic Wish: Popular Participation and the Limits of American Government* (New York: Basic Books, 1990), 16.
5. Robert H. Wiebe, *The Search for Order, 1877–1920* (New York: Hill and Wang, 1967), 72.
6. Morone, *The Democratic Wish*, 1.
7. Lawrence Goodwyn, *The Populist Moment* (New York: Oxford University Press, 1978), xv.
8. Wesser, "George W. Norris," 321.
9. Morone, *The Democratic Wish*, 109.
10. Morone, *The Democratic Wish*, 106.
11. John Senning, *The One-House Legislature* (New York: McGraw-Hill, 1937), 43–44.
12. Senning, *The One-House Legislature*, 43–44.
13. James C. Olsen, *History of Nebraska* (Lincoln: University of Nebraska Press, 1955), 291.
14. Paul W. Glad, "Progressives and the Business Culture of the 1920s," *Journal of American History* 53 (1966): 81.
15. Nye, *Midwestern Progressive Politics*, 361, 369.
16. Alaska State Legislature, Legislative Research Agency (July 8, 1991).
17. Herbert J. Storing, ed., *The Anti-Federalist: Writings by the Opponents of the Constitution* (Chicago: University of Chicago Press, 1981), 16.
18. Alvin W. Johnson, *The Unicameral Legislature* (Minneapolis: University of Minnesota Press, 1938), 76.
19. George Norris, *Fighting Liberal: The Autobiography of George Norris* (New York: Macmillan, 1945), 353.
20. Senning, *The One-House Legislature*, 16–26.
21. Senning, *The One-House Legislature*, 34.
22. Senning papers Box 2, Folder 19, Nebraska State Historical Society.

23. *Sunday Journal and Star*, February 12, 1933.
24. Arthur Holcombe, *State Government in the United States* (New York: Macmillan, 1916), 267.
25. Senning, *The One-House Legislature*, 36–38.
26. *Congressional Record*, February 7, 1935, 1636.
27. Senning papers Box 5, Folder 47.
28. Senning, *The One-House Legislature*, 43.
29. *Congressional Record*, February 7, 1935, 1636; *Sunday Journal and Star*, February 12, 1933.
30. Norris papers Box 7, Folder 3, Nebraska State Historical Society.
31. *Congressional Record*, February 7, 1935, 1635.
32. *Lincoln Star*, October 30, 1934.
33. Senning, *The One-House Legislature*, 50.
34. George Norris, "Only One House," *State Government* 7, no. 10 (1934): 210; *Sunday Journal and Star*, February 12, 1933.

2. Power to the People

1. Gordon Wood, *The Creation of the American Republic, 1776–1787* (New York: W. W. Norton, 1969), 606.
2. Olsen, *History of Nebraska*, 130; Addison Sheldon, *Nebraska*, vol. 1 (Chicago: Lewis Publishing, 1931), 452.
3. Sheldon, *Nebraska*, 446.
4. John H. Hicks, *The Populist Revolt* (Minneapolis: University of Minnesota Press, 1931), 33.
5. Olsen, *History of Nebraska*, 221.
6. Sheldon, *Nebraska*, 671.
7. Olsen, *History of Nebraska*, 226, 227.
8. Sheldon, *Nebraska*, 688.
9. Norris, *Fighting Liberal*, x.
10. Bernard Kolasa, *The Nebraska Political System: A Study in Apartisan Politics* (Lincoln: University of Nebraska, 1968), 116.
11. Kolasa, *The Nebraska Political System*, 149.
12. Sheldon, *Nebraska*, 824.
13. Nye, *Midwestern Progressive Politics*, 319, 321, 322.
14. Senning, *The One-House Legislature*, 63; Dorothy Weyer Creigh, *Nebraska: A Bicentennial History* (New York: W. W. Norton, 1977), 198; Patrick O'Donnell, "A Unicameral Legislature,"*Journal of the American Society of Legislative Clerks and Secretaries* (Spring 1996): 6.
15. David Judge, *The Politics of Parliamentary Reform* (Rutherford NJ: Fairleigh Dickinson University Press, 1984), 132.
16. Harrison Boyd Summers, *Unicameralism in Practice: The Nebraska Legislative System* (New York: The H. W. Wilson Co., 1937), 29.
17. Senning, *The One-House Legislature*, 49.
18. Senning, *The One-House Legislature*, 50.
19. Creigh, *Nebraska*, 198.
20. Norris, *Fighting Liberal*, xiv.

21. Oswald Garrison Villard, "Pillars of Government: George W. Norris," *The Forum* (April 1936): 110.
22. Senning, *The One-House Legislature*, 49, 51.
23. Senning, *The One-House Legislature*, 51.
24. Senning, *The One-House Legislature*, xii.
25. Norris, *Fighting Liberal*, 346.
26. Wesser, "George W. Norris," 315.
27. Norris, *Fighting Liberal*, 349.
28. *The Nebraska Beacon*, May 3, 1934.
29. Senning, *The One-House Legislature*, 63; Creigh, *Nebraska*, 198; O'Donnell, "A Unicameral Legislature," 6.
30. Phillip K. Tompkins, *George W. Norris's Persuasion in the Campaign for the Unicameral Legislature* (University of Nebraska: unpublished thesis, 1957), 79.
31. Robert Miewald, ed., *Nebraska Government and Politics* (Lincoln: University of Nebraska Press, 1984), 25.
32. Senning papers Box 4, Folder 17.
33. *Time*, January 11, 1937.
34. Olsen, *History of Nebraska*, 316; Luebke, 289.
35. *Grand Island Independent*, November 7, 1934.
36. Senning papers Box 5, Folder 47.

3. Let the Sun Shine In

1. Adam C. Breckenridge, "Innovations in State Government: Origin and Development of the Nebraska Nonpartisan Unicameral Legislature." *Nebraska History* (Spring 1978): 33.
2. *New York Times*, January 28, 1923, 12.
3. George Norris, "The One House Legislature," *National Municipal Review* (February 1935): 88.
4. Norris, "The One-House Legislature," 88.
5. *New York Times*, January 28, 1923, 12
6. William Riley, "Nonpartisan Unicameral—Benefits, Defects Re-examined," *Nebraska Law Review* 52, no. 3 (1973): 383.
7. Norris papers Box 7, Folder 3.
8. Galen Saylor, *The Unicameral Legislature: Its Operation in Nebraska* (Lincoln: Nebraska State Teachers' Association, 1937), 37.
9. *Lincoln Star*, December 9, 1936.
10. *St. Louis Post-Dispatch*, June 26, 1937.
11. Walter Johnson, "Politics in the Midwest," *Nebraska History* 32, no. 1 (1951): 139.
12. *Arkansas Gazette*, May 18, 1937.
13. Cortez Ewing, "Organized Groups: Lobbying in the Nebraska Legislature," *The Public Opinion Quarterly* (July 1937): 104.
14. Senning, *The One-House Legislature*, 82.
15. Saylor, *The Unicameral Legislature*, 6.
16. Senning papers Box 4, Folder 25.
17. Norris, *Fighting Liberal*, 352.
18. *St. Louis Post-Dispatch*, June 26, 1937.
19. Saylor, *The Unicameral Legislature*, 8.

20. Saylor, *The Unicameral Legislature*, 38.
21. Personal interview, January 31, 2003.
22. Saylor, *The Unicameral Legislature*, 16.
23. *Lincoln Star*, January 7, 1965, 22.
24. Personal interview, March 4, 2002.
25. Senning papers Box 4, Folder 37.
26. *Lincoln Evening Journal*, January 13, 1975, 4.
27. *Nebraska Legislative Journal* (1953), 730.
28. *Nebraska Legislative Journal* (1953), 732.
29. *Lincoln Evening Journal*, January 7, 1971, 8.90. *Nebraska Legislative Journal* (1980), 157.
30. *Record of Floor Debate* (January 13, 1981), 184.
31. *Christian Science Monitor*, July 15, 1947.
32. *Lincoln Evening Journal*, February 19, 1975, 4.
33. *Record of Floor Debate* (January 8, 1996), 9499.
34. *Record of Floor Debate* (January 8, 1996), 9505.
35. *Record of Floor Debate* (January 8, 1996), 9510.
36. *Lincoln Journal*, July 29, 1987, 6.
37. Kim Robak, "The Nebraska Unicameral and Its Lasting Benefits," *Nebraska Law Review* 76, no. 4 (1997): 810.
38. Personal interview, September 4, 2001.
39. Personal interview, September 18, 2001.
40. Personal interview, September 6, 2001.
41. Personal interview, October 9, 2001.
42. Personal interview, August 28, 2001.
43. Personal interview, September 25, 2001.
44. Survey response, Nebraska Legislators Survey, 2001.
45. Personal interview, September 25, 2001.
46. Personal interview, September 25, 2001.
47. Personal interview, July 29, 2001.
48. Personal interview, October 14, 2001.
49. Personal interview, September 18, 2001.
50. Personal interview, September 18, 2001.
51. Personal interview, October 14, 2001.
52. Bureau of Sociological Research (NASIS), 2000.
53. Personal interview, September 4, 2001.
54. Personal interview, September 25, 2001.
55. Personal interview, September 27, 2001.
56. Personal interview, August 28, 2001.
57. Personal interview, September 25, 2001.
58. Personal interview, October 9, 2001.
59. Personal interview, October 14, 2001.
60. Samuel Popkin, *The Reasoning Voter: Communication and Persuasion in Presidential Campaigns* (Chicago: University of Chicago Press, 1991), 51.149. Bureau of Sociological Research (NASIS), 2000.
61. Personal interview, September 20, 2001.
62. Survey response, Nebraska Legislators Survey, 2001.

63. Personal interview, September 17, 2001.
64. Personal interview, October 2, 2001.
65. Personal interview, September 17, 2001.
66. Bureau of Sociological Research (NASIS), 2000.
67. Personal interview with Mary Campbell, June 27, 2001.
68. Personal interview, September 18, 2001.
69. Personal interview, August 30, 2001.
70. Survey response.
71. The Citizens' Conference on State Legislatures, 384.
72. Personal interview, September 4, 2001.
73. Survey response, Nebraska Legislators Survey, 2001.
74. Personal interview, September 27, 2001.
75. Survey response.
76. Personal interview, March 4, 2002.
77. The Citizens' Conference on State Legislatures, 385.
78. Survey response.
79. Survey response.
80. Survey response.
81. Personal interview, October 14, 2001.

4. Forty-nine Independent Contractors

1. *New York Times*, January 28, 1923, 12.
2. Peter Bachrach, *The Theory of Democratic Elitism: A Critique* (Boston: Little, Brown, 1967), 27.
3. *Sunday Journal and Star*, February 12, 1933, C4.
4. *Sunday Journal and Star*, February 12, 1933, C4.
5. Alvin W. Johnson, *The Unicameral Legislature* (Minneapolis: University of Minnesota Press, 1938), 76.
6. Letter to Calvin Coolidge, December 6, 1923, Norris papers.
7. Senning, "*One House, Two Sessions,*" 844.
8. Saylor, *The Unicameral Legislature*, 39.
9. Saylor, *The Unicameral Legislature*, 40.
10. *San Antonio (TX) Express*, April 29, 1937.
11. *Lincoln Star*, May 29, 1937.
12. James Johnson, *The Nebraska Legislative System: Legislative Roles in a Nonpartisan Setting* (Ann Arbor MI: University Microfilms International, 1972), 27.
13. Saylor, *The Unicameral Legislature*, 40.
14. Kolasa, *The Nebraska Political System*, 356.
15. *Lincoln Journal*, January 16, 1937.
16. *Lincoln State Journal*, May 19, 1936.
17. *Arkansas Gazette*, May 18, 1937.
18. Senning papers Box 3, Folder 6.
19. *New York Times* editorial; reprinted in *Amsterdam (NY) Recorder*, May 15, 1937.
20. *Lincoln Journal*, March 22, 1937.
21. *Hay Springs News*, June 4, 1937.
22. *Journal of the Nebraska Legislative Council*, 1937, Senning papers Box 20, Folder 2.

23. *Journal of the Nebraska Legislative Council*, 1937, Senning papers Box 20, Folder 2.
24. The Citizens Conference on State Legislatures, 234.
25. *Record of Floor Debate* (March 7, 1979), 1281.
26. *Record of Floor Debate* (January 11, 1983), 69.
27. *Record of Floor Debate* (January 9, 1996), 9661–9662.
28. *Record of Floor Debate* (January 9, 1996), 9665.
29. *Record of Floor Debate* (January 9, 1996), 9666.
30. *Record of Floor Debate* (January 9, 1996), 9666.
31. *Record of Floor Debate* (January 9, 1996), 9668.
32. *Record of Floor Debate* (January 9, 1996), 9670.
33. *Record of Floor Debate* (January 9, 1996), 9671.
34. *Record of Floor Debate* (January 10, 1996), 9742.
35. *Record of Floor Debate* (January 10, 1996), 9758.
36. *Record of Floor Debate* (January 10, 1996), 9762.
37. *Record of Floor Debate* (January 10, 1996), 9767.
38. *Record of Floor Debate* (January 10, 1996), 9763–9764.
39. *Record of Floor Debate* (January 10, 1996), 9765.
40. *Record of Floor Debate* (January 10, 1996), 9769.
41. *Record of Floor Debate* (January 10, 1996), 9770–9771.
42. *Record of Floor Debate* (January 10, 1996), 9777.
43. *Record of Floor Debate* (January 11, 1996), 9799. 44. *Record of Floor Debate* (January 11, 1996), 9825.
45. *Nebraska Legislative Journal* (1994), 264.
46. *Lincoln Journal Star*, January 15, 2002, 1A, 2A.
47. Jim Pappas personal interview, September 4, 2001; Don Dworak personal interview, August 30, 2001; Don Wesely personal interview, September 18, 2001; Tim Hall personal interview, September 20, 2001.
48. *Lincoln Journal Star*, April 29, 2001.
49. Robert Sittig, "The Nebraska Legislature: Policy Implications of Its Organization and Operation," *Nebraska Policy Choices* (1987):22.
50. Personal interview, October 9, 2001.
51. Personal interview, September 25, 2001.
52. Personal interview, September 6, 2001.
53. Personal interview, September 18, 2001.
54. Personal interview, August 28, 2001.
55. Personal interview, October 9, 2001.
56. Personal interview, October 14, 2001.
57. Personal interview, August 30, 2001.
58. Personal interview, September 25, 2001.
59. Personal interview, August 28, 2001.
60. Personal interview, September 4, 2001.
61. Personal interviews, October 14, 2001, and October 2, 2001.
62. Personal interview, September 27, 2001.
63. Personal interview, September 25, 2001.
64. Personal interview, July 24, 2001.
65. Personal interview, September 6, 2001.

66. Personal interview, October 14, 2001.
67. Personal interview, July 5, 2001.
68. Personal interview, October 2, 2001.
69. Personal interview, July 5, 2001.
70. Personal interview, September 13, 2001.
71. Personal interview, September 27, 2001.
72. Personal interview, October 2, 2001.
73. *Record of Floor Debate* (January 10, 1996), 9764.

5. We, the People

1. Senning papers Box 9, Folder 84.
2. O. Douglas Weeks, "Two Legislative Houses or One?" *Arnold Foundation Studies in Public Affairs* (Winter 1938):22.
3. Weeks, "Two Legislative Houses or One?" 22.
4. Senning papers Box 9, Folder 84.
5. Senning papers Box 12, Folder 34.
6. Senning papers Box 2, Folder 24.
7. *Official Debate Handbook* (Lincoln: Nebraska High School Activities Association, 1937), 54.
8. Senning papers Box 4, Folder 24.
9. Senning papers Box 4, Folder 18.
10. *New York Times*, January 10, 1937.
11. *Omaha World-Herald*, January 17, 1937.
12. Tvrdik papers Box 2, Folder 2, Nebraska State Historical Society.
13. *Congressional Record*, January 23, 1940.
14. *Lincoln Star*, December 28, 1936; *Arkansas Gazette*, May 15, 1937.
15. *Journal of the Nebraska Legislative Council*, 1937, September 13 proceedings.
16. *Lincoln Journal*, February 22, 1937.
17. *Lincoln Star*, July 14, 1935.
18. *Congressional Record*, April 25, 1938.
19. *El Paso (TX) Herald Post*, March 27, 1937.
20. Senning, *The One-House Legislature*, 74.
21. *Lincoln Evening Journal*, September 14, 1937.
22. *St. Louis Post-Dispatch*, June 26, 1937.
23. Miewald, ed., *Nebraska Government and Politics*, 40.
24. Senning papers Box 5, Folder 54.
25. Senning papers Box 4, Folder 17.
26. *St. Louis Post-Dispatch*, June 27, 1937.
27. Tvrdik papers Box 1, Folder 1.
28. *Arkansas Gazette*, May 21, 1937.
29. *Sunday Journal and Star*, December 27, 1937.
30. Senning papers Box 4, Folder 18.
31. Senning papers Box 4, Folder 37.
32. Personal interview, January 27, 2003.
33. Charlyne Berens, *Leaving Your Mark: The Political Career of Nebraska State Senator Jerome Warner* (Nebraska Times, 1997), 60–61.
34. Personal interview, September 6, 2001.

35. Personal interview, September 27, 2001.

36. Personal interview, August 28, 2001.

37. *Arkansas Gazette*, May 15, 1937.

38. Virginia Gray and Herbert Jacob, *Politics in the American States: A Comparative Analysis* (Washington DC: CQ Press, 1996), 237.

39. Personal interview, July 2, 2001.

40. Personal interview July 2, 2001.

41. Personal interview September 18, 2001.

42. Personal interview, September 27, 2001.

6. "You Lie, You're Gone"

1. Alan Rosenthal et al., *The Case for Representative Democracy* (Denver: National Conference of State Legislatures, 2001), 22.

2. *Washington Post*, May 24, 1934.

3. Norris, "The One-House Legislature," 88, 89.

4. *Congressional Record—Senate*, February 7, 1935, 1636.

5. *Associated Press*, July 27, 1937.

6. *Omaha World-Herald*, September 26, 1934.

7. Senning, "One House, Two Sessions," 846.

8. Alan Rosenthal et al., 36.

9. Senning, *The One-House Legislature*, 89.

10. *Arkansas Gazette*, May 20, 1937.

11. Senning papers Box 9, Folder 80.

12. Johnson, *The Unicameral Legislature*, 76.

13. Ewing, "Organized Groups," 104.

14. *Arkansas Gazette*, May 19, 1937.

15. Personal interview, March 21, 2002.

16. Personal interview, July 24, 2001.

17. Personal interview, July 24, 2001.

18. Personal interview, July 2, 2001.

19. Personal interview, June 27, 2001.

20. Personal interview, July 5, 2001.

21. Personal interview, July 20, 2001.

22. Personal interview, August 30, 2001.

23. Personal interview, Sept. 20, 2001.

24. Personal interview, July 18, 2001.

25. *Omaha World-Herald*, January 10, 1993.

26. Personal interview, July 2, 2001.

27. Personal interview, September 6, 2001.

28. Personal interview, July 2, 2001.

29. Personal interview, July 5, 2001.

30. Personal interview, July 2, 2001.

31. Personal interview, June 27, 2001.

32. Personal interview, July 20, 2001.

33. Personal interview, July 24, 2001.

34. Personal interview, July 18, 2001.

35. Personal interview July 2, 2001.
36. Personal interview, September 20, 2001.
37. Personal interview, July 18, 2001.
38. Personal interview, July 2, 2001.
39. Personal interview, September 6, 2001.
40. Personal interview, July 2, 2001.
41. Personal interview, June 27, 2001.
42. Personal interview, July 29, 2001.

7. Promises Fulfilled?

1. James G. March and Johan P. Olsen, "The New Institutionalism: Organizational Factors in Political Life," *American Political Science Review* 78 (1984): 741.
2. Miewald, ed., *Nebraska Government and Politics*, 130.

Bibliographic Essay

A number of authors and their works were the primary sources for information on Nebraska history. They include, in alphabetical order: Dorothy Weyer Creigh, *Nebraska: A Bicentennial History* (New York: W. W. Norton, 1977); James C. Olsen, *History of Nebraska* (Lincoln: University of Nebraska Press, 1955); Addison Sheldon, *Nebraska*, vol. 1 (Chicago: Lewis Publishing, 1931).

Other works provided information specifically about Nebraska's political system, including its one-house legislature. Those include Adam C. Breckenridge, "Innovations in State Government: Origin and Development of the Nebraska Nonpartisan Unicameral Legislature."*Nebraska History* (Spring 1978); Robert W. Cherny, *Populism, Progressivism and the Transformation of Nebraska Politics* (Lincoln: University of Nebraska Press, 1995); John C. Comer and James B. Johnson, *Nonpartisanship in the Legislative Process: Essays on the Nebraska Legislature* (Washington: University Press of America, 1978); Alvin W. Johnson, *The Unicameral Legislature* (Minneapolis: University of Minnesota Press, 1938); James Johnson, *The Nebraska Legislative System: Legislative Roles in a Nonpartisan Setting* (Ann Arbor MI: University Microfilms International, 1972); Bernard Kolasa, *The Nebraska Political System: A Study in Apartisan Politics* (Lincoln: University of Nebraska, 1968); Robert Miewald, ed., *Nebraska Government and Politics* (Lincoln: University of Nebraska Press, 1984); *Official Debate Handbook* (Lincoln: Nebraska High School Activities Association, 1937); and John Senning, *The One-House Legislature* (New York: McGraw-Hill, 1937).

Several authors offered valuable information about Senator George Norris—including the senator himself, in his autobiography. These works include Richard Lowitt, *George W. Norris: The Triumph of a Progressive, 1933–1944* (Urbana: University of Illinois Press, 1978); George Norris, *Fighting Liberal: The Autobiography of George Norris* (New York: Macmillan, 1945); Robert F. Wesser, "George W. Norris, the Unicameral Legislature and the Progressive Ideal," *Nebraska History* (December 1964).

The following authors and works were sources for the history of and theory behind Populism and Progresivism: Peter H. Argersinger, *The Limits of*

Agrarian Radicalism: Western Populism and American Politics (Lawrence: University Press of Kansas, 1995); Thomas Cronin, *Direct Democracy: the Politics of Initiative, Referendum and Recall* (Cambridge: Harvard University Press, 1989); Lawrence Goodwyn,*The Populist Moment* (New York: Oxford University Press, 1978); John H. Hicks,*The Populist Revolt* (Minneapolis: University of Minnesota Press, 1931); Richard Hofstadter, *The Age of Reform: From Bryan to F.D.R.* (New York: Alfred A. Knopf, 1955); Arthur Holcombe, *State Government in the United States* (New York: Macmillan, 1916); Arthur S. Link, "What Happened to the Progressive Movement in the 1920s?" *American Historical Review* 64 (1959); George McKenna, ed., *American Populism* (New York: G. P. Putnam's Sons, 1974); Russell B. Nye,*Midwestern Progressive Politics: A Historical Study of Its Origins and Development, 1870–1958* (Lansing: Michigan State University Press, 1959); Jeffrey Ostler, *Prairie Populism: The Fate of Agrarian Radicalism in Kansas, Nebraska, and Iowa, 1880–1892* (Lawrence: University Press of Kansas, 1993); Robert H. Wiebe, *The Search for Order, 1877–1920* (New York: Hill and Wang, 1967).

In addition, nearly thirty current and former Nebraska state senators as well as lobbyists and other legislative observers provided information and observations about the unicameral in personal interviews. Their names, alphabetically, and the dates of the interviews are: Dennis Baack, September 6, 2001; Douglas Bereuter, October 14, 2001; Ardyce Bohlke, October 2, 2001; Mary Campbell, June 27, 2001; Frank Daley, March 21, 2002; Don Dworak, August 30, 2001; Tim Hall, September 20, 2001; Peter Hoagland, October 9, 2001; Lowell Johnson, September 18, 2001; Vard Johnson, September 25, 2001; Jim Jones, January 31, 2003; Douglas Kristensen, July 29, 2001; Howard Lamb, September 13, 2001; David Landis, September 18, 2001; Scott Moore, September 25, 2001; Bill Mueller, July 2, 2001; Patrick O'Donnell, March 4, 2002; Paul O'Hara, July 2, 2001; James Pappas, September 4, 2001; Walter Radcliffe, July 24, 2001; Jenny Robak, October 2, 2001; Kim Robak, July 20, 2001; Larry Ruth, July 18, 2001; DiAnna Schimek, August 28, 2001; January 27, 2003; Herb Schimek, July 24, 2001; Sandy Scofield, September 27, 2001; Roger Wehrbein, September 17, 2001; Don Wesely, September 18, 2001; Robert Wickersham, September 27, 2001; Ronald Withem, July 5, 2001.

I should also mention that James Morone's *The Democratic Wish: Popular Participation and the Limits of American Government* (New York: Basic Books, 1990) provided a jumping off point for much of the underlying theory in this book.

Index

Page numbers in italics indicate illustrations, which follow page 102.

Accountability and Disclosure Act (1976), 166, 168–69, 178
agriculture. *See* farming
Alaska Legislative Research Agency, 9
Allen, William V., 28
Appropriations Committee (unicameral), 59, 101, 109

Baack, Dennis, 138; and bill reading, 61; and committee chairs, 109, 110; on legislator participation, 138; on nonpartisanship and lobbying, 164, 168; on openness, 71; on power of speaker, 174; on rural-urban split, 104–5
Baker v. Carr (reapportionment), 52
Barrett, Bill: on openness, 63; on the unicameral, 71
Bereuter, Doug, 105, 107, 108; on George Norris vision realization, 172; on openness, 65; on partisanship, 66; on the unicameral, 71, 105, 107, 108; on unicameral size, 64
Bernard-Stevens, David: on power of the speaker, 92
Betts, Curtis, 126
Beutler, Chris: on power of the speaker, 92–93
bicameral last legislature session, *102-2*
bicameral legislatures: Alexander Hamilton, on, 37; and battling

houses, 42; and class, 12, 43; complexity of, 12–13; and conference committees, 9, 11, 42, 43; and direct democracy, 9–10; as divided responsibility, 42; and efficiency, 16; as favoring "quiet" deals, 9; George Norris attack of, 9, 73–74; and Great Britain, 43; legislative statistics for, 16; and populism, 9; reinstating, 133
big business: and control of government, 152; and populism, 4
Bohlke, Ardyce: on committee chair power, 109; on power of the speaker, 107, 108; on rural-urban split, 104
Boyd, James, 27–28
Brady, Frank, 124
Bromm, Curt, 92–93
Bryan, Charles, 16, 32
Bryan, William Jennings, 29
Budget Committee (unicameral), 59
Burdette, Franklin, 11
Burke, Edmund, 144
Burlington railroad, 25, 30. *See also* railroads

calendar, legislative: Executive Board oversight, 87–88, 90–93, 94–95; legislature oversight of, 88; and lieutenant governor, 76–77; and speaker, 87–88, 91–95, 107
campaign finances: contribution influence and, 165–66; and disclosure, 157; and special interest contributions, 165–66

Campbell, Mary, 162, 163, 165, 166, 168
capitol (Nebraska): construction of, *102-1*; tower, *102-3*
Carpenter, Terry, 156
Cavanaugh, John, 56
Chambers, Ernie: and bill amending, 62, 97; on leadership power, 92–95; "Lola" amendment of, 93, 94; on media coverage, 57; on partisan affiliation, 102
Christian Science Monitor: first unicameral session, 48; on unicameral first decade, 59
Citizens' Conference on State Legislatures (1971): and accountability of the unicameral, 53, 71; and functionality of the unicameral, 87; and openness of the unicameral, 53; and representativeness of the unicameral, 132
coalitions: and coalition building, 173; and "communities of interest," 104–5, 118, 120, 173; and nonpartisanship, 104–7; philosophical underpinnings of, 105; rural/urban basis for, 104; and self-interest, 105
Cochran, Robert, 49, 50, 124, 125
Committee of the Whole (unicameral), 46, 121–22, 131
Committee on Committees (unicameral), 77–79, 88, 98–99, 104
Committee on Enrollment and Review (unicameral), 77
Committee on Legislative Administration (unicameral), 128
Committee on Order and Arrangement (unicameral), 88
committees (unicameral): authority granted to, 79–80; authority of, 101; bill referral, 86; bills killed in, 100; chairs of, 78–79, 92, 109, 112, 174; chairs of standing, 86, 98; and change over time, 59; and the first unicameral session, 80–81; importance of, 111–12, 184–85; and lieutenant governor, 77; member-

ship in, 78; number of, 47, 59; and oversight of entire body, 100–101; overview of, 98–101; and public hearing requirement, 100; and public testimony, 54–55; and regional interests, 104; Rule VI.4 (committee definition), 48; second-guessing of (by legislature), 80; standing, 100, 123, 131–32, 142; and unicameral simplification, 59. *See also* rules (the unicameral); *specific committees*
conference committees, legislative, 73–74, 149–50, 163, 164, 171–72, 197–200; and lobbying, 149–50, 163, 164. *See also* bicameral legislatures; Norris, George
Congressional Record: George Norris interview in, 149
constitutional amendments (Nebraska): bill reading rule and, 61; early progressive, 31; initial unicameral (1913–1915, 1917), 6, 8, 13, 34, 42; and legislative proceeding openness, 58–59; and legislative sessions (1971), 134–35; Norris attempt (1919), 34; Norris successful unicameral (1933–1934), 36–37, 46; post–World War I unicameral attempt (1919–1920), 32, 34; and press access, 58–59; and roll call vote recording, 58; unicameral enacted (1933–1934), 36–37, 46, 76
Coolidge, Calvin, 32
Council of Defense (Nebraska), 31
Council of State Governments: and legislator salaries in Nebraska, 143
Crosby, Lavonne, 62
Cuming, Thomas B., 19–20

Daley, Frank, 157–58, 159
Damn Yankees, 94
DeCamp, John, 66
Declaration of Independence, 72
Democratic Party: and nonpartisanship, 101–7; partisan planks, 50; and People's Party, 5, 20, 28–29; post–World War I, 32, 33

Diers, W. H., 155
Douglas, Stephen A., 19
Drainage Committee (unicameral), 59
Dworak, Don: on committee system, 69; on lobbyists, 163; on vote trading, 105

efficiency *versus* equality/openness, 55, 60, 84–85, 90, 93, 98, 101
Executive Committee (unicameral), 55, 86

The Farmers' Alliance, 4; and People's Party formation, 27; roots of, 25–27
Farmers Cooperative and Educational Union: unicameral proposal for (1924), 8, 34
farming: and early statehood (Nebraska), 25–27; interests of, 51–52, 119–20, 130, 145; and monopolies, 25, 26; and populism, 26–27, 33; post–World War I economic collapse of, 31; and progressivism, 7; and societal rank, 26; and unicameralism opponent claims, 14. *See also* unicameral: rural/urban divide
FDR. *See* Roosevelt, Franklin D.
frontier foundations (Nebraska): and early growth, 19; and the Homestead Act, 20; and the Kansas-Nebraska Act, 19; and Lincoln as capital, 20; and Nebraska Territory, 18–21; and Northwest Ordinance of 1787, 19; and partisan politics, 20; and the Platte River, 19, 20; and Republican Party, 20; and statehood, 20–21 (*see also* statehood, early); and Thomas B. Cuming, 19–20; and transcontinental railroad, 18–19, 21; and voting rights, 21

Government Committee (unicameral), 82
governor (Nebraska), 115; and 2002 fiscal problems, 140–41; authority of, 134; constitutional powers of, 134; and legislature, 123–26, 133–35,

139–41, 144–45, 176; and nonpartisanship, 140; opinion poll of, 140, 186; veto, 140–41
grassroots organizing, 166
Great Britain, 43
Great Depression, 34–36. *See also* New Deal

Hall, Tim: on accountability, 67; on lobbying, 163, 167
Hamilton, Alexander, 37
Hastings Tribune: on the unicameral amendment, 37
Highways and Bridges Committee (unicameral), 59
Hoagland, Peter: on coalitions, 105; on party labels, 66; on rural-urban split, 104; on the unicameral size, 64
Hudkins, Carol, 67

initiative procedure (Nebraska constitution), 31; secret session ban, 46; and unicameral success, 37–40
Internet access, 70

Jefferson, Thomas, 72
Johanns, Mike, 102–3
Johnson, Andrew, 21
Johnson, Lowell, 65
Johnson, Vard: on nonpartisanship, 66; on party discipline, 104; on the unicameral size, 64
Jones, Jim, 52–53

Kristensen, Doug, 87; and bill amending, 62; and bill reading, 61; on collegiality, 106; on lobbyists, 168–69; on power of speaker, 108; on staffing, 142; on unicameral size, 64

LaFollette, Robert, 33, 35
Lamb, Howard, 112
Landis, David: on citizen access, 171; on coalitions, 105; on efficiency, 93; on power of the speaker, 108–9; on public testimony, 68; and unicam-

eral staffing, 142–43; on unicameral
virtues, 65

leadership (unicameral), 86–95, 107–
14, 174–75; need for, 107; and seniority, 111, 184–85; and speaker,
86–88, 107–9, 174–75 (see also
speaker); and term limits, 145

legislation: amending bills, 61–62;
amount of, 55, 107; bill reading, 60–
61; bill referral, 77, 86; bills killed in
committee, 100; complexity, 54; debate limits, 90, 95–96, 132, 137–38;
deliberation, 46–47, 60, 77, 132; filibusters, 95–98, 108; and functionality, 87; germaneness, 54, 70, 88–89;
logrolling, 105; "Lola" amendment,
93–93, 94; and number limits, 55–
56; Omnibus bills, 43; as participatory process, 93; priority bills, 89–90;
public hearings, 45–46, 53–54, 55,
62, 68–69, 80, 100; quality, 43–44;
statement of purpose/germaneness,
54, 70; super-priority, 91–95; tracking of, 63; vote trading, 105–6, 183.
See also calendar, legislative

Legislative Council, 15; bill introduction, 55; and budget background,
124; Executive Board, 109–10; and
professionalism, 81–84; research director, 127

Legislative Journal: and lobbyist disclosure, 158

lieutenant governor, 76–77; and committees, 77; and legislative calendar,
76–77; as presiding officer, 87

Lincoln Evening Journal: on bill introduction limit, 56; on bill reading,
60

Lincoln Journal: on committee membership, 78; on speaker, 77

Lincoln Journal Star: on party affiliation, 102–3; on pride of the unicameral, 170; on unicameral virtues, 63

Lincoln Star: on gubernatorial control,
125; on legislative deliberation, 127;
on unicameral amendment, 37; and
nonpartisanship, 45; on nonparti-

sanship, 124, 125; on seating in the
legislature, 154; on unicameral leadership (letter to editor), 75

lobbying, 13; Accountability and Disclosure Act (1976), 166, 168–69,
178; and bicameralism, 164; versus citizen influence, 167–68; and
conference committees, 149–50, 163,
164; and disclosure, 158–60; ethics,
disclosure, regulation and, 153; and
expenditures of lobbyists, 157–58;
and First Amendment, 152; general-
ization of, 152–53; from government
to private sector, 160; and grassroots
organizing, 166; and influence, 147,
154–55, 160–61; as information provision, 153, 160–62, 177; and legislator access, 166, 167–68; legislator
attitude toward, 160–61; legislators
on, 166–67; and lying, 159, 161–62;
and Nebraska Accountability and
Disclosure Commission, 157–58; and
nonpartisanship, 150–51, 161, 163–
64; and Norris, George, 147–49, 168,
177, 178; and openness, 149–50,
155, 158–59; overview of, 147–48;
and professionalism, 126; and public
hearings, 155, 167; of railroads, 30–
31; and registration with the unicameral, 157, 158, 160; and regulation,
30–31, 161–62; and relationships,
162; Ron Withem and, 156–57, 161–
62, 164–65; and trust, 162, 177; and
truth, 161–62; and the unicameral,
149–50; the unicameral first session,
153–54; and unicameralism, 164–
65, 177–78; and unicameral rules,
155–60. See also lobbyists; special
interests

lobbyists: Dennis Baack, 164, 168;
Mary Campbell, 162, 163, 165, 166,
168; Paul Mueller, 142, 162, 164–65,
167; Paul O'Hara, 141–42, 162, 164,
168; Walt Radcliffe, 107, 142, 162,
164, 166; Kim Robak, 163, 164, 165,
167; Larry Ruth, 163, 164, 166, 167;

Herb Schimek, 161, 163, 166; and seating, 153–54

Madison, James, 144
Maher, John, 48
Marvel, Richard, 87
Matzke, Gerald, 69
Maurstad, Dave: and authority of speaker, 94; on efficiency, 93; on nonhierarchical structure, 113
McCarthyism, 57
McKelvie, Samuel, 32
media. *See* press
Miscellaneous Appropriations and Claims Committee (unicameral), 59
Miscellaneous Subjects Committee (unicameral), 59
Model Legislature Committee, 36, 40, 128
The Model Legislature speech (George Norris, 1934), 3, 19, 73, 147; on evils of bigness, 13, 116–17, 148; nonpartisanship, 15, 45; text of, 195–208
monopolies: and populism, 4; and railroads, 25, 30; and unicameralism, 16
Moore, Scott: on accountability, 64, 65; on collegiality, 106, 173; on committee chair power, 109; on committee hearings, 68–69; on media coverage, 70; on nonpartisanship, 65; on openness, 171; on power of the speaker, 107, 174
Mueller, Paul, 142, 162, 164–65, 167

The National Municipal League, 34
Nebraska Accountability and Disclosure Commission, 157–58
Nebraska Farmer: and the unicameral amendment opposition, 38, 119
Nebraska Legislative Journal: and lobbyist registration, 160
Nebraska State Education Association (NSEA), 166
Nebraska State Teachers Association (NSTA) 1937 legislative report, 75, 76, 80–81

Nebraska voters: independence of, 7
Nelson, Arlene, 64
Newberry, Fred, 27
New Deal: and progressivism, 7–8, 33; and unicameralism, 40, 152
Newell, Dave: on media access, 58
News-Week, 63
New York Times, Norris full-page unicameral piece (1923), 9, 10, 13, 16, 34, 116–17; text of, 189–94
Non-Partisan League, 31
nonpartisanship, 14–15, 172, 173, 193, 205–6; and accessibility, 63, 68; and accountability, 66–67; and coalitions, 104–7 (*see also* coalitions); concerns about, 38, 44–45, 49–51, 65–66, 67–68, 75; constitutional amendment (Nebraska), 65–66; and decision making, 85, 132; and district apportionment, 130–31 (*see also* reapportionment); efficiency of, 38, 67, 106; and gubernatorial power, 125–26; and judges' election, 31; and leadership, 75–76; and lobbying, 150–51, 161, 163–64; and openness, 65; and opinion polling, 67, 68, 106, 137, 181–82, 183; overview, 74–76; and party line voting, 101–7; and party organization, 44–45; and special interests, 151; in successful unicameral amendment, 36–37; and voting participation, 67. *See also* partisanship
Norris, George, 64, 102-4; and accountability, 1, 62–63, 70, 72, 151; and achieving the unicameral, 39–40; Arthur M. Schlesinger Jr. on, 35; and bicameral reform, 2–3; on big business, 16; on checks and balances, 43; and Committee of Whole flap, 122, 131; on conference committees, 11–12, 42, 43, 73, 147, 164, 172, 197–200; on corruption, 193–94, 207–8; and efficiency, 72, 84–85; and egalitarian priorities, 72, 83–84, 91, 93, 113–14, 138; and faith in people, 35, 36, 42; farm policy, 7; on ideal legislature, 10 (*see also*

The Model Legislature speech); on legislative "checking," 12; and legislative disclosure, 57; on legislative

Norris, George (*continued*)
independence, 123–24; on legislature size, 10, 13–14, 44, 73, 116–18, 148–49, 175, 201–2; and lobbying, 147–49, 168, 177, 178; The Model Legislature speech by(1934), 3, 11–13, 15, 45, 116–17, 148, 195–208; on monopolies, 16; *New York Times* unicameral piece by (1923), 9, 10, 13, 16, 34, 116–17; and nonpartisanship, 14–15, 36–37, 44–45, 50–51, 67–68, 74–75, 85, 193, 205–6; and ongoing unicameral improvement, 170; on openness, 190–92; overview of, 1–2, 72; partisan affiliations of, 35, 39–40; and partisanship, 10; professionalism of, 115–16, 126, 129, 143–44, 176–177; as progressive, 2–3, 31, 137; and promises, 178–80; on public hearings, 80; on quality legislators, 16, 17; reflected in the unicameral history, 85; and representativeness, 115–17; as Republican, 31; as Rural Electrification Associations father, 40; and salary as legislator, 126, 128, 129, 135–36, 146, 149, 176–77, 192, 202–4; and "selling" the unicameral, 9–11; and simplification, 12–13, 48, 151; and special interests, 16, 147–48, 150, 168, 169, 177; on state as corporation, 200; as Tennessee Valley Authority father, 40; term of, as legislator, 126, 129, 206–7; and unicameralism as economical, 204–5; after the unicameral first session, 149; unicameralism foundations, 48–49; on U.S. Constitution, 37, 189; and vision realization, 172–73; and World War I, 39

Norton, John: and Committee of the Whole, 121; and equality, 91; and Legislative Council, 81–83; on lobbying, 155; and ongoing unicameral improvement, 170; on openness, 45, 155; and promises fulfilled, 178–80; and the unicameral committee organization, 48, 79; and unicameral establishment, 34

Nuernberger, L. C.: on the speaker, 77

O'Donnell, Patrick, 56; and bill limits, 56; bill reading habits of, 61; openness of, 70–71; and public hearings, 54

Official Debate Handbook, 154

O'Hara, Paul, 141–42, 162, 164, 168

Omaha Morning Bee News: on unicameral leadership, 75

Omaha World-Herald: and unicameral support, 37–38

opinion polls: on committee importance, 111–12, 184–85; on constituent legislative influence, 167, 187; of governors, 139; interpersonal legislator relationships, 182; legislator, 65, 68, 71, 102, 105, 111–12, 181, 182–87; on legislator salaries, 143, 187; on legislator staffing, 142, 186; Nebraska citizens, 65, 67, 106, 113, 138, 166, 181–83, 185–87; on nonpartisanship, 181–82, 183; party influence, 182; on representativeness, 138, 176, 186; on seniority, 111, 184–85; on special interest influence, 166, 178, 187; on unicameral popularity, 65, 181; on unicameral power, 138, 185; vote trading, 183

Pappas, Jim: on amendment limits, 69–70; on hierarchy lack, 110; on openness, 63; on power of speaker, 107; on the unicameral size, 64–65

partisanship: and decision making, 85, 132; Nebraskan, 32; positive view of, 66–67; reinstating, 133, 140. *See also* nonpartisanship

People's Party, 5, 20, 31; and Democratic Party, 5, 20, 28–29; and established parties, 27–28; and The Farmers' Alliance, 27; first platform

of, 27; formation of, 27; legacy of,
29–30; legislative work of, 27–28; as
political institution, 28; and railroad
reform, 27–28. *See also* populism
political parties. *See* Democratic Party;
nonpartisanship; partisanship; Republican Party
polls. *See* opinion polls
populism, 1, 118, 126; and bicameral
legislatures, 9; and decision-making
process, 81; and farming, 26–27, 33;
and leadership, 75; and "the people,"
2, 4; and political structure, 4–5; and
populist revolt (1880s-1890s), 3–4;
and progressivism, 2; and Republican Party, 27; roots of, 3–5; and
Thomas Jefferson, 72; and World
War I, 31. *See also* People's Party;
progressivism
press: and access, 58–59; and confidentiality, 57–59; and unicameral
policies, 46, 56–59
private gain, legislator, 158
professionalism, 6, 54, 115–16, 135–36,
146; Clerk of the Legislature, 126–
27; Committee on Enrollment and
Review, 127; and Legislative Council, 81–84; Legislative Reference Bureau, 126; and lobbyists, 126; Office
of Constitutional Reviewer, 127; and
support staff, 141–43, 176–77
Progressive Party, 32–33
progressivism, 1, 118, 126; and farmers, 7; and government growth, 31;
ideals of, 5–6; influence growth, 31–
32; and institutional perfectibility,
6; and legislative reform, 33; and
machine politics, 5; and Nebraska
as leader, 31; and New Deal, 7–8,
33; and New Freedom (Woodrow
Wilson), 7; and open government,
2; and "the people," 7; and political structures, 5; and populism, 2;
post–World War I decline of, 32;
and professional bureaucracy, 6; and
professional expertise, 129; and reform, 6; and Republican Party, 30,

31; roots of, 5–8, 30; and sunshine
reforms, 9; and World War I, 7. *See
also* populism
Proud, Richard, 53–54
Public Works Committee (unicameral),
59

Radcliffe, Walt, 107, 142, 162, 164, 166
railroads: Board of Railroad Commissioners, 31; breakup of, 30; Burlington railroad, 25, 30; lobbyists of,
30–31; as monopolies, 25, 30; and
People's Party, 27–28; regulation of,
31; as special interests, 30–31, 33,
152; Union Pacific railroad, 21, 25,
28, 30
Rasmussen, Jessie, 69
reapportionment, 129–31; 1962, 51;
court cases, 52; and geography, 175–
76; post-2000 census, 52; for the
unicameral, 118–19
Reference Committee (unicameral),
54, 86
referendum procedure (Nebraska constitution), 31
reform: bicameral, 2–3; and Great
Depression, 34–36; legislative, 33–
34; Nebraska as leader in, 31; and
progressivism, 6; sunshine, 9; and
Woodrow Wilson, 6–7
regulation, 30; of lobbyists, 30–31; of
railroads, 31; by state, 161–62
Republican Party, 29; frontier foundations (Nebraska), 20; and nonpartisanship, 101–7; partisan planks, 50;
and populism, 27; post–World War I,
32–33; progressivism, 30, 31
Reutzel, Barry: on public participation,
69
Revenue Committee (unicameral), 109,
141
Reynolds v. Sims (reapportionment),
52
Robak, Jenny, 113
Robak, Kim: on lobbying, 163, 164,
165, 167; on openness, 63; on the
unicameral structure, 164

Roosevelt, Franklin D.: and New Deal,
8, 33
rules (the unicameral): closed rule,
55; initial rules, 45–48; on lobbyists,
155–56; power of, 109. *See also spe-
cific rules*
Rule I.4 (presiding officers), 78
Rule II.10 (speaking turns), 95
Rule III (media access), 57–58
Rule III.2 (unicameral staff), 128
Rule III.18 (pulling bill from commit-
tee), 100
Rule IV.10 (speaking turn limits), 95
Rule V (legistation/member limit), 55
Rule V (priority bill deadlines), 89
Rule V (senatorial priority bill desig-
nating), 89
Rule V (speaker relieved from standing
committee service), 86
Rule V.2 (speaking turns), 95
Rule VI (committees), 98
Rule VI (proceeding confidentiality),
57
Rule VI.4 (committee definition), 48
Rule VII (cloture [filibuster limita-
tion]), 96–98, 108
Rule VII (committees), 98
Rule VII (public hearing notice), 45
Rule VII (reporting of bills), 80
Rule VII.3 (public hearings), 80
Rule VII.5 (committee report require-
ments), 101
Rule VII.6 (committee legislation rec-
ommendations), 80
Rule VII.9 (committee roll call votes),
46
Rule VII.10 (final committee action),
46
Rule XII.2 (bill introduction), 47
Rule XII.3 (legislative order change),
77
Rule XII.15 (bill subject), 47
Rule XIII (bill process), 77
Rule XIII.6 (Committee on Enroll-
ment and Review), 127
Rule XVI (lobbyist literature), 155
Rule XVI (press accuracy), 56–57

Rule XX.1 (bill re-referral), 77
Rules Committee (unicameral), 45–46,
79–80, 90, 122, 155–56
Rural Electrification Associations fa-
ther, 40
Ruth, Larry, 163, 164, 166, 167

salary, legislator, 126, 128, 129, 135–36,
146, 149, 176–77
Schimek, DiAnna: on accountability,
64; bicameral proposal of, 133; on
coalitions, 105, 106; on committee chair power, 109; on nonpartisanship, 65, 66; on policy making,
138
Schimek, Herb, 161, 163, 166
Schultz, O. Edwin: on lobbyists, 150;
on the speaker, 77
Scofield, Sandy, 138
secrecy: initiative procedure, 46; legislative, 56–59
Senning, John, 11, 16, 35, 42, 48, 64,
102-4; on achieving the unicameral,
39; and Committee of the Whole,
131; and committees, 47, 81; on
communities of interest, 118, 120;
and egalitarian decision making, 91;
on gubernatorial power, 125; on legislation quantity, 55; and Legislative Council, 81–82, 127; on legisla-
tive/executive dynamics, 124; on legislature size, 117; on lobbying regulation, 153; on lobbyists, 150, 151–
52, 154; mapping the initial unicameral districts, 40–41; on nonpartisanship, 75; and ongoing unicameral
improvement, 170; and professionalism, 126; and promises fulfilled,
178–80; on reapportionment, 120,
121; on representativeness, 118
Sheldon, George, 30–31
Shumate, Roger, 15, 127
small is beautiful, 13–14
Smith, Al, 35
Sorensen, C. A., 40
The Sower (Nebraska capitol), *102-1,
102-3*

speaker (unicameral): and agenda setting, 107; and bill referral, 86; checks on, 91–95; compared to same post for other bodies, 108–9; and coordination of standing committee chairs, 86; debate structuring authority of, 137–38; early days of, 77–78, 86; Executive Committee membership of, 86; as "guiding force," 107–9; and leadership, 86–88; and legislative calendar, 87–88, 91–95, 107; legislature oversight of, 88; one-term limit lack, 87; and order of bills/amendments, 90–92; power of, 88–89, 107–9, 108, 173–75; as presider, and 86–87; priority bill designation, 89; and Rule V (speaker relieved from standing committee service), 86; super-priorities, 91–95; weak by principle, 92, 107

special interests, 30; campaign contributions, 165–66; of citizens, 168; George Norris on, 16, 147–48, 150, 168, 169, 177; history for negative view of, 152; legislators on, 166–67; and nonpartisanship, 151–60; and public hearings, 167; railroads as, 30–31, 33. *See also* lobbying

St. Louis Post-Dispatch, 45, 49

statehood, early (Nebraska): agriculture/farming, 21–24 (*see also* farming); and class chasm, 26; and constitutional machinations, 23–24; and deflation, 25–26; and the Farmers' Alliance, 25–27; growth and, 22–23, 24; hardships and, 24–26; land distribution and, 21–23; and monopolies, 25, 26; and People's Party, 27–30; People's Party formation and, 27; and railroad, 22, 23, 24, 25, 27–28; William Jennings Bryan and, 29

Strong, Allen, 82–83

suffrage, woman (Nebraska constitution), 31

Sunday Journal and Star: George Norris interview in, 149

sunshine legislative reforms, 9

Swanson, Bill: on party affiliation, 66

Tennessee Valley Authority, 40

term limits, 144–45

Tvrdik, Charles: on Committee of the Whole, 122; and Legislative Council, 127

two-house model (Nebraska), 1

the unicameral: and 1935 districting, 44; and 2002 fiscal problems, 140–41; and accessibility, 63, 64, 68, 166, 167–68 (*see also* the unicameral: and openness); and accountability, 3, 47, 62–63, 145, 172; and Accountability and Disclosure Act (1976), 166, 168–69, 178; in action, 102-2; annual sessions of, 55, 134–35; Appropriations Committee, 59, 101, 109; and authority delegation, 46; bill amendment process of, 61–62(*see also* legislation); and bill deliberation, 46–47, 60, 77, 132; and bill reading, 60–61 (*see also* legislation); and bipartisanship, 74–76; and budget, 124, 140–41 (*see also* Appropriations Committee); and bureaucracy, 128; cable television coverage of, 70; calling sessions of, 124–25; and campaign finance disclosure, 157; and caucuses, 98; challenge to (1954), 49; and citizen access/influence, 167, 168–69; citizen knowledge of, 171; and Clerk of the Legislature, 15, 126–27; and cloture, 97–98, 138; and coalitions, 104–7 (*see also* coalitions); collegiality and, 106, 110; Committee of the Whole, 46, 121–22, 131; Committee on Committees, 77–79, 88, 98–99, 104; Committee on Enrollment and Review, 127; committees, 46, 47–48, 54 (*see also* committees); and communities of interest, 104–5, 118, 120, 173; and conference committee lack, 64–65, 163, 171–72; and consensus, 107, 132; constitutional

the unicameral (*continued*)
amendment enabling, 36–37, 46–47;
and Constitutional Reviewer Office,
127; and debate limits, 90, 95–96,
132, 137–38; decentralization of, 92;
and decision making, 83–85; district
apportionment for, 40–41, 52–53;
and district makeup, 129–31(*see also*
reapportionment); and division of
labor, 81–84; early *versus* contemporary, 75–76; economics of, 2, 40; efficiency of, 46, 55, 61, 62, 84–85; and
efficiency *versus* equality/openness,
55, 60, 84–85, 90, 93, 98, 101; egalitarian aspects of, 76–81, 93, 113–
14; election for, 38–39; and equal-
ity/openness *versus* efficiency, 55, 60,
84–85, 90, 93, 98, 101; established,
1; establishing operation of, 40–41;
Executive Board, 56, 86, 88–93, 94–
95, 99, 109–10; executive sessions,
46, 57–58; and Farmers Cooperative
and Educational Union (1924), 8,
34; and filibusters, 95–98, 108; first
session of, 53, 75–76, 80–81; and
functionality, 87; George Norris as
prime evangelist for, 39–40; Government Committee, 82; and governor,
103, 115, 123–25, 123–26, 133–35,
139–41, 144–45; and hierarchy, 76–
81, 91, 110, 113, 173–74; influence
within, 108, 110–11; initiative attempt (1923–1924), 8; initiative as
successful (1934), 37–40, 46; internal procedures of, 131–32; and
interpersonal legislator relationships,
182; and leadership, 75, 86–95, 107–
14, 145 (*see also* leadership); and
leadership/power, 76–81, 138, 185;
Legislative Council (*see* Legislative
Council); and the legislative calendar, 76–77, 87–88; and the legislative
process, 46–47; Legislative Reference Bureau, 15, 126; and legislator
aides, 142; and legislator participation, 138; and legislator salaries, 16–
17, 128, 129, 135–36, 143–44, 146,
176–77; and lieutenant governor, 76–
77 (*see also* lieutenant governor);
lobbyist influence and, 154–55, 160–
61; and lobbyist rules, 155–60; and
media coverage, 46; and member
voting records, 57; and New Deal,
40; and noncontroversial bills, 53;
and notice for public hearings, 45,
69, 80 (*see also* the unicameral: public hearings); and Omnibus bills, 47;
opening day for, 45; and openness,
47, 56–61, 62–71, 171, 172; original
apportionment for, 118–19, 129–30,
175–76 (*see also* the unicameral: district apportionment for); overriding
bills killed in committee, 100; and
partisan proposals, 49–50; path to establishment of, 33–39; power in, 76–
81, 107–13; president pro tem (*see*
the unicameral: speaker); presiding
officer of, 76–77; and press policies,
46, 56–57; and procedure manipulation, 108; and proceeding records,
172; and professionalism, 126–36,
141–42 (*see also* professionalism);
and progressive ideal, 137; and progressivism *versus* representativeness,
144; and proposal opponents, 37–39;
and public hearings, 45–46, 53–54,
55, 62, 68–69, 80, 100, 155, 167;
public scrutiny of, 53; and reapportionment, 120–21; and regional interests, 104; and representativeness,
131–32, 137–39, 144, 145–46, 175–
76; and resolution number limits, 56;
review of history of, 179–80; reviews
of, 49–53; roots (*see* frontier foundations); and rural interests, 51–52,
119–20, 130, 145; and rural/urban
divide, 104, 119–20; and secrecy, 56–
58; "selling" of, 9–11; and seniority,
111, 184–85; and session limits, 55–
56, 135; simplified procedure of, 48,
59–60; size of, 41, 51–53, 63–64, 67,
121, 140, 148–49, 171, 175; speaker
of, 77–78, 86–88 (*see also* speaker);
and speaking turns, 95; and special-

ization, 81–84; and special sessions, 124–25; and staff support, 127–28, 141–43, 144, 176–77, 186; structure of, 76, 81–85; and "substitute bill" mechanism, 61–62; and supermajority (cloture), 97–98; and term limits, 144–45; timing to achieve, 40

unicameralism: and amendment making, 43–44; and attracting quality legislators, 16, 17; and bipartisanship, 74–76; Centinel (eighteenth-century Anti-Federalist) on, 9–10; and checks and balances, 43, 150; committee strengthening and, 78; as demystifying process, 9; of early American colonies, 48; efficiency of, 15–16, 46, 72; and equality, 91, 173; and expert/specialist reliance, 15; fostering openness/accountability, 63–71, 171, 190–92; frugality of, 16–17; and gubernatorial power, 133–34; initial constitutional amendment (1913–1915) for, 6, 8, 13, 34, 42; and legislation quality, 43–44; and legislative independence, 123–24; and legislator terms, 126, 129, 206–7; legislature attempt at (1925), 34–35; and legislature size, 43–44, 63–64, 67, 73, 116–18, 121, 171, 175–76; and lobbying, 13, 147, 154–55, 160–61, 164–65, 177–78; national attention for, 34; and nonpartisanship, 14–15, 36–37, 44–45, 49–51, 205–6; Norris constitutional amendment (1919), 34; opponents of, 14, 37–39, 43, 44, 45, 47, 49; path to establishment of, 33–39; and petition drive (1923), 34; and professionalism, 115–16; and public scrutiny, 45, 46; and reapportionment, 120–21; and reform attempts (1912–1934), 8; and representativeness, 115–18; as simplification, 12–13, 48; smallness advantage of, 13–14; and tracking legislation, 63; and vote-trading, 34

Union Pacific railroad, 21, 25, 28, 30. *See also* railroads

U.S. Constitution, 37, 189
U.S. Supreme Court, 52
utility regulation, 30

Van Wyck, Charles, 28
Von Seggern, Emil: on Legislative Council, 83; on lobbyists, 155

Warner, Charles, 45, 49; on Committee of the Whole, 122
Warner, Jerome: on annual sessions, 135; and authority of speaker, 94; on lobbyists, 154, 163–64; on nonpartisanship, 163–64
Washington Post: George Norris interview in, 148–49
Weeks, Douglas: on representativeness, 117–18
Wehrbein, Roger, 67, 68
Wesely, Don, 89; on accountability, 64; on coalitions, 106; on Executive Board, 110; on legislator responsibility, 71; on media access, 58; on the unicameral size, 64
Wickersham, Bob: on accountability, 65, 70; on committee chair power, 109; on leadership, 112; on legislator salary, 143; on power of the speaker, 107
Will, Eric: on amendment limits, 97; on debate streamlining, 90
Wilson, Woodrow: and New Freedom policy, 7; as reformer, 6–7, 32
Witek, Kate, 65–66
Withem, Ron, 87; and bill amending, 61–62; and committee system, 111–12; lobbying, 156–57, 161–62, 164–65; on power dispersal, 107–8; on power of the speaker, 90–92, 174
woman suffrage (Nebraska constitution), 31
World War I, 31–32; conservative response to, 31–32; and populism, 31; and progressive movement, 7

York Republican: and special interests, 155

CPSIA information can be obtained at www.ICGtesting.com
Printed in the USA
BVOW08s0321081113

335739BV00001B/1/P